COMBAT READY!

by

Alastair Goodrum

published by GMS Enterprises

in association with The Aero Book Co.
P.O. Box 1045, Storrington, West Sussex

'OMBAT READY!

First published 1997

by GMS Enterprises
67 Pyhill, Bretton,
Peterborough,
England PE3 8QQ
Tel and Fax (01733) 265123

ISBN: 1 870384 60 1

The author and publisher are indebted to many people and organisations for providing photographs for this military history, but in some cases it has not been possible to identify the original photographer and so credits are given in the appropriate places to the immediate supplier. If any pictures have not been correctly credited, the author and publisher apologise.

Printed and bound for GMS Enterprises by
Woolnough Ltd, Express Works, Irthlingborough, Northants

Acknowledgements

During my years of research I have had the pleasure of meeting and corresponding with many individuals and members of organisations across the globe. I wish to thank them all and without wishing to diminish any single contribution, the following deserve particular mention.

Gp. Capt. Allen Wright DFC AFC RAF(retd)., Douglas Broom, Peter Montgomery, Eric Raybould, Bill Whitty (Canada) and the late Air Cdre. Alan Deere DSO OBE DFC, for detailed accounts of their time at RAF Sutton Bridge.

Lt. Col. James A. Gray USAF(retd) and the US Eagle Squadron Association for information about American volunteers in the RAF.

Peter Green for his special help and advice with photographic material.

Dave Stubley, Ian Blackamore and the Lincolnshire Aircraft Recovery Group.

Bill Welbourne and the Fenland Aircraft Preservation Society.

Paul Sortehaug (NZ) for 486 Sqn information.

Ray Sturtivant. Don Hannah. Tony Hancock .

Air Britain Historians.

The Editors and staff of:

Lincolnshire Free Press and Spalding Guardian newspapers,

Stamford Mercury,

Lynn News & Advertiser.

The Staffs of MOD Air Historical Branch; Public Records Office, Kew and RAF Museum Library, Hendon for access to Crown Copyright material, from which extracts and references made are by kind permission of the Controller of HM Stationery Office.

Lincolnshire and Cambridgeshire County Library Services for access to archive material.

Graham Simons for his advice and the practical help which has gone into the planning and production of this book.

Contents

Front Cover

"One Man and a Bridge"

by Edmund Miller G.Av.A.

As a result of his breathtaking mid-day interval aerobatic display at the 1926 Hendon Air Display, Flying Officer Richard 'Batchy' Atcherley became a *'...legend in his own lunchtime'.*

Edmund Miller's cover painting depicts 'Batchy' as the consummate fighter pilot, returning to RAF Sutton Bridge from the Holbeach Range in July 1930, putting his skill - and career - on the line having just flown his 23 Squadron Gamecock under the Cross Keys Bridge.

Introduction

The area I have defined for the purposes of this book is the region known as the Fens. It covers some 2000 square miles, loosely conforming to the geographic fenland of South Lincolnshire, North Cambridgeshire and West Norfolk, clustered around and including The Wash itself. This landscape is almost entirely flat and featureless, save for ruler-straight rivers and dykes and the distinctive outline of The Wash. Many airfields, some still active, are scattered around the periphery of the region, with evocative names such as Alconbury, Coningsby, Cranwell, Digby, Downham Market, East Kirkby, Feltwell, Glatton, Mildenhall, Upwood, Wittering and Wyton, to remind us of a long association with military flying.

Dealing with these counties, steeped as they are in aviation history, it is hard to conceive an aspect of that history which has not yet been analysed to exhaustion. And yet there is such an area left to be examined and it is that which is dealt with in this book.

In the centre of the region is the site of another airfield, little known yet with a history almost as long as the very oldest of those mentioned above. The former RAF Sutton Bridge, whose grassy acres have long since returned to farmland - itself shortly to be covered by a power station - and its buildings demolished or converted to agricultural use, is the focal point for this story about air combat training.

If the battle of Waterloo was *"...won on the playing fields of Eton"*, then it can be argued that the aerial battles of France and Britain were won in the skies around RAF Sutton Bridge and The Wash ranges. Sir Hugh Trenchard's own target was a professional Air Force based on quality of men, machines and training. It was RAF Sutton Bridge's role to put the latter into the most devastating effect

Much has been written about battles in the air, airmen who fought them, and the aeroplanes and airfields involved. But little is known about how those airmen learned their deadly trade and the organisations that tried to make them ready for combat.

In *Combat Ready!* I have tried to redress the balance a little but it is a vast subject area. How fortunate we are, then, to have such a splendid example, because in the history of RAF Sutton Bridge can be found a microcosm of that very subject. The role of aerial gunnery and operational training in the RAF can therefore be conveyed easily to the reader by telling the story of this small station, the ranges that have been established In The Wash and the effect of both upon the surrounding area. The reader will now have a much better prospect of grasping what was taking place in the RAF without becoming lost in the complexities into which a larger, more wide-ranging analysis would devolve.

This book is about a subject and a station both set in the context of events played on a world stage, all of which played vital roles in moulding the history, tradition and professionalism of the Royal Air Force in peace and war. But even more, it presents and remembers the men and women who contributed in so many different ways, sometimes paying the highest price for human fallibility.

Alastair Goodrum
Spalding
1st August 1997

Foreword

by

Group Captain Allan Wright DFC & Bar, AFC. RAF(retd)

An operational Spitfire pilot with 92 Squadron during Dunkirk and the Battle of Britain and Chief Instructor, Pilot Gunnery Instructor Training Wing, Central Gunnery School, RAF Sutton Bridge,1942.

When the manuscript of this book arrived in the post, I flipped through the pages and began reading. Half an hour later I made myself put it down to finish the work I had been doing but for the rest of the day I found myself picking it up again and again. For several reasons it is a fascinating read.

I was only six months at Sutton Bridge, under the determined marksman 'Sailor' Malan, facing the challenge of setting up and running a new concept. For me the immediate attraction of this book is to discover what went before and after my time there and 'meeting' again my former contemporaries. Such will be the interest for so many others.

Combat Ready! is also much more than that. The author has chosen to write about an RAF station which, although not engaged on operations (except for one notorious night) was as near as could be. The OTU and CGS was staffed by men exceptionally experienced and up-to-date in their field of aerial gunnery, either as fighter pilots or bomber gunners. For most of the Second World War their students were either already experienced in combat, eager and able to improve their techniques and so be able to pass these on to the rest of the fighter pilots or gunners in their own squadrons, or destined to become so. The Central Gunnery School itself was the first of its kind in the world.

Then again, the story covers just twenty years. But that period takes us from the 'stick and string' aircraft left over from the First World War to the most developed all-metal aircraft of the Second. The book is enlivened by copious illustrations of men and machines covering every period - a great variety there, too.

Finally - and perhaps here is where the greatest interest lies - the author has not only obtained first hand stories from those who taught and learned the fighting skills but has knitted these in with the stories of those, perhaps closer to the feel of the place. I refer to the crews that mended and kept the aircraft flying and the people living close by, observing and being involved in the intense activity in their midst.

Alastair Goodrum must be congratulated on collecting together in one book, the many detailed facets that reflect the life of a small but vital RAF training station which spearheaded the art of front and rear gunnery, both before and especially during the Second World War, until bullets gave way to guided missiles.

Abbreviations

Abbreviation	Meaning
1st. Off.	First Officer (ATA rank)
1/Lt.	First Lieutenant
2/Lt.	Second Lieutenant
A.A.	Anti-aircraft
A&AEE.	Aircraft and Armament Experimental Establishment
A/.	Acting/(rank)
AAF.	Auxiliary Air Force
AAS.	Air Armament School
ABA.	Amateur Boxing Association
AC.	Aircraftman
(AC).	Army Co-operation
AC1.	Aircraftman First Class
ACM.	Air Chief Marshal
ADGB.	Air Defence of Great Britain
AFC.	Air Force Cross
AFS.	Advanced Flying School
AFU.	Advanced Flying Unit
AG.	Air Gunner
Air Cdre.	Air Commodore
AM.	Air Marshal
AOC.	Air Officer Commanding
ATA.	Air Transport Auxiliary
ATC.	Air Training Corps.
ATC.	Armament Training Camp
Aus.	Australian
AVM.	Air Vice Marshal
BAe.	British Aerospace
BBMF.	Battle of Britain Memorial Flight
BEM.	British Empire Medal
Bf.	Bayerische Flugzeugwerke (Messerschmitt)
BG.	Bombardment (Bomb) Group
BS.	Bombardment (Bomb) Squadron
BSTU.	Bomber Support Training Unit
C&M.	Care and Maintenance
Capt.	Captain
Cat.	Category
CBE.	Commander of the Order of the British Empire
CCGS.	Combat Crew Gunnery School
CFI.	Chief Flying Instructor
CFS.	Central Flying School
CGS.	Central Gunnery School
CI.	Chief Instructor
C-in-C.	Commander-in-Chief
CO.	Commanding Officer
(C) OTU.	Coastal Command OTU
Cpl.	Corporal
DI.	Daily Inspection
DFC.	Distinguished Flying Cross
DFM.	Distinguished Flying Medal
DH.	De Havilland
Do.	Dornier
DSC.	Distinguished Service Cross
DSO.	Distinguished Service Order
E&RFTS.	Elementary and Reserve Flying Training School
EFTS.	Elementary Flying Training School
ETO.	European Theatre of Operations.
f.l.	Forced landing
FAA.	Fleet Air Arm
FAPS.	Fenland Aircraft Preservation Society
FBW.	Fighter Bomber Wing
FG.	Fighter Group
FIS.	Flying Instructor School
Flg. Off.	Flying Officer
Flt.	Flight
Flt. Lt.	Flight Lieutenant
Flt. Sgt.	Flight Sergeant
FPP.	Ferry Pilot Pool
Fr.	French
FS.	Fighter Squadron
FTS.	Flying Training School
Fw.	Feldwebel
G&TTF.	Gunnery and Target Towing Flight
Gp. Capt.	Group Captain
GSU.	General Service Unit
hp.	Horsepower
HCF.	Heavy Conversion Flight
HCU.	Heavy Conversion Unit
He.	Heinkel
HE.	High Explosive
HQ.	Headquarters
I.	Injured
Ju.	Junkers
Kfg.	Kustenfliegergruppe (Coastal Aviation Group)
KG.	Kampfgeschwader (Bomber Wing)
KIA.	Killed in Action
K.	Killed
LAC.	Leading Aircraftman
LARG.	Lincolnshire Aircraft Recovery Group
Ldg. Airm.	Leading Airman (RN)
LFS.	Lancaster Finishing School
Lt.	Lieutenant or Leutnant
Maj.	Major
MG.	Machine gun
MIA.	Missing in Action
Mid.	Midshipman
MC.	Military Cross
MM.	Military Medal
Mk.	Mark
MO.	Medical Officer
MOD.	Ministry Of Defence
MT.	Motor Transport
MTU.	Mosquito Training Unit
MU.	Maintenance Unit
N/K.	Not Known
NAFDU.	Naval Air Fighting Development Unit
NATO.	North Atlantic Treaty Organisation
NF.	Night Fighter
NJG.	Nachtjagdgeschwader (Night Fighter Wing)
NZ.	New Zealander
Oblt-z-s.	Oberleutnant-zur-see
Obs.	Observer
Ofw.	Oberfeldwebel
Ogefr.	Obergefreiter
ORTU.	Operational Refresher Training Unit
OTU.	Operational Training Unit
PAFU.	Pilot Advanced Flying Unit
Plt. Off.	Pilot Officer
PRU.	Photographic Reconnaissance Unit
Q-Site.	Decoy airfield lighting installation
RAE.	Royal Aircraft Establishment
RAFC.	Royal Air Force College (Cranwell)
RAFR.	Royal Air Force Reserve
RCAF.	Royal Canadian Air Force
RFC.	Royal Flying Corps
RLG.	Relief Landing Ground
RN.	Royal Navy
RNAS.	Royal Naval Air Service
RP.	Rocket Projectile
S/Lt.	Sous Lieutenant (Fr)
S/M.	Sous Matelot (Fr)
SFTS.	Service Flying Training School
Sgt.	Sergeant
Sqn.	Squadron
Sqn. Ldr.	Squadron Leader
Sub. Lt.	Sub-Lieutenant
(T).	Trainer
TT.	Target Tug
TCG.	Troop Carrier Group
TEU.	Tactical Evaluation Unit
TFS.	Tactical Fighter Squadron
TFW.	Tactical Fighter Wing
TRW.	Tactical Reconnaissance Wing
uc	Undercarriage
Uffz.	Unteroffizier
U.	Uninjured
US.	United States (ofAmerica)
USAAF.	United States Army Air Force
VIP.	Very Important Person
VR.	Volunteer Reserve
W/T.	Wireless Telegraphy
WAAF.	Women's Auxiliary Air Force
Wg. Cdr.	Wing Commander
Wimpey.	Wellington Bomber
WO.	Warrant Officer
Wop/AG.	Wireless Operator/Air Gunner
WW1.	First World War 1914-1918
WW2.	Second World War 1939-1945

Prelude

One man and a Bridge...

Did Schneider Trophy ace Richard 'Batchy' Atcherley really fly under the Cross Keys bridge? Local legend certainly has it so, even though no official evidence has been found to corroborate the story.

This bizarre tale first surfaced when a former airman who, between 1929 and 1931, served at RAF Sutton Bridge just a stone's throw from the swing bridge, described an aeroplane accident and suggested that the unfortunate pilot "..*might be the same fellow who flew under the bridge.*"

He was referring to a 23 Squadron contemporary of Atcherley, Flying Officer Charles Jones, killed near the airfield in 1929. This diminutive Scotsman joined the RAF in 1925 and by March 1927 was a fighter pilot with 23 Sqn. based at RAF Kenley. He had made a name for himself by winning the RAF Fighter Aerobatics Competition, held at Northolt in May 1929. Furthermore, with fellow officer, Flg. Off. Purvis, he had represented the Squadron at Hendon airshow, performing synchronised aerobatics for the public's enjoyment. Further investigation revealed that Jones died prior to the alleged 'bridge' incident.

One of twins serving in the RAF - his brother David became the Commanding Officer of 25 Sqn., one of the crack night fighter squadrons in World War Two - Flight Lieutenant Richard 'Batchy' Atcherley was revered by many as an outstanding aerobatic pilot. His name arose, as a more positive candidate for the dubious honour of flying beneath the Bridge, during conversations with former Aircraftman Jack Flint, who was stationed at Sutton Bridge Camp during the time in question and now is one of the best known residents in the village having retired from the RAF in 1945.

Jack, while admitting he did not witness the incident personally, is most emphatic in his claim that: "*Richard Atcherley of 23 Squadron flew under the Bridge in 1930. Atcherley was returning from the Gunnery Range and claimed he wanted to pull out - he would have to be flying well below the bank top - but had got too close to the bridge to do so. He was not court-martialled but was hauled over the coals for it.*"

Richard 'Batchy' Atcherley, as a Flying Officer and member of the 1929 Schneider Trophy team.

Richard Atcherley certainly appears to have all the right credentials for pulling off such a prodigious feat. Winner of many aerobatic competitions, a member of the 1929 RAF Schneider Trophy team (and holder of the fastest lap time), he constantly pulled - nay, tugged hard- at the reins of authority. In his autobiography no less a person than the C-in-C Fighter Command, Air Marshal Sholto Douglas spoke thus of Richard Atcherley:

"*...I was well aware that one of my responsibilities...was to keep a tight rein on the natural exuberance of my fighter pilots. Of all of them, the most colourful were the Atcherley brothers. They were exceptionally fine pilots and had become well known during the 1930's...for their astonishing feats in aerobatics; but their force of character, or the ways in which they expressed it, were always getting them into scrapes which on several occasions resulted in first-rate rows and losses of seniority. Dick Atcherley was perhaps the slightly better pilot of the two... eventually both reached Air rank. After the war David disappeared on a jet fighter flight over the Mediterranean. Richard went on to become Air Marshal with a knighthood before retiring as C-in-C Flying Training Command.*"

Such was Atcherley's reputation that even the *Spalding Guardian* was moved to report on 12 July 1930:-

"*Sutton Bridge Local Notes; RAF; Flt. Lt. Atcherley, winner of the King's Cup in 1929 and also a member of the Schneider Trophy Team last year, is now at Sutton Bridge with the 23rd Squadron. It is likely that aero-acrobatics will be frequent at Sutton Bridge until the end of the month."*

On his way up the RAF ladder, Richard Atcherley attended wartime Air Ministry meetings at which Sholto Douglas was present and in another recollection by the latter, Atcherley's forthright character is again illustrated graphically.

Adolf Galland was reported to have shocked Goering when he uttered his now legendary request for "*...a squadron of Spitfires.*" Sholto Douglas writes: "*At our conference... Atcherley came up with much the same idea in reverse. When he was asked for his views about which aircraft we should use for night fighters he suggested the twin-engined Messerschmitt Bf.110. The Germans were angry with Galland but at the Air Ministry we just guffawed at Atcherley and there was chalked up to his credit yet another of those remarks that were so typical of him.*"

Versions of the 'airman under the bridge' tale abound among Sutton Bridge residents who were children back in the 1930's and '40's. In 1942 or '43 for example, a Canadian instructor at Central Gunnery School, was also said to have been "*..the man who flew beneath the bridge*", but more of that later.

No official evidence - probably for the sake of maintaining discipline - of this earlier escapade has yet come to light but there are several Sutton Bridge residents who claim to have witnessed it while playing as children on the river bank near the bridge.

One official sequel, however, does seem to lend a little weight to the story. It seems odd, to say the least, that the foremost single-seat fighter pilot of his day, a known aerobatic 'wizard' and a pilot to whom speed and daring were the spice of life, should within two months of the alleged 'offence' find himself posted to a lumbering bomber squadron in the stifling heat of the Trans-Jordan desert! The incident may have been hushed up but was it a 'punishment posting' to put the brake on a wild spirit?

Daredevil exploits are, however, the stuff by which reputations are made and perpetuated. As to whether the feat could be done at all, depends on whether certain measurements would allow it.

Gloster Gamecocks operated by 23 Sqn. in Atcherley's day had a wingspan of 30 feet and a height of 10 feet, while Supermarine Spitfires

Royal Air Force Sutton Bridge in the mid-1930s, looking towards the Cross Keys bridge. It is under this bridge that 'Batchy' Atcherley is supposed to have flown. [via Vic Goodman]

At readiness for another air-firing sortie! A Bristol Bulldog outside the canvas hangars of 3 Armament Training Camp, Sutton Bridge. Visible above the the upper wing of the Bulldog is a camera gun used to record the pilots efforts. [*AJG Collection*]

operating at Sutton Bridge during WWII had a 37 foot wingspan and in flight, would also occupy 10 feet vertically. With a gap beneath the main bridge span, at low tide, estimated as 70 feet wide and 20 feet vertically, the probability of success by any candidate is best left to the imagination!!

Bravado is all very well but what about Opportunity? Fenland tidal rivers, particularly the Nene, are noted for their high, banked outfalls which, at low tide, create ruler-straight, deep, wide canyons. How tempting it must have been for a budding fighter 'tyro' to 'dice' as low as he dare, skimming the turgid water until that Bridge and the presence of 'officialdom' forced him to pull out.

Naturalist Sir Peter Scott, a man gifted with an eye for detail, provides an eyewitness account of an incident in 1936, which in turn offers an interesting perspective on the issue of temptation. For a number of years during the 1930's Sir Peter lived in the East Lighthouse, one of a pair of dwellings set opposite each other atop the Nene banks, three miles down river from the Camp.

Acting Pilot Officer J. W. H. Radice, a distant relative of the present day Labour M.P., Mr. Giles Radice, was detailed to fly a weather test over the Range. He took off from Sutton Bridge in Bristol Bulldog K1683 but failed to return. What happened to him is the subject of two differing stories - an official and an unofficial version. The former runs thus:

"This pilot was returning from a weather test flight over Holbeach Range. It is thought he may have stalled in cloud at about 300 feet, leaving the cloud in a dive. The neutral colour of the river may also have caused him to think he was still in cloud. He failed to level out before hitting the water with great force. The aeroplane sank and was not recovered until next day, with the pilot still strapped inside. The only eyewitness was Mr. Peter Scott, the naturalist, who was outside his lighthouse-home by the river at the time."

Fifty years later and just a few years before his death, that gentleman, now Sir Peter Scott sent this writer his recollections of that day.

"I remember this accident very clearly indeed," he wrote. *"There was a target bombing range lying just to the west of the mouth of the river Nene. Aircraft coming back from practice bombing or machine-gunning would frequently drop down over the river in between the straight banks at low tide and fly back up to RAF Sutton Bridge below the level of the banks on each side. This was a fairly common practice and on the day in question I happened to be standing outside my lighthouse door, looking down-river and saw this aircraft low over the water. I looked down for a moment and when I looked up again the aircraft was not there. We took a boat down to the spot and hoped that the pilot might be found alive but a floating object seen earlier turned out to be one of the wheels, which had been torn off and was bobbing in the waves. I do not recall any particularly low cloud on that day and for a significant period before the accident the aircraft was flying at wave-top height. The pilot must have gone just a little bit too low, hit a big wave and that was the end."*

Although memory can play tricks, particularly after many years have elapsed, this eyewitness would undoubtedly be considered reliable. Sir Peter's version differs significantly in two ways. First, in that he refers to the aeroplane flying at wave-top height *"...for a significant period"* and secondly that he refers to aircraft *"...frequently dropping down over the river in between the straight banks at low tide and flying back up (river) to Sutton Bridge."*

Does Sir Peter's statement give credence to that 'legend' relating to flying beneath the Bridge? If such an eyewitness as this, with his reputation for a keen eye and attention to detail, living for several years in a house perched on the river bank itself saw the practice of flying between those high banks as a regular occurance - then might not one intrepid pilot, braver (or more foolhardy!) than the rest, take the next step...?

The Cross Keys bridge at Sutton Bridge as it was in the 1930s. The scene has little changed today. The span under which Atcherley is supposed to have flown is on the right, with the tidal River Nene being about 'half full'.[Wisbech Museum]

Whichever is the accurate version, Acting Plt. Off. Radice's aeroplane sank into the mud where the Lutton Leam outfall joins the main river at Guy's Head a few hundred yards from the two dwellings.

Are the stories just a 'line-shoot', or did someone really pit his skill and nerve against that tempting structure....? After much probing among the many hearsay accounts, an eyewitness to this hair-raising event, was located in 1992, still living in the village.

Resident in Custom House Street, close by the river, Mrs Muriel Morley looked back with enthusiasm to the day she vowed she watched an aeroplane fly under the Bridge. As a 15 year old girl (in 1930), *"...standing with my friends on the west bank, at the top of Lime Street, I saw this aeroplane go by below our level. To my astonishment it went right under the bridge, tilting sideways a bit as it passed under. I thought he must have been a crazy man and everyone said afterwards that he was a real daredevil pilot."*

Muriel went on to name two of her friends still believed to be in the area and a third who lives in the Corby area now who also witnessed the stunt.

Whatever happened, it cannot be stated categorically that Richard Atcherley performed this feat but it seems indisputable that it was actually done. Suffice it to say that 23 Sqn., with Atcherley in attendance, was at Sutton Bridge between July 8 and July 20, 1930. Why then, on October 8, was Flt. Lt. Atcherley an expert fighter pilot posted to 14 (Bomber) Sqn. in Amman, Jordan, to fly the Fairey IIIF....?

Chapter One

Silver Wings and Black Clouds

Royal Air Force Sutton Bridge is generally perceived to have played a minor, unglamourous Air Force role in a quiet backwater of eastern England. While the latter point may be conceded, to persist with the former view is to ignore or, at best, seriously undervalue the true situation.

For more than a quarter of a century just the sheer variety of aeroplanes - whose evocative names conjure up and chart the changing fortunes of the RAF - will be seen as evidence of a vital role played by this Station in peace and as will be seen later, in war too. Flying personnel from all front line Squadrons passed through its portals at one time or another to hone the skills of air gunnery and fighter tactics which were their stock in trade. Some, sadly were never to leave, as the line of military headstones in the parish churchyard testifies. Further evidence of the intense aeronautical activity over the Ranges still turns up in the sand in the form of remnants of millions of spent cartridge cases of various calibres; the detritus left by generations of pilots and air-gunners.

From RFC to RAF

After 1918 the legacy of peace, as far as the RAF was concerned, was a massive cutback in the quantity of active squadrons and a woefully limited financial budget. Of the 188 front-line squadrons active at the end of hostilities, Hugh Trenchard, to whom as Chief of the Air Staff fell the task of trimming and re-shaping the post-war 'junior' service within the constraints allowed, had by the end of 1919 dwindled to just 25 at home and overseas, with which to begin his task. His personal vision was, however, to achieve long term quality in men, machines, training and organisation, in spite of politicking by the Army and Navy to strangle the RAF as an independent service.

In 1923 it was reported by the national press and repeated in local newspapers, that Trenchard envisaged an establishment of 52 squadrons for Home Defence. At the time of the reports, however, only 18 were actually in being. In that same year clear evidence of the enormity of the political in-fighting with which Trenchard had to contend, emerged into the light of day through the medium of the Press.

Under a heading: *"The Costly Air Force - Admiralty control or Air Board"* the following report appeared in the *Wisbech Advertiser,* culled from the nationals in July 1923.

"The agitation by the Admiralty for control of their own branch of the Royal Air Force has assumed almost the air of a political crisis. The rumour that the Board will resign if their claims are not allowed is not taken seriously. The Committee of Imperial Defence is understood to have reported to the Cabinet in favour of a separate Air Force. A statement on the subject by the Prime Minister is expected shortly. A manifesto, supporting the claims of the Admiralty, was signed by fifty Conservative MP's.

An airman's first view of 3 Armament Training Camp Royal Air Force, Sutton Bridge. The main entrance with Guardroom and visiting airman's parking area for cars and motorcycles and, disappearing towards the airfield proper, the MT shed. [Wisbech Museum]

Above: A trio of Hawker Woodcocks of 3 Sqn. become airborne. [MoD Air]

Right: J8646, a Siskin IIIA belonging to 41 Sqn. An interesting, possibly local piece of equipment is what is almost certainly an aircraft state board hanging just below the cockpit with its single pointer. [via C.F.E.Smedley]

SUTTON BRIDGE VISITORS

Above:A Gloster Grebe J7581 of 25 Sqn. [Sqn Archive]

Right: Gloster Gamecock J7910.

In 1916, when the struggle was waging between the RNAS (Naval Wing) and the RFC (Military Wing) for the supreme control of a unified Air Force, a report was circulated among certain MP's prior to the appointment of an Air Board in which both Services were represented to co-ordinate the control on a business basis. Before the establishment of this unified control it was revealed that the two Services were paying something like 200% above the intrinsic value of each aircraft purchased, and that they were actually bidding against one another in the open market for essential spare parts and supplies. A manufacturer supplying engines and fuselages would put in tenders for the supply at different prices to each Service. Naturally, the higher priced order was preferred and the Service making the lower offer had to go without machines that were urgently required. When next a tender came to be made, prices quoted were even higher. In both cases the price was paid without question."

Improving one's targetting skills...

By 1925 Trenchard had consolidated this cadre of the RAF, having fought off predators and survived. The success story of his policies and the performance of the RAF during that crucial gestation period is a matter of history. Now he could plan expansion, albeit still constrained by a miserly budget. Emphasis for this new phase was on the Air Defence of Great Britain (ADGB) with additional fighter and bomber squadrons being re-activated in the case of the former, equipped with a variety of types, such as Hawker Woodcock, Gloster Grebe and Gamecock and Armstrong Whitworth Siskin. Being fighters, too, it was very important for their pilots to be brought to the highest state of proficiency and this included gunnery. An integral part of Trenchard's plan made provision to establish permanent live firing and bombing ranges to keep his aircrew efficient in the skills fundamental to their roles.

Indeed it would, by the end of the decade, be enshrined within the pages of The RAF Flying Training Manual (Air Publication 928), in that part relating to Applied Flying (Pt.II). This document put it succinctly that: *"the utmost skill in flying is...of no avail unless pilots and gunners attain complete efficiency in the use of their weapons and sights and they receive continual practice in firing and aiming while in flight, at stationary and moving targets."*

The miserly budget, however, was particularly evident in the context of armament. Practice with 'live' ammunition was severely limited, its use being confined usually to the annual two-week detachment to armament practice Camp. Pretty 'aerial evolutions' are all very well, but if the effect of firing at a target is not experienced a pilot, particularly a fighter pilot, will have a serious handicap.

It was some years before squadron diaries made reference to individual firing performances but, at random, 19 Sqn's. overall score average in 1928 was just 22%. It rose to 39% in 1929, with top scorer Flt. Lt. Openshaw achieving 68%. In 1930 Sgt. Cleland scored 83% and 1931 saw Flt. Lt. Lart with 82%. Note of scores lapsed for a time until, in 1935, with justifiable pride, the squadron recorded Flt. Lt. Harry Broadhurst as winner of the Brooke-Popham Trophy, competed for as usual at Holbeach Range. Broadhurst repeated the feat in 1936 with a score of 89% and went on to earn, in addition to high rank, acclaim in the RAF as an exceptional aerial marksman whose prowess was proven in combat in WW2.

...by practicing on a range.

Sites for this potentially dangerous facility were duly investigated, with a prerequisite being to select a location which, while accessible for use, would minimise danger and disturbance to both public and military personnel and property. The Wash outmarsh adjacent to Gedney Drove End was one such site meeting these criteria and during 1925 plans were set in hand to acquire the necessary area of the Marsh for Air Ministry use, together with a site on the edge of Sutton Bridge village for use as an airfield to act as a base from which to serve the range.

Sutton Bridge Armament Practice Camp opened officially on September 1, 1926 and Flt. Lt. A. R. Mackenzie became its first Commandant, supported by Flg. Off. E.R.H.Coombes as adjutant, Flg. Off. J. O. Priestley, Medical Officer and thirty airmen. Mackenzie was ordered to establish a base camp and landing ground on farm land acquired by the Air Ministry to the east of the swing bridge across the river Nene at Sutton Bridge, near the Lincolnshire/Norfolk boundary. His team was responsible for setting up, operating and maintaining ground targets for machine gun firing and bomb dropping by aeroplanes. The location of this range was at the edge of the salt marshes adjacent to the village of Gedney Drove End, about five miles from the Sutton Bridge Camp.

Accomodation on the airfield for both men and machines was quite basic, being Bell tents for the former and canvas 'Bessoneau' type hangars - also known as 'H' type - for the latter. Some Officers were fortunate to be billeted in the village, for Autumn in the

Early accomodation at Sutton Bridge was quite basic - Bell tents, Marquees and Bessoneau hangars. [Spalding Guardian]

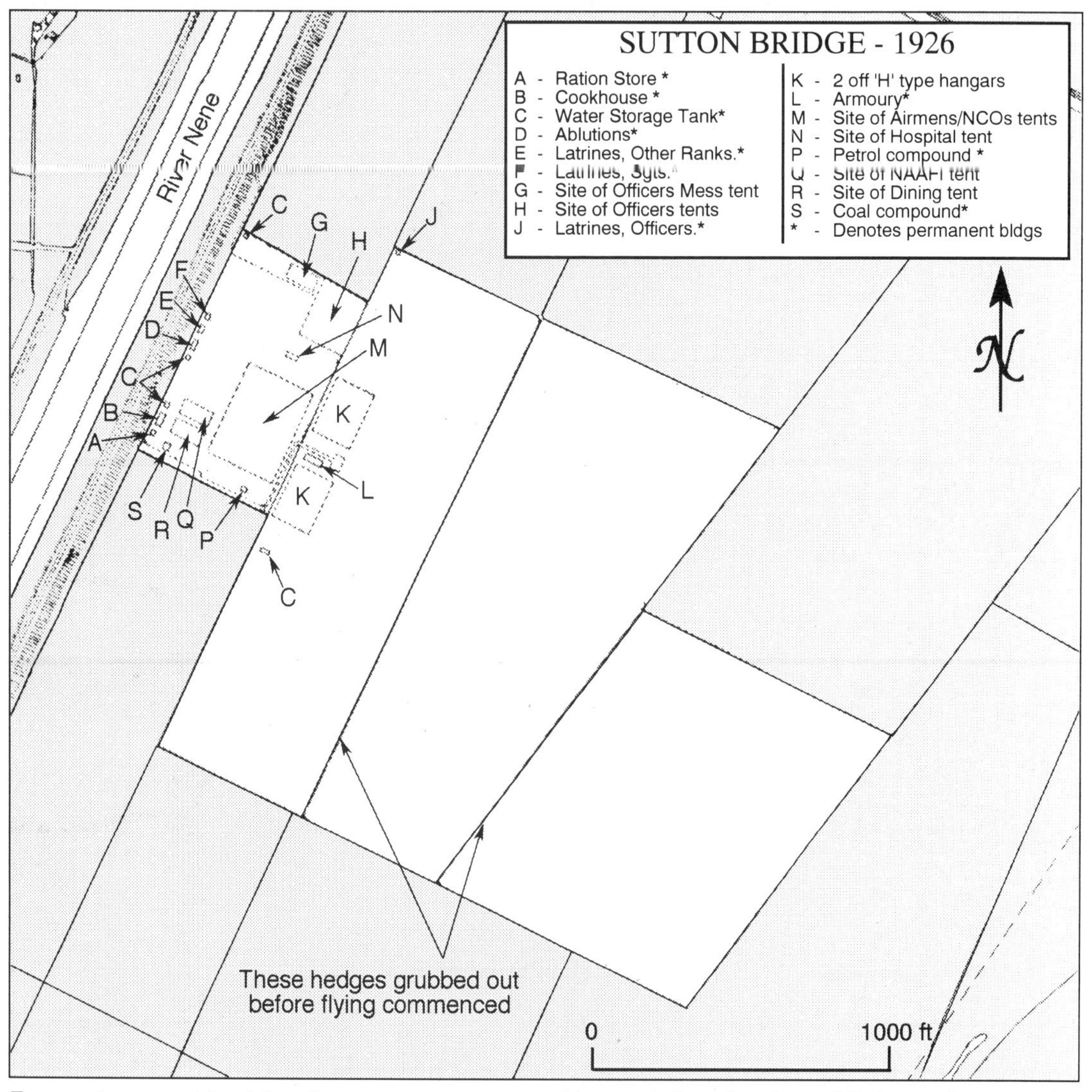

Fens can be very cold and damp!

Jack Flint, arriving at the Camp in 1929 found living conditions, even a few years after it opened, still somewhat primitive. *"Drinking water was not laid on to the Camp as it was on the opposite side of the river from the village. Twice daily a water tanker journied back and forth to Kings Lynn to bring in supplies. Electricity was generated on the Camp and the generator was shut down prompt at 21.30 each evening."*

Mobilised at RAF Bircham Newton, the embryo unit proceeded in convoy, on September 1, to its new abode to begin the task of target building. By September 27 all was ready and the first 'customers' fired over the area known as Holbeach Marsh.

So it was that a long line of evocative names, Grebe, Siskin, Flycatcher, Woodcock, Bulldog, Fury, Hart and so on began an association with The Wash marshes and air firing. Still, after nearly seventy years this association, though modified over time, remains active and seems set to continue into the 21st. Century.

Flying continued for just one month that first year. By October 31 the weather was grim and firing was halted for the 'season'. In that time numbers 19, 23, 29, 43 and 111 Squadrons had passed through the Camp.

As an experiment, 19, 29, and 111 Sqns worked their spells at the range by flying from their home station, Duxford, landing at Sutton Bridge daily. Due to the time this consumed in flying back and forth, these three Squadrons failed to fully complete their firing programme. Operating from a base other than Sutton Bridge was proving most unsatisfactory, a situation which contributed to the subsequent development of the airfield facilities as time wore on.

Further critical evaluation of the range operating procedure suggested it, too, was unsatisfactory. The system was for a formation of six aeroplanes to approach the range in line astern, flying a left-hand

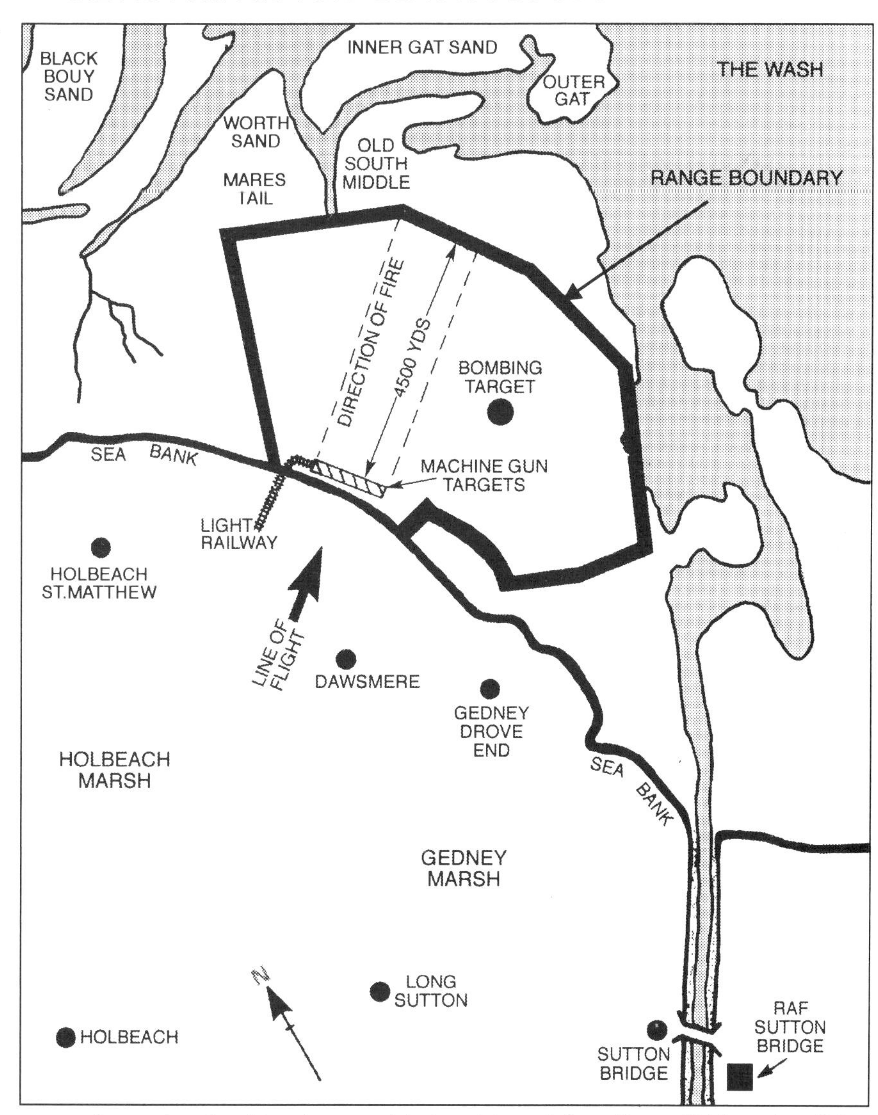

The general area of the WesternWash, showing the Range and location of the airfield at Sutton Bridge in 1927.

circuit during firing passes, each aeroplane breaking to starboard and leaving the formation. This was found to be neither safe nor efficient and was discontinued at the close of the Camp that year.

It was April 1, 1927 when Sutton Bridge Practice Camp reformed, with Sqn. Ldr. A. R. Arnold DSC, DFC posted in as Commandant, together with three officers and 49 airman. Air firing began on the 19th. of that month just in time for an inspection by Air Marshal Sir John Salmond.

A change in working practice.

Once again working practices were examined to try to improve the efficiency of the operation. In June, accomodation for the Range working party was on ground adjoining the range itself, in Durham's Road, Gedney Dawsmere, just to the landward side of the sea bank. Subsequently this became a permanent arrangement - in use even to this day - to obviate the need to travel to and from Sutton Bridge when firing was in progress. The precise nature of the 'accomodation' is not recorded but it could not have been a popular posting in view of the uninviting, wind-swept countryside out there at the edge of The Wash.

At the close of firing operations in 1926 a brief resume of the byelaws and range procedure appeared in local newspapers, principally as a warning to the public to keep well away when firing re-commenced. A plan of the range was printed, showing the position of targets and the line of fire. The public was advised that there were nine warning flags and danger notices. On the seaward side markers had been erected to warn ships and boats of the danger area limits. Six canvas firing targets would be permanent features on the seaward side of the marsh bank.

Air to ground gunnery was planned to take place between April 1 and October 31, between the hours of 07.00 and 18.00 on weekdays and 07.00 to 12.00 on

"...occasional clouds of white smoke could be seen"

Looking back over the tail of an A.W. Atlas to the bombing target circle. The puff of smoke indicates the fall of a practice bomb on the Wash range.

[P.H.T. Green collection]

Saturdays. Thirty minutes before firing began range staff would raise red flags, post sentries and bar public access to that part of the marsh.

Aircraft, flying singly or in flights fired .303 ammunition from a height of 500 feet (e.g from a two-seater carrying a gunner) or by diving onto targets from 800 feet down to about 100 feet. Bomb dropping was with practice smoke or alternatively with light to medium weight HE bombs.

It was not until July 1927 that the local population first gained a peep behind the scenes at RAF Sutton Bridge. Official secrecy was lifted to allow a visit by a 'Special Correspondent' and photographer from the *Spalding Guardian* whose report provides further enlightening details of life at the station.

"Abutting upon the southern bank of the Nene, the camp, with Bell tents arranged in orderly rows, covers 80 acres, of which 70 acres are devoted to the landing ground itself.

A solitary aeroplane, indulging in a clear case of 'loop-itus', flew overhead as we began our tour, while others were being readied for the firing range. Bombs, painted white and of light calibre, could be seen being fitted to racks beneath their wings. Airmen were scurrying about loading belts of cartridges into machine guns. Our presence on the airfield co-incided with the arrival of three flights of Bristol Fighters, from Andover and Old Sarum, about to begin their 14-day visit to the Range facility. Together with Woodcocks of 17 Sqn. from Upavon, the Bristol Fighters brought the total of aeroplanes at the camp to 21, well within the capacity of the four spacious hangars."

According to the station 'Form 540' these arrivals seem to confirm entries referring to 13 (Army Co-operation) Sqn, at that time based at Andover and to 16 (AC) Sqn., from Old Sarum. The third 'flight' might actually refer to the arrival of a detachment from 4 (AC) Sqn. which operated Bristol F2B Fighters at Farnborough and which is also recorded as using Sutton Bridge that summer. Since there were no aeroplanes on the station establishment at that time, it can be reasonably assumed that 17 might bring a full squadron complement of twelve Woodcocks, suggesting that the other three 'flights' witnessed represented a flight of three aeroplanes from each Army Co-op Squadron.

The 'Corresponent' continued: *"Our attention was drawn to a firing butt, for static testing of the alignment of aeroplane gun-sights. Another butt, containing innumerable sand-bags, was in the course of construction.*

Vickers Vimy J7447 of 9 Sqn, which crashed at Gedney Drove End on 6 October 1924 was from the same batch as J7445 here photographed at Farnborough between October 1925 and March 1926 when it was used for various flying experiments, including the attachment of a large drogue seen here at the rear of the fuselage. [J.M. Bruce/G.S. Leslie collection]

Left: The first post World War One accident in the region. Bristol F2B Fighter F4420 of 2 FTS, after crashing near Ely on 8 April 1922.

Under the guidance of Sqn. Ldr. Leacroft we were then conveyed to Gedney Drove End, to the firing range itself."

Sqn. Ldr. John Leacroft MC was Officer Commanding 17 Sqn. at that time. He was a pilot with considerable operational experience having been credited with 22 air victories while flying with 19 Sqn. in France during WW 1.

The report continued: *"Here we took up position on the sea bank behind the machine gun targets. Soon aeroplanes began swooping down, spattering the targets liberally with bullets. After each firing exercise is complete, the target is repaired by range staff.*

Bombing practice was also demonstrated but since that target was well out on the marsh, only occasional clouds of white smoke could be seen. The machine gun targets are easily served by a light railway but repairs to the distant bombing target is a far more troublesome matter it consisting of a raft in a large white circle, submerged at high tide. To reach the target a repair squad is compelled to go out by boat from Kings Lynn dock.

Public access is barred by stringent laws, sentries and warning flags, with dire penalties for those who dare to wander onto the range. In general, however, our visit was most hospitable. The health of the troops seems reasonably good, while the landing ground has not fulfilled the forbodings of numerous local farmers, who were of the opinion that the ground would be too soft for the aeroplanes."

Incidents and accidents

Observing that only two minor mishaps had occurred during its first two years of operation, 'Special Correspondent' was perhaps tempting fate. The first of these two occurred on October 19 as the result of a pilot raising the tail of his aircraft too high during take off. The propeller was smashed when it struck the ground, causing the aeroplane to end up ignominiously on its nose. It was not long before that same newspaper was reporting the first of what was to become a sad litany of accidents.

Between the Wars the area around The Wash was to become a mecca for fighters but an assortment of bombers too made some spectacular appearances from time to time. As early as August 1924, for example, Blackburn Kangaroo G-EAMJ (ex-B9977) came to grief during a forced landing near Spalding. Operated for the RAF Reserve by North Sea Aero Co of Brough, near Hull, its Reserve pilot, became lost on a cross-country flight and ran into a dyke when he landed to find his whereabouts.

The antics of Vickers Vimy J7447 alarmed villagers in Gedney Drove End on October 6, 1924 when it circled their homes at roof-top height. This 9 Sqn. crew, also lost, were on a cross-country from Manston and according to locals, were *"...low enough to read the signposts!"*. The pilot stalled trying to avoid hedges and dykes and crashed heavily, burying

John Leacroft MC is on the extreme right of this picture, whilst still a Captain and an Instructor at the Turnberry School of Air Fighting in Scotland. Others in the picture are (from L. to R) Captains Le Gallais, Atkinson DFC, G. C. Maxwell MC and Taylor.

All are standing in front of a Bristol M.1 Monoplane Scout.

SPALDING FREE PRESS. AUGUST 19, 1924. 5

AEROPLANE'S LITTLE SMASH IN COWBIT WASH.

A concealed dyke brought to grief an aeroplane which landed on Cowbit Wash on Wednesday to discover its whereabouts. Damage was done to the undercarriage and fuselage and the 'plane had to be dismantled. The machine was a private one engaged on R.A.F. Reserve instruction, and the little picture inset shows the damage to the nose of the 'plane's body. Fuller particulars appear in this issue.

—"Free Press" Photograph.

AEROPLANE MISHAP ON COWBIT WASH.

Descends to Find Whereabouts,

AND DISCOVERS A DYKE.

SLIGHT DAMAGE.

Attracted by the apparently ideal nature of the landing ground, an aeroplane, which lost its bearings over the town on Wednesday, descended on Cowbit Wash. Whilst taxiing along a grass field, and just before pulling up, the plane struck a dyke and sustained damage to the undercarriage. The nose of the plane was torn, part of the fuselage broken, the under-carriage damaged, and a propeller shaft snapped off in the ground. A picture appears amongst our illustrations.

As the machine was travelling slowly, the pilot, who was alone, was unharmed. Fortunately, he was seated in the second seat from the nose of the aeroplane, otherwise he might have been severely shaken.

The pilot was Mr. G. Eley, of the Aerodrome Club, Brough, East Yorkshire, and the machine (numbered G-EAMJ) was the property of the North Sea Aero and General Engineering Company, Ltd. It was being used for instructional purposes for the R.A.F. Reserve, and, curiously enough, this was Mr. Eley's last trip in this connection this season. The aeroplane was a heavy twin-engined one, of a type used for submarine spotting during war time. The type is known as the "Blackburn Kangaroo."

"I was on my way from Brough to Grantham and came down to discover my whereabouts," said the pilot to our representative, "and instead of finding my whereabouts I found this dyke," he added humorously.

"Were you bruised?"

"No, I received a jolt, but nothing much. I sat there stuck in the dyke

Above: A Blackburn Kangaroo 'hops' into trouble. Kangaroo G-EAMJ, an RAF Reserve trainer brought to an abrupt halt by one of the notorious Fenland dykes near Spalding in August 1924. [Spalding Free Press]

Left: The ungainly lines of Kangaroo G-EAMJ before the accident..

Below:DH9A J7074, marked '4' is second from the left in this 39 Sqn line-up at its Grantham base. This aircraft crashed near Spalding on 25 July 1927.

the nose of the Vimy almost up to its engines fortunately without injury to the crew.

Perhaps the most spectacular incident was the loss of a brand new 99 Sqn. Handley Page Hyderabad in The Wash on May 14, 1927. En route North Coates to Bircham Newton J7751 suffered port engine failure and the pilot, Sgt. Mitchell, force landed on Bulldog Sand at low tide. The crew was rescued unharmed by local fishing boats but the Hyderabad was submerged by the rising tide. Later, found drifting in a shipping lane by the crew of *SS Max Weidtmann,* the remains were winched aboard and handed over to the RAF at Kings Lynn.

The worst year for RAF accidents was 1927 when no less than eighteen Gamecocks were lost in crashes. Really a development of Gloster's Grebe, the Gamecock was a relatively sleek and agile design. However, it was not devoid of similar wing flutter problems to those currently being experienced by its contemporary, the Woodcock. This livliness brought with it a reputation as a handful in a spin and when landing. Nevertheless it was considered a popular aeroplane with its pilots, even though records suggest its other qualities contributed to a 25% attrition rate - and only 90 were built!

A typical example of one of those mishaps occurred at Sutton Bridge on July 20, 1927, the first to befall that type at the camp. On that day, too, Flg. Off. R.G.Pace of 32 Sqn., Kenley, became the first fatality associated with the range when he was killed flying Gamecock J7907.

Two pictures of the shattered Gloster Grebe J7850 from which Flg. Off. Andrews escaped with his life on Holbeach Marsh Range on 20 July 1927. [Spalding Guardian]

Making several firing passes at No.1 target, each time the pilot turned away seawards. After this final pass the aeroplane had climbed to 700 feet. Its engine seemed to falter then it dived, without warning, into the mud-flats. So hard was the impact that its force shattered the machine completely, broke the pilot's seat straps and pitched him some distance through the air.

Just three hours later a second aeroplane crashed in similar circumstances but fortunately with less tragic consequences. Having been at the camp since July 9, 19 Sqn, too, was nearing the end of a two week detachment when its safety record became blemished.

Gloster Grebe, J7580, from 19 Sqn. was flown to the range by Flg. Off. Andrews. Circling, after making a firing pass, he appeared to lose control of the aeroplane at low altitude and it was seen to dive at high speed. Crashing into about three feet of water from the incoming tide, the Grebe sent up a huge fountain of spray as it went in at a shallow angle. Luckily for Andrews, water cushioned the impact and undoubtedly saved his life. In the process of turning over, as its nose dug in, his harness snapped catapulting him sixty yards through the air. His parachute partially opened, whether by accident or design he could not remember and in streaming out behind him further broke his headlong flight. He was quickly rescued from the rising water by range staff who found him soaked to the skin, bruised, shaking like a leaf - but alive!

Business returned to normal after the mishaps of July and almost inevitably, to add incentive and appeal to the natural instincts of the fighter pilot, it was not long before a competition was introduced. At the end of September, when the firing 'season' was complete, the best shots from each of the Fighting Area Squadrons passing through Sutton Bridge competed for the Brooke-Popham Trophy, named after the AOC-in-C Air Defence of Great Britain, Air Marshal (AM) Sir

Twelve Gamecocks of 32 Sqn. on parade! The third aeroplane from the front is J7907 - the first machine lost on Holbeach Marsh Range when flown by Flg. Off. Pace.

Young Sidney Clifton thought it was "...wizard" the day Plt. Off. P.K.Bone from 7FTS dropped into a stubble field near his house on 5/9/38. Hawker Hart K5797 developed engine trouble during a cross country training flight and Plt. Off. Bone had to force land near Pinchbeck. Sidney is seen here with a neighbour Mrs C. Shotbolt in front of K5797. [S.Clifton].

Sir Robert Brooke-Popham and awarded for the overall top scorer. In that inaugural year it was won by Flt. Lt. H. C. Calvey of 23 Sqn.

Even from the limited records kept, it is clear that the armament camp was well into its stride, with men and aircraft from 1, 3, 4, 13, 16, 17, 19, 23, 25, 29, 32, 41, 43, 56 and 111 Sqns. all completing a two week stay at Sutton Bridge that year. From this list of fifteen squadrons it can be seen that silver, gaudily-painted fighters from all front line fighter units must have kept the air above South Lincolnshire fairly buzzing with noise for seven months of the year - so, in the 1990's what's new? With the onset of Winter all staff returned to Bircham Newton.

Spring 1928 brought the arrival of the usual convoy, this time under the leadership of Sqn. Ldr. W. Sowrey DFC, AFC with three officers and 52 airmen. The camp re-opened on March 28, with air firing beginning by mid-April and continuing unabated until the end of September.

By the close of operations, the same units as recorded in the previous year, with the further addition of 2 (AC) Sqn., had passed through the camp. October brought the end of 'season' competition to find the best overall shot, won this year by Flg. Off. C.W.McK.Thompson from 43 Sqn.

Sadly 1928 did not pass without mishap. Flg. Off. G. Bradbury, 41 Sqn., was fatally injured on May 8. Bradbury was considered a proficient pilot, who had been in the RAF for just over three years. By the time of the accident, though, he had accumulated only 171 solo flying hours.

It was midday when Flg. Off. Bradbury, in company with another aircraft, took Siskin IIIA, J8402, down to the range. He made several firing passes at No.4 target, pulling up into right-hand circuits after each dive. His method of approach appeared to follow a flat glide, with the engine throttled back, continuing as he put the nose down towards the target. By keeping the approach speed down, could this have been his 'wheeze' of achieving a longer, better-aimed and thus higher scoring, firing pass?

It was from one of these slow dives that Bradbury failed to pull out. At first it seemed his aeroplane would recover but the undercarriage hit one of the many creeks which criss-crossed the marsh and it was torn away. J8402 staggered, disintegrating in an explosion which ripped the engine from the fuselage.

Pinned beneath the wreckage, Flg. Off. Bradbury lay unconscious for nearly an hour before rescuers reached him through the maze of creeks. He was rushed to Kings Lynn hospital where, after fighting bravely, he succombed to his injuries twelve days later.

Asked for an opinion at the inquest, the Range Control officer considered Flg. Off. Bradbury ought to have lined up on the targets with the engine power on and then only throttle back during the firing dive itself. Due to the gliding approach, the aeroplane appeared to lose even more speed and may have either stalled or the engine failed to respond quickly enough when the throttle was eventually re-opened.

In May, to provide a Squadron 'hack', Avro 504N H2434, was allocated to the camp. Arriving at Sutton Bridge on 28th, it did not, however, last long. Flt. Lt. Calvey, 23 Sqn., who it will be recalled was the winner of the first Best Shot competition, was killed en-route Kenley to Sutton Bridge. With him in H2434 when it crashed near Henlow, was Flt. Sgt. W.Holker who also lost his life in the accident.

Tragedy continued to punctuate operations at the camp, rearing its head again just a few days later. Flt. Lt. Lance Browning MC DFC, another veteran WW 1 pilot now a flight commander with 3 Sqn., took off for the firing range in Woodcock, J7974.

Emerging from the ashes of the old Sopwith Aeroplane Company, a victim of the immediate and deep post-WW1 decline in British aircraft production, Hawker Engineering Company's first offering, the Woodcock, was its attempt to meet a government specification for a single-seat night fighter.

The Woodcock, a contemporary of those Gloster products Grebe and Gamecock and Armstrong Whitworth's Siskin, was not without its share of teething problems, which seemed to dog its short, unimpressive, service life. Displaying a tendency to wing flutter at high speed and a reputation for weakness in the main spar, it was considered unsuitable for aerobatics and spinning was definitely discouraged. In the event, only two squadrons were allotted this fighter, the first being 3 Sqn. at Upavon, relinquishing its aging Sopwith Snipes for the Woodcock in May 1925. Another year elapsed before 17 Sqn. took delivery of its allocation.

In service for three years, by 1928 3 Sqn. was the only Woodcock unit remaining, as 17 Sqn. had converted to Gamecocks.

The elegant but flawed Hawker Woodcock J7974 suffered a wing failure in a dive over Holbeach Marsh on 2 August 1928, killing 3 Sqn. pilot Flt. Lt. Lance Browning. [Hawker Siddeley]

Having acquired a reputation for being accident-prone, what happened at Holbeach Range on August 2 was an extreme case but seemed to seal the type's service fate.

Flying alone, Browning approached the range, lining up on No. 2 target. Completing his firing pass he brought the nose up, flattened out then began to climb for another circuit. At that point a sudden crackling noise, heard by watchers on the ground, followed the spectacle of the starboard upper wing folding back. It broke clean away, causing the aeroplane, stricken as if it had been shot like one of the birds after which it was named, to roll and spiral inverted to the ground, giving the pilot no chance of escape.

With 1928 only seven months old, Flt. Lt. Browning's became the 52nd serious accident sustained by the RAF that year. As a matter of interest, in the three years up to 1911 there were 9 recorded fatalities in Britain as the result of aeroplane accidents. By comparison, the RAF total at the beginning of the post-WW1 era was 57 in 1921, of which 22 were fatal. A total of 55 serious accidents were recorded in 1927.

The rapidly escalating demands of Trenchard's air force development scheme had its human price. On the positive side, however, although quantity was increasing, the rate at which flying accidents occurred was, fortunately, decreasing as the following table shows.

	1921	1931	+/-
Military flying hours	50,000	340,000	+600%
Serious accidents	57	97	+70%
Fatalities	22	40	+80%
Rate of serious accidents	1 in 900hrs	1 in 3500hrs	-300%
Rate of fatal accidents	1 in 2200hrs	1 in 8600hrs	-300%

Following an investigation into Browning's accident and in the light of its poor record, on August 21 an Air Ministry order grounded all Woodcocks. Subsequently 3 Sqn. was re-equipped with Gamecocks.

So, another busy and eventful year drew to a close. Sixteen fighter squadrons, virtually the entire fighter squadron strength of the RAF, had passed through the camp, whose sterling work was rewarded by a visit from Marshal of the Royal Air Force Sir Hugh Trenchard on September 27, 1928.

In 1928 the Armstrong Whitworth Atlas was re-equipping Army Co-Operation Squadrons such as 4 (AC) Sqn. Here can be seen NCO aircrew - and four 20lb Cooper practice bombs - on summer camp at Sutton Bridge.

[P.H.T. Green Collection]

Air Accidents in the Fenland Region - 1922 to 1936.

Date	Aircraft	Serial	Sqn	Location	Pilot/Crew	Fate
08/04/22	Bristol Fighter	F4420	2FTS	Chettisham	Unknown	K
19/08/24	Kangeroo	G-EAMJ	RAFR	Spalding	Mr. G. Eley	U
06/10/24	Vimy	J7447	9	Gedney Drove End	5 x Unknown	U
21/11/24	Bristol Fighter	C4685	2FTS	Warboys	Unknown	U
28/01/25	Bristol Fighter	F4949	?	Kings Lynn	Unknown	U
29/06/25	Avro504K	E3760	99	Stamford	Unknown	U
29/09/26	DH9A	J7812	39	Gosberton	Fg. Off. B.Bethune	I
19/10/26	Unknown	Unknown	?	RAF Sutton Bridge	Unknown	U
14/05/27	Hyderabad	J7751	99	The Wash	Sgt. Mitchell + 4 crew	U
20/07/27	Gamecock	J7907	32	Holbeach Range	Flg. Off. R.G.Pace	K
20/07/27	Grebe	J7580	19	Holbeach Range	Flg. Off. Andrew	I
25/07/27	DH9A	J7074	39	Wykeham, Spalding	Flt. Lt. Gibb / LAC. Hutchins	U
27/03/28	Bristol Fighter	F4836	2	Stamford	Unknown	
28/01/28	DH9A	Unknown	2FTS	Gosberton	2 x Unknown	
08/05/28	Siskin	J8402	41	Holbeach Range	Flg. Off. G.Bradbury	K
30/05/28	Bristol Fighter	F4965	2	RAF Sutton Bridge	Unknown	
31/05/28	Atlas	J8793	13	RAF Sutton Bridge	Unknown	
13/06/28	Atlas	J8789	13	RAF Sutton Bridge	Unknown	
31/07/28	Unknown	Unknown	RAFC	Cowbit, Spalding	Unknown	I
02/08/28	Woodcock	J7974	3	Holbeach Range	Flt. Lt. L.Browning	K
14/08/29	Gamecock	J7914	23	RAF Sutton Bridge	Flg. Off. Jones	K
26/05/30	Avro504N	J8728	CFS	Barholm, Stamford	Flg. Offs. V.H.Nicholay / P.F.Laxton	K
29/05/30	Bulldog	J9586	17		Unknown	
15/07/30	Siskin	J8896	111		Unknown	
16/07/30	Gamecock	J7894	23	Gedney Dawsmere	Flg. Off. Roger	K
? /04/31	Gordon	Unknown	207	RAF Sutton Bridge	Sgt. Hudson / LAC. Molyneaux	U
09/04/31	Atlas	J9540	2FTS	RAF Sutton Bridge	Flt. Lt. Davies	U
24/04/31	2 x Siskin	J8404/J9874	1	RAF Sutton Bridge	Storm damage	
20/07/31	2 x Siskin	J9873/J9910	41	RAF Sutton Bridge	Unknown (taxying)	
01/08/31	Bulldog	Unknown	54	Holbeach Range	Unknown	
17/03/32	Avro504N	J8568	CFS	Barnack, Stamford	Sgts. N.W.Nicholls / J.Richardson	K
06/05/32	2 x Avro504N	Unknown	CFS	Stamford	Flg. Offs. D.S.McDougall /N.E.White	K
?/ 06/32	Bristol Bulldog	K2173	19	RAF Sutton Bridge	Flg. Off Foster?	
11/07/32	Fairey IIIF	J9144	3ATC	Holbeach Range	Unknown	I
11/07/32	Fury I	Unknown	25	RAF Sutton Bridge	Unknown	U
12/07/32	Wapiti	Unknown	3ATC	Terrington St.Clements	Sgt. Nunnerby / Cpl. Dobson	I
20/09/32	Bulldog	K2160	19	Holbeach Range	Flg. Off. B.Matson	U
26/09/32	Flycatcher	N9929	401Flt	Holbeach Range	Lt. H.M.King RN	K
06/06/33	Bulldog	Unknown	29	Holbeach Range	Flt. Sgt. Starr	I
07/04/34	Demon	Unknown	23	Holbeach Range	Flg. Off. Rough / Plt. Off. Gillman	I
18/05/34	Bulldog	K2194	41	Holbeach Range	Flt. Sgt. F.Baker	K
03/07/34	Gordon(ex-IIIF)	J9681?	3ATC	Gedney Drove End	Unknown	U
21/07/34	Gordon	K1763	207	Crowland	Sgt.Goodwin/ LACs.McCabe, Easton	U
15/01/35	Hart	Unknown	3FTS	Surfleet	Unknown	
01/03/35	3 x Gauntlets	K4086/?/?	19	Dry Drayton/Smithy Fen	Sqn. Ldr.Cassidy / Flt.Lt.Broadhurst./ Flt.Sgt. Bignall	U
03/07/35	Gordon	K1766	3ATC	RAF Sutton Bridge	Flg. Off.C W.Williams	U
14/08/35	Unknown	Unknown	17?	Not known	2 x Unknown	
18/08/35	Hart	K2985	600	RAF Sutton Bridge	Unknown	U
11/09/35	Gauntlet	K4083/K4085	19	RAF Sutton Bridge	Flg. Off. J.R.MacLachlan	U
10/01/36	Bulldog	K2209	111	RAF Sutton Bridge	Flt. Lt. H.A..Simmonds	U
05/05/36	Bulldog	K1683	111	R. Nene, Sutton Bridge	Flg. Off. J.W.H.Radice	K
06/05/36	Bulldog	K2208	111	Nr RAF Sutton Bridge	Plt. Off. G.C.Cornwall	U
14/05/36	Bulldog	K1672	111	Holbeach Range	Plt. Off. M.S.Bocquet	U

Gloster Gauntlet K4086 at the end of a practice sortie for 19 Sqn's. Hendon aerobatic team. All three team aircraft ran out of fuel in thick fog which blanketed eastern England on 1 March 1935. All crashed at Smithy Fen, north of their Duxford base. [Cambridgeshire Collection]

39 Sqn. DH9A J7812 came of worst after it's encounter with a haystack in Gosberton on 29 September 1926. [Spalding Guardian]

Another season, and more facilities.

Winter was still much in evidence when, on February 19, an advance party of two Corporals and seven airmen unlocked the Camp gates to begin the 1929 'season'.

Sqn. Ldr. C. B. Cooke assumed command with an establishment split with 3 officers and 45 other ranks at the main camp and 2 officers, 12 other ranks and a civilian warden at the range. It is indicative of the advancing status of RAF Sutton Bridge's role that the commandant's rank was shortly to be upgraded to that of Wing Commander.

At the range, the quantity of ground targets remained at the six of previous years but a second bombing circle was constructed. Such was the pressure on the range facilities that practice bombing was even permitted over the airfield itself.

This year also saw the introduction of a Station Flight, formally recorded in the '540' in April 1929, a further indicator of the developing nature of aerial gunnery training in line with Trenchard's quest for quality. This was perhaps rather a grandiose title at this stage since its sole aeroplane appears to have been a venerable Bristol F2B Fighter MkIV. The identity of this 'Brisfit', adapted to carry RAE Sleeve target towing gear, is not recorded but H1634, of 1918 vintage modified to 'J' model standard, is believed to have arrived at Sutton Bridge in July of the previous year. Although not recorded by the camp diarist of 1928 as being on the establishment, this may simply reflect the generally sparse nature of the diary entries for that year. 1929's diarist was clearly a different person, which is reflected by the, relatively, more comprehensive entries - which include, at the start of 'business', the comment about a Bristol Fighter.

It is worthy of note that, from that example and from a multitude of similar sources examined in the course of this project, the usefullness of unit diaries to the researcher is directly in proportion to the time, effort and personal interest each diarist was prepared to put into that task all those years ago.

Brisfit H1634 appears to have left Sutton Bridge at some point, possibly at the close of the 1929 season, as this serial turns up on the establishment of 5 FTS at Sealand in 1930. Scrutiny of other Bristol Fighter serial records indicates this type was still in use at the camp for sleeve target towing until at least the end of 1931. For example, D7835, F4741 and F4845 are noted as allocated to Sutton Bridge in early 1931. First 'customers' and taking up the whole of April 1929, were the Army Co-operation Squadrons, Nos. 4, 13 and 26, bringing with them a mixture of Bristol F2B Fighters and the new Armstrong Whitworth Atlas. May saw them give way to a steady stream of fighter boys, which seems to confirm the events of previous years.

In the first week of May, 29 and 43 Sqns. arrived, followed by 41 and 17 at the end of that month.

It appears the 'management' was always striving to become more organised, with the objective of maximising the amount of gunnery time at the range for all pilots. A Pilots Room was established at the camp as a focal point for briefing and information. Regular weather charts were displayed - a wise move in view of the fickleness of The Wash - so that interruptions to the programme could be planned around. Range plans and firing procedures were also displayed, so that pilots could manage their firing time effectively. All small changes in their own right but collectively, professionalism was becoming the order of the day.

Meanwhile, down at the range, pilots were able to assess and correct their gunnery more quickly now that

The crew were lucky to escape from this DH9A, J7074 of 39 Sqn. when it rolled over into a dyke in a force landing near Spalding on 25 July 1927. [Spalding Guardian]

a new system of ground to air 'position of burst' signals was introduced.

At least it could not be said that the 'top brass' were not taking an interest in the expenditure of all this hot lead, for there was yet another VIP visit in June when AVM's Ellington and Scarlett kept the camp on its toes. An outcome of their inspection was a conference at 23 Group HQ to hammer out even more ideas for speeding up air firing procedures. Flt. Lt. Crawford, the camp Armament Officer, came up with a design for a new type of target frame. Made of steel, he believed it would be resilient to the ravages of machine gun bullets, thus taking less time to repair. In the event, his steel-framed target, when tested, proved to be *"...very bad."* No reason is recorded but in view of the modern practice of still using stout, wooden telegraph poles to support 30 mm cannon targets, it is reasonable to surmise the reason might be the danger from ricochets. That is a very real danger now but even in those early days the smaller velocity and spatial factors would produce relatively similar dangers.

On June 26, the range played host to a more splendid visitor in the form of a 101 Sqn. 'Sidestrand' bomber, over for the day from its base at Bircham Newton. The reason given for its arrival was: *"to carry out Backfire Tests on the range"* but no further enlightenment as to what that involved was forthcoming.

Halcyon summer days saw a steady flow of fighters through camp, with 19 Sqn. being followed by Nos. 1, 25, 23 and 111.

In August that year 23 Sqn. was detached to RAF Sutton Bridge for its two weeks annual gunnery practice. Commanding the unit at this time was Sqn. Ldr. Jones-Williams, a pilot famous for his record non-stop flight from Cranwell to Karachi earlier that year, in the Fairey Long-range Monoplane.

It was now August 14, 1929. Bathed in the noonday sun, the camp lay quiet, with little outward sign of the tragedy which had occurred. A flag outside the Adjutant's hut fluttered sadly at half-mast.

Clutching a sheaf of papers and attended by three grim-faced officers, a trench-coated Air Ministry crash investigator hurried purposefully past hangars where mechanics worked quietly upon their charges. Nearby, a cluster of pilots discussed gunnery scores just received from the ammunition store.

Crossing the camp perimeter, the little group moved on into an adjoining arable field. Here lay a twisted heap of charred metal, the object of their attention, casting an ugly scar among a broad expanse of green carrot tops. It was all that remained of J7914, the single-seat Gloster Gamecock fighter in which Flg. Off. Jones had taken off at 09.20 that morning.

He and Flg. Off. Purvis, both considered 'crack shots', were briefed to fly to the firing range on the desolate marshes at Gedney Drove End. Both aeroplanes were loaded with 200 rounds of ammunition each with which to fire at ground targets.

Purvis took off first. Then his friend opened the throttle of J7914 and followed in his wake. Jones had climbed about forty feet in the air when he banked the machine steeply. Sgt. James Hickling, a pilot with 111 Sqn., also at the camp, witnessed what happened next.

"I was standing on the 'drome, not more than 200 yards from the crash, when the Gamecock took off. It rose quite normally but soon after crossing the airfield boundary, turned steeply to the right and the nose dropped. In an instant the aeroplane dived into the ground with its engine full on and burst into flames."

Later, when asked by the Coroner for an opinion as to the cause of the accident, Sgt. Hickling replied, *"I should say it was through turning too soon after leaving the ground. He should not have tried to turn at all at that height."* Another eyewitness referred to the aeroplane being in *"...a sixty degree turn"*, before the crash. Bursting ammunition, intense heat and flames prevented would-be rescuers from approaching the stricken pilot but it was soon clear to all that he was beyond help.

Stunned by the sight, Flg. Off. Purvis circled the scene twice before landing to have his worst fears

Although a close neighbour to Sutton Bridge, 101 Sqn Boulton Paul Sidestrands based at Bircham Newton were rare visitors to the range facility. [P.H.T. Green Collection]

A portrait of Flg. Off. Charles Henry Jones of 23 Sqn.

[Lincs free Press]

confirmed. It was now that Air Force discipline and camaraderie prevailed. Purvis was ordered to carry on with his gunnery practice but first, as a mark of respect, he and other 23 Sqn. pilots flew over the crash site.

Alone, Flg. Off. Purvis flew off to the range, fired his 200 rounds and came away to find he had made the highest score of any pilot in 23 or 111, since both squadrons arrived at the Camp.

Much discussion ensued at the inquest, held in sombre mood in the pilots briefing room. The verdict of accidental death was inevitable and thus did the official curtain fall on the all too short life of Flg. Off. Charles Jones.

There was a lull in the programme when the next two squadrons, 56 and 32, departed at the beginning of September. This was to allow Permanent Staff officers an opportunity to attend the Schneider Trophy Competition, held over the Solent on 6th and 7th. No doubt they much enjoyed their well earned break, rejoicing in a second successive win for Britain.

The gunnery year drew to a close with the arrival of 3 Sqn. with its new mount, the Bristol Bulldog, a beautiful sight which would grace the sky around The Wash for many years to come. Finally, competitors began to arrive at Sutton Bridge on September 25 for the annual Brooke-Popham Cup competition. After an intensely competitive two days Flg. Off. Thomson of 56 Sqn. was declared the winner with a score of 88%.

It only remained now for the events of the year to be analysed so that the lessons learned could be incorporated into next years programme. It was considered that the trial use of airborne sleeve-targets by two pilots from each squadron, was a success and would be expanded upon next year. Final, tangible, confirmation of the success of the Camp and Range facility was evident from the visit, in October 1929, of Sqn. Ldr. P. Huskinson, an Air Ministry staff officer, to select suitable adjacent fields for the expansion of the aerodrome. In addition to the camp facilities it was vital to enlarge the range itself.

The reasons underpinning this expansion are a matter of simple logistics. New aeroplane types, such as the Bulldog and soon the Fury, would be entering service and fighter squadrons were anxious to reach proficiency as quickly as possible. Even more units, for example Fleet Air Arm Fighter Flights and coastal defence squadrons, like the Fairey III's of 35 at Bircham, were bidding for time on the range. Coupled with this pressure was the constraint placed upon the time available for operations by the weather - bear in mind aeroplanes in those days did not have 'all-weather' capability and The Wash has a reputation for its mists.

In consequence, more targets were needed to allow more aeroplanes to use the range simultaneously. The spatial effect of this was a need to disperse the targets over a larger area of the Marsh to avoid hazarding pilots. From the experiments with sleeve targets in 1928 and 1929 it seemed that air to ground targets would increasingly be supplemented by air to air, towed targets and this will be seen to be the case in subsequent years.

All in all, 1929 can be considered a watershed in the life of Sutton Bridge Camp and the Holbeach Range in terms of expansion. As the 1930's unrolled and black clouds of war loomed, this camp would play a vital role in training fighter pilots and air gunners in their science. The soundness of Trenchard's system, the methods evolved at the Range and the beneficial effects of regular practice would be seen by quality of

23 Sqn's finest! Gamecock J7914 - nearest the camera - in which Flg. Off. Charles Jones met his death at Sutton Bridge on 14 August 1929.

pilots who had to bear the initial brunt of air fighting in France and Britain in 1940. The quality of men and aeroplanes is usually undoubted but can the same be said of aeroplane armament...?

It is interesting to note that this same Range played a role in the 'feedback' system when the Central Gunnery School spent several years based at Sutton Bridge.

Into a new decade...

The majority of Permanent Staff had re-assembled at Sutton Bridge by March 10, 1930, under the command of Wg. Cdr. D.L. Allen AFC. The remainder of March was spent preparing both the Camp and the Range for the coming training season. Most onerous of these tasks was that of putting canvas onto the four Bessoneau hangar frames, left bare over the previous winter months. Much grumbling was inevitable as all airmen were obliged to work on Saturday afternoons and Sundays to complete the work in time for the April 1 opening date.

Two Army Co-operation squadrons, 4 and 13, were first to use the camp facilities. Between April 1 and October 12, they were followed by most of the squadrons from Fighting Area.

Representative of these was 23 , whose CO, Sqn. Ldr. Woolett DSO MC, a Great War veteran with 35 air victories to his credit, brought the Squadron from Kenley in July. For the second year running it would return to Kenley with less than it came.

Line of approach to the ground targets was from the landward side of the sea bank and those aeroplanes waiting their turn to fire manouevered in the vicinity of the Range between the village and the sea bank.

Although aeroplanes wheeling above their heads had become an everyday occurrance, they still provided a welcome diversion to land-workers toiling among the thousands of acres bordering Holbeach Range. Hoeing sugar beet was tedious at the best of times when, on 16th, the sight and sound of Flg. Off. Roger's silver Gamecock, J7894, caught the eye as it fell into a left hand spin, flashing in the sunlight, twisting in it's death throes.

Its brief plunge from 400 feet ended abruptly in Caudwell's beet field where, in the words of Mr. Arthur Edgley of Lutton: *"... it looked just like an enormous heap of crumpled silver paper"*. Rescuers uncovered Rogers to find him dead but with his seat straps unfastened, leading them to believe he had tried in vain to bale out. This was the only major accident at the camp that year.

During the final week of the 1930 season, representative pilots from the fighter squadrons competed for the annual Air Firing Trophy, won this year by Sgt. Cleland of 29 Sqn.

The competition heralded the closure of the camp and the Permanent Staff set about the job of removing canvas from the hangars once more. Sutton Bridge then took on a desolate air as the staff drifted back to their units and the camp was left in the care of Station Warden, Mr. Pettit and another civilian assistant, Mr. Barnshaw who settled in for the long winter vigil.

According to the RAF Flying Training Manual, referred to earlier, among the qualities required of pilots and air gunners was: *"...a considerable amount of practice in developing their judgement of distance in the air, so that they can manouevre close to the enemy without risk of collision."*

Misjudging one's attack approach was indeed a very real hazard now that air to air targets featured strongly in the range training programme. Bulldogs were not a great deal faster than the fighters they replaced (20mph above Gamecocks and Siskins) but they were substantially heavier aeroplanes (+25% loaded). Because of this, extra care was needed when cavorting around at low level as they were not so responsive as their lighter predecessors. From time to time, therefore, during their earlier years a few came to grief on The Wash range.

On September 20, 1932, for example, during the annual Brooke-Popham Competition, Flg. Off. B. Matson representing 19 Sqn. misjudged the approach speed of a target-towing Wapiti and flew into the drogue. The latter was, of necessity, quite a sturdy affair and did substantial damage to the upper starboard wing of Bulldog K2160 forcing Matson to make a very hasty but successful, landing on Durham's Farm close to the range.

29 Sqn. was halfway through its annual air firing practice when, on June 6, 1933, a similar mishap befell Flt. Sgt. Starr. Diving from 2000 feet towards a drogue, he 'over-cooked' it and, in his efforts to swerve out of danger, hit the towing cable with the lower starboard wing. His Bulldog fell into an uncontrollable spin but,

The Bristol Bulldog began to be seen on the Range from 1930, and 111 Sqn, whose K220? is seen here, were to loose a number of the type as the decade wore on.

"...it looked like an enormous heap of crumpled silver paper'. Gamecock J7894 in a sugar-beet field near the Range.

[Spalding Guardian].

keeping his head, Starr baled out with just sufficient height to deploy his parachute safely. Landing heavily he hurt his right foot but considered this a small price to pay for his life, bearing in mind his Bulldog lay completely wrecked just a short distance from where he came down.

It was perhaps inevitable that the odds - or luck - would would change against some unfortunate pilot. Flt. Sgt. Frank Baker, newly posted to 41 Sqn. just a month earlier, was flying the first detail to Holbeach range on May 18, 1934. The target drogue was being towed at 1500 feet when he dived on it. Misjudging his dive sent Bulldog K2194 crashing into the steel-framed neck severing it completely from the towing cable. This time there was no escape from the resultant spin for the pilot and Flt. Sgt. Baker perished in a plume of spray four miles offshore. A fast-rising tide hampered rescuers who had to wait six hours for the water to recede sufficiently for his body to be recovered.

Strange to relate that, apart from these three Bulldog incidents, there is no evidence of any further mishaps, at Holbeach range, involving collision with towed targets during the remainder of the decade. Maybe the difficulty simply arose as a transient situation marked by the arrival of this significantly heavier fighter coinciding with the introduction of the new practice of manouevring with towed targets. The subject raises its head again during WW2 but under somewhat different circumstances.

Of all the many aeroplane types to use Holbeach Range between the Wars, the Bristol Bulldog features most frequently in accidents. This is no reflection on its record as a frontline aeroplane however, as most of the incidents fall into the category of 'pilot error' rather than through some fundamental flaw in the design.

In addition to the three accidents involving collision with towed targets, mentioned earlier, Flt. Lt. H.A.Simmonds of 111 - the famous 'Treble-One' - Squadron bent K2209 when he landed at Sutton Bridge on January 10, 1936. In common with many grass airfields, Sutton Bridge in wet weather could become a quagmire trapping the unwary pilot. On this occasion it might have been wiser to have sent out more than just one airman to guide a wingtip as Simmonds taxied in. One wheel sank into a soft patch while the aircraft was moving quite quickly and over it went in a somersault as the nose dug in. Flt. Lt. Simmonds clambered out unscathed but his aeroplane was severely damaged.

111 returned to Sutton Bridge for annual firing practice in May 1936 and left, no doubt, more subdued than when it arrived. The squadron returned to Northolt with three Bulldogs and one pilot fewer than when it set out. First to go, on May 5, was K1683 in the fatal accident near the mouth of the River Nene. Just one day later, May 6, K2208 was next to go. Plt. Off. G.C.Cornwall choked the engine after take off, forcing him to make a hurried return to earth. On his way to the range it seems he opened the throttle a bit too quickly while climbing away from the airfield and the engine spluttered to a halt. To his credit Plt. Off. Cornwall got the nose down swiftly and landed straight ahead in a ploughed field. The aeroplane, however, ran headlong into a hedge, turned over and came to rest, completely wrecked by the side of the Midland & Great Northern Railway line a few hundred yards from the airfield perimeter. On this occasion Plt. Off.

There are time when having a carthorse around proves to be very handy!

The damage caused by collision with a target drogue is very evident here, even in this poor photograph. Flg. Off Matson was lucky to land Bulldog K2160 in such a dangerous condition. [Spalding Guardian]

Heeeave!

Judging by the similarlity between the shade of the chequers with the blue outer ring of the roundel, this badly damaged Bristol Bulldog K2173 is from 19 Sqn.

The photograph is noted as being taken at Sutton Bridge in 1931 or 1932. There was a Bulldog crash-landing recorded near the Range on 1/8/31, but the ORB states '54' not 19 Sqn. However, the 1931 entries seemed to have been scrawled in particular haste and, not for the first time, could be in error at that point.

[Air Britain Archives]

Cornwall escaped injury but just over a year later, his luck ran out, for he was killed in an accident on July 16, 1937 while flying a Gloster Gauntlet.

A great deal of effort, over many decades, has been put into raising awareness of the dangers of 'foreign object damage' (FOD). This is not a modern phenomenon by any means since a little carelessness on the ground at any time may become lethal in the air. Such was the verdict of an enquiry into the loss of another 111 Sqn. Bulldog, K1672, only a week later, on May 14. Acting Plt. Off. M.S.Bocquet not only joined the ranks of the 'Caterpillar Club' that day but could also count himself fortunate to be alive to do so.

Over the range on a firing exercise, the controls of K1672 jammed at an altitude of 1500 feet. The aeroplane became uncontrollable and began to lose height rapidly. Plt. Off. Bocquet kept his head though and baled out with sufficient height remaining to land safely on the foreshore, watching his Bulldog hurtle into the sea nearby. Subsequent enquiry considered the controls probably locked due to a loose machine gun cleaning plug, rolling about and fouling the base of the control column. Thus ended one of the most eventful and costly two-week practice camps for any single squadron since Sutton Bridge opened.

On the other hand by the end of 1936, the prospect of war loomed greater with each new year. Not only would the pace of activity at the Camp and the Range move into top gear but the volume of mishaps that increased activity brought with it, would increase substantially upto the beginning of WW 2.

March 1931 saw the familiar sight of an advance party arriving at Sutton Bridge, followed on the 10th by the main body of Staff, this year drawn from 2 Flying Training School (FTS), RAF Digby. Only the bare minimum of effort seems to have been spent this year by the Station official diarist. Hiding behind an illegible signature his record of events take up a mere sixteen lines of scrawling text on a single page of the Form 540.

The demise of one of 2 FTS's Armstrong Whitworth Atlas's, J9540, which crashed on landing at the airfield on April 9 was considered sufficiently noteworthy. Flt. Lt. Davies, pilot, was unhurt although his unnamed passenger received slight injuries.

More aerial tow-target gear was installed in the Station Flight Brisfits during April under the watchful eye of a certain Mr Ashworth from the Royal Aircraft Establishment (RAE).

Fierce storms hit the district towards the end of April, causing damage to a hangar, requiring a week long repair by MOD 'Works and Bricks' Department. Hangarage at this time was still of the steel-framed canvas-covered variety but later, in 1933, the first rigid hangar, an 'Hinaidi' design, was erected. This structure still exists (1995) and is believed to be the only surviving example of its type in Lincolnshire and possibly the UK.

Among the litany of accidents to equipment and personnel, attached to the station and associated target range, one diary item stands out: *"30/4/31 A horse, property of Mr.H.C. Wright, wounded by shot from Lewis gun near range"!.*

Over the next three months not a single entry described events at the Station and apart from a Bulldog of 54 Sqn. force-landing at the range on August 1, 1931 seems to have been accident-free.

It has been noted elsewhere that 25 Sqn. visited Sutton Bridge from May 25 to June 12 and their representatives in the Brooke-Popham competition, in September, Flt. Lt. C.R. Hancock DFC and Flg. Off. H. St G.Burke tied for 4th and 7th places respectively.

Whilst 25 seemed pleased to record that event in their own ORB, the parsimonious Sutton Bridge diarist deigned not to record the eventual winner.

Closing officially on October 26, the clearing-up party departed on the 30th and the Camp was left silent and deserted once more.

Sutton Bridge Station Flight, the permanent (at least while the Camp was open) flying unit employed

Bulldog K2210 shows off the distinctive markings of 29 Sqn. K2210 survived, where '08 and '09 did not.

to tow aerial targets over The Wash range, expanded rapidly from the venerable Bristol F2B Fighter of the 1929 to 1931 period. As mentioned earlier, that lone Brisfit of 1929 appears to have been augmented later, since at least three were in use by 1931.

The precise aircraft establishment for 3 Armament Training Camp, as it was known from 1932, is obscure but following the Bristol Fighters the principal towing types in use during the 1930's were Westland's Wapiti and Wallace, Fairey's IIIF and Gordon with the Hawker Henley arriving just prior to the War.

Judging by the amount of flying these tugs were required to perform it is not surprising to find mishaps occurring in their ranks occasionally, in addition to those among the visiting units. In 1932, for example, Fairey IIIF, J9144, crashed at the Range on July 11, injuring the pilot. Next day a replacement Wapiti was flown up from Eastchurch but that, too, failed to reach its destination intact. Nearing The Wash, Sgt. Nunnerby, became lost in low cloud and mist. Spotting what he thought was a suitable grass field he decided to land to establish his whereabouts. Unfortunately the 'grass' turned out to be a field of barley the stems of which clogged the propeller and undercarriage to such an extent that the Wapiti turned somersault. Both Nunnerby and his observer, Corporal Dobson, pinned beneath the wreckage, were injured by the impact and when released were admitted to Kings Lynn hospital.

More visits, more VIPs.

In contrast to 1931, 1932 exudes activity and in particular a resurgence of interest from the 'brass', the latter being evidenced by a procession of VIP's visiting the Camp that year.

Flt. Lt. Connelly brought in the advance party on March 3, which soon had the transportable Wireless (W/T) Station set up in time for the arrival of the main party, whose staff was drawn from a variety of units. Station Commander, Wg.Cdr. W. Sowrey arrived a day later, bringing 3 ATC under the control of the Air Armament School (AAS) with its HQ located at RAF Eastchurch.

Under the watchful eye of Flg. Off. Hooper, the range party began their own task of erecting targets out on Holbeach Marsh and March 16 saw two Fairey IIIF's fly in to Sutton Bridge, bringing Flg. Off.'s Hales and Hyland to assist with range duties.

The procession of VIP's included three visits by Sqn. Ldr. Ivens from Eastchurch, Sqn. Ldr. MacKenzie from HQ Fighting Area, Air Commodore Brock, Brigadier Wavell and several visits each by AM Higgins, Major General Jackson, Gp, Capt. Tedder, Air Commodores Bowen, Masterson and Gossage, a group of Danish Air Officers ... and so the list went on. The SWO must have had a field day for hardly a month seemed to pass without VIP visits of some sort, a pattern which continued for many subsequent years. It had taken a long time - ten years - but these visits were a visible sign of the changing mood among the Service higher echelons in general. War was coming and Sutton Bridge was a vital cog in the machinery of war.

As far as the 'real' business of the camp was concerned, first to fly in on March 26 was Sqn. Ldr. Simpson with 4 (AC) Sqn. Staying until April 29, 4 was followed by the shiny new Hawker Furies of 1 and the Bulldogs of 3 Sqn.

Deliberations by the 'Brass' seemed to bring about a short experiment to lengthen the Range opening hours. Peacetime 'working hours' of the RAF have traditionally been Monday to Friday plus Saturday mornings but on two weekends, May 7/8 and 14/15, the Range was kept open from 07.00 to 18.00 on both Saturday and Sunday. There is no sign of longer hours occurring again that year and setting a precedent for present day objectors, it may be due to the local population and fishermen in particular, voicing disapproval. On several occasions the diary notes meetings and visits by senior officers with Boston fishermen, local community representatives, wildlife and countryside protection groups.

May 21 saw the departure of Nos.1 and 3 Sqns., this pair being replaced by Bulldogs of 19 and Siskins of 29 Sqn.

During their first week 29 had a spot of bother with their gun synchronising gear. Reports of bullets hitting propellers filtered back to the Air Ministry, two of

Above and left: What's the serial then? Siskin J9874 of 1 Sqn, following the storm of April 1931. There is evidence of an earlier repair that married the port lower wing of J992- to J9874 to suggest J9924 (the'4' being the remainder of the aircraft's true serial painted on the centre section) but the latter was a DH60 Moth serial.

[P.H.T. Green Collection]

Right: J8404, a Siskin of 1 Sqn left in a very sorry state following storm damage at Sutton bridge in April 1931.

Below: A further view showing J9874 and the storm damage.

[P.H.T. Green Collection]

whose inspectors hurried north to investigate the cause. No explanation was recorded in the station diary and although the reason for the trouble remains a mystery, 29 Sqn. left with 19 on June 11 at the end of its allotted time. In his biography, Douglas Bader recalled a narrow escape when he, too, shot off part of his propeller over Holbeach Range during Summer Camp with 23 Sqn. in 1931. A couple of days later 23 (minus its 'A' Flight which is believed to have been detached for duty at the Hendon Pageant) and 56 Sqns. flew in to Sutton Bridge. The latter squadron is actually written in the diary as '54', the error coming to light through closer examination of an unusual incident noted on June 18.

The River Nene flows close by the airfield, the camp entrance perimeter, for example, being separated only by the huge bank surmounted by a tarmac road. Ruler straight for mile after mile, the banks at this point have broad, gently sloping grassy tops dropping away suddenly to an extremely deep cut channel. It was on this day that Sgt. L.H. Holman of 56 Sqn. became a local hero by helping to save a child from drowning in the fast flowing tide. Reported in the *Spalding Guardian,* the story went as follows:

"Little Owen Burton fell into the river while playing on the airfield-side bank, near the swing bridge. Shouts for help brought railway porter Mr J. R. Harper running from the nearby station. Although in poor health and practically exhausted by his run from the station, Harper plunged into the river and brought the boy to the surface. A strong current was running though and had not Sgt. Holman also dived fully clothed into the river and gone to Mr Harper's aid, in all probability both he and the boy would have perished. Good fortune prevailed, however, and the boy was brought out unconscious but alive."

56 Sqn. left Sutton Bridge on July 1 followed next day by 23. With its sleek Fury I's, 25 Sqn. had the camp to itself until replaced by 17 Sqn. on July 16, which itself was joined shortly after by 'A' Flight of 23 Sqn. on July 23. Then came 41, 111, 32 and 54 Sqns. in turn throughout the summer, the latter leaving Sutton Bridge on September 9. Of these units only 25 Sqn. suffered one minor landing accident, that occurring on July 11.

Extending the Holbeach Marsh Range boundaries brought the opening of No. 2 Air Firing Range for business on July 25. This additional facility heralded the arrival of the Fleet Air Arm (FAA) to use the range simultaneously with the RAF. First to arrive were 402 and 407 Flights FAA, using the Camp at the same time as 43 Sqn. RAF. What a feast of fighters to be seen over The Wash in those days!

On September 21 while 402 flew north to join HMS *Courageous* at Invergordon, 407 Flight left for RAF Netheravon. These two were replaced by 404 Flight coming in from Netheravon and 401 Flight direct from HMS *Furious.*

But tragedy struck in the afternoon of September 26. One of 401 Flight's Fairey Flycatcher aeroplanes, N9929, loaded with four 20lb Cooper bombs swooped repeatedly over the bombing targets. Three times Lt. Henry Maitland King RN released a single bomb at the white circle floating below. He was seen to circle twice more but without releasing the remaining bomb. As the silver biplane dived for a third time there was a flash followed a second later by the dull, flat report of an explosion. Engulfed by flames, the stricken Flycatcher fell vertically onto the wild marshland below, burying itself in the oozing mud. Running and stumbling 500 yards across the mudflats the NCO in charge of the range reached the wreckage only to be held at bay by intense flames. It took twenty minutes for the blaze to subside, too late to be of any help to the poor pilot. Returning a verdict of 'Accidental death' the jury brought this sad episode to a close in sombre mood at an inquest held in the Camp Education Hut next evening. In the best tradition of the Service Lt. King's body, escorted by his friend Lt. Garnett RN, was conveyed by rail to his home in Llanfairfechan for burial.

With the air firing 'season' drawing to a close, October 3 saw an experimental demonstration of a 'Flag' towed target, arranged by the Station Flight for the benefit of Gp. Capts. Tedder (OC AAS Eastchurch), Bradley and Baldwin with Mr Howarth a civilian from RAE Farnborough in attendance. 401 and 404 Flights returned to their bases that week and 25 Sqn. flew in to complete its period of practice, having been interupted in July by its participation in the RAF Pageant at Hendon. When it departed on October 12 this signalled the arrival of pilots for the two-day

The sturdy Atlas, mainstay of Army Co-Op squadrons in the early 1930's, was a regular summer visitor to Sutton Bridge. Here J9541 of 4 (AC) Sqn in seen in front of the canvas hangars and mess tent. [P.H.T. Green Collection]

Fleet Air Arm Fairey Flycatcher N9928, stable-mate of 401Flight's N9929 which crashed at Holbeach Range in 1932 when one of its bombs exploded prematurely. [Westland Ltd]

annual Brooke-Popham Trophy competition, won this year by Sgt. J. Williams of 3 Sqn. As usual the competition drew the 1932 season to a close. Post season conferences, reviewing events at the Range, were held at AAS HQ Eastchurch at the end of the month and the Camp closed down officially with the departure of Wg. Cdr. Sowrey on November 14.

On March 3, 1933 he was back at Sutton Bridge in command for a new firing season.

Bombs and Bullets...

It is difficult to estimate the quantity of .303 ammunition fired annually at the Holbeach Range but it could easily have been of the order of 500,000 rounds. If, for example, 15 squadrons attended, each with 12 aeroplanes, these 180 pilots are known to fire off 200 rounds per sortie thus they would consume 36,000 rounds. It would not be unreasonable to assume each pilot might complete at least ten sorties during his two-week camp. If this were the case that alone would produce an overall expenditure of 360,000 rounds. Allowing for the annual firing competition and a margin of error it is reasonable to suggest that at least half a million rounds would need to be stocked at the Camp, all of which was brought in by railway to the village station. Bearing in mind the range also catered for bombing, villagers might have been quite alarmed had they been aware of such a large quantity of explosive ordnance moving through their back yard. It is also a sobering thought to remember that the .303 round was in regular use in aeroplane weapons being fired at the range for about thirteen years prior to WW2, so that the quantity of spent cartridges deposited on the outmarsh over those years must run to many millions. The more intensive wartime use would add several million more.

The annual ordnance quota usually arrived with the main party, this year being March 3. The Officer's and Airmen's Messes were opened up, telephones laid on to Camp and Range and the wireless station set up once again as 3 ATC blossomed into life like a new plant in the Fenland springtime.

Three Fairey Gordons were brought in from AAS Eastchurch to form the Station Flight. Notices circulating in the locality announced the imminent opening of the Range.

In the months from March 27 2 (AC) Sqn. lead a procession of Nos. 32, 54, 29, 41, 56, 17 (after the Hendon Pageant), 111, 800 Sqn FAA (ex HMS *Courageous*), 801 (HMS *Furious*), 3, 25, 1, 43, and

WINNERS OF
THE BROOKE-POPHAM TROPHY
FOR AIR-FIRING MARKSMANSHIP.

Year	Name	Squadron
1927	Flt. Lt. H. C. Calvey	23
1928	Flg. Off. C.W.McK. Thompson	43
1929	Flg. Off. Thomson	56
1930	Sgt. Cleland	29
1931	Not known	-
1932	Sgt. J. Williams	3
1933	Flg. Off. E. M. Donaldson	3
1934	Flg. Off. E. M. Donaldson	3
1935	Flt. Lt. H. Broadhurst	19
1936	Flt. Lt. H. Broadhurst	19

SUMMER CAMP 1932

Sleek Fury I's of 25 Sqn are drawn up in front of the Watch Office and canvas hangars at Sutton Bridge, whilst pilots and ground crew pose for the camera - one can almost imagine the caption "Armament Practice Camp, Sutton Bridge 1932"!

[Cambridgeshire Collection]

finally 19 Sqn. On September 11 the Camp even managed to squeeze in a four-day visit by four Bulldogs from AAS for air firing practice (these were probably K1638, 1648, 1669 and 1670).

Activity at Sutton Bridge was now subject to almost continuous direct interest by the 'Top Brass', led by the AOC-in-C ADGB, Air Marshal Sir Robert Brooke-Popham who made no less than five visits to the Camp during the year. One of these was to present his Air Marksman trophy personally to Flg. Off. E.M. Donaldson of 3 Sqn. The latter was destined to achieve prominence as a WW2 fighter pilot, a post-war air-speed record holder and in more recent times, the respected air correspondent of the *Daily Telegraph.*

Station Flight aircraft flew back to Eastchurch on October 30 but unusually, there was an air of indecision about closure of the Camp for the winter. Posting of all Airmen was placed in abeyance on November 3 then, just a week later, was reinstated for all except a group detailed to keep the Camp open during winter.

Having completed its alloted two weeks on October 7, the Hawker Demons of 23 Sqn. were held back to undertake a significant experiment involving air-firing at night, with tracer ammunition at illuminated targets. To help accomplish this exciting new task a detachment of soldiers arrived on October 9, complete with two lorries on each of which was mounted a large searchlight.

Positioned on the sea bank at each end of the Range, these searchlights sought out and illuminated towed drogues, holding them in their beams while the two-seaters let fly with tracer rounds. Night trials continued under the watchful eye of Gp. Capt. Tedder from HQ AAS until October 18 when at last 23 Sqn. departed, making way for the annual firing competition.

There is no record of the success or otherwise of the 1933 night firing trial but from the reappearence of 23 Sqn. in a similar role for a week in October 1934, it is reasonable to assume it would be only a short time before practical operating problems were ironed out and more squadrons would fire at night.

Not least of these difficulties (apart from the obvious one of actually piloting an aeroplane in the dark) was the co-ordination needed to bring the target tug into close proximity to its 'attacker' over the desolate Holbeach Marsh. No mean feat even with the aid of searchlights!

By the time the 1935 season got under way it was clear that night firing was to remain an established feature of training at Sutton Bridge. Lengthening the

In July 1933, 801 Sqn.was aboard HMS Furious operating the Hawker Nimrod, an example of which, K2824, is seen here. 801 Sqn. was one of several FAA units to visit RAF Sutton Bridge that year and amongst its pilots was Lt. J. A. T. Ryde, RN. Lt. Ryde flew Nimrod K2827 into RAF Sutton Bridge on 20/7/33 and remained there until 28/7/33. In that period he made 17 air firing sorties over the range in a total of 9 flying hours, before making a 90 minutes transit flight back to Furious. Lt. Ryde was posted to RAE Farnborough for experiemental flying duties which earned him an AFC and her rose to the rank of Gp. Capt. [P.H.T.Green Collection]

Range programme in this way brought with it problems of manning and organisation, matters which were delegated to Wg. Cdr. De Crespigny from HQ Fighting Area who arrived in March to sort out more formal administration, accomodation and personnel arrangements.

Returning now to 1934, aerial towing duties were taken over by Fairey Gordon aircraft, a few examples of which were involved in accidents at the airfield and range. Equipped with 'Drogue' boxes, these Gordons had cable reels installed inside and beneath their long cockpit. Boxes containing 'Flag' targets were attached to the fuselage sides. Drogues resembled an oval wind-sock in shape with the dimensions of a fighter fuselage, while Flags consisted of a flat length of canvas which could be towed in the vertical or horizontal plane. Targets were streamed on a Bowden cable, winched out to a distance of 1,000 feet behind the Gordon flying at heights varying between 1,500 and 2,000 feet.

All in a days work...

Towing aircraft cautiously prescribed a large circle over the Range, in order to avoid being in a direct line of fire. Attacking pilots were briefed to begin their practice upon a hand signal from the observer in the towing aircraft. Up to three targets were carried and on completion of each attacking section's session against a target, that target was released to float down to the range below for marking. Ammunition for each attacker was smeared with a distinctive colour paint prior to take-off. This colour would later show clearly round each shothole, thus enabling the performance of a particular pilot or gunner to be identified.

The training routine began with each pilot or air-gunner firing at the wooden framed, canvas ground targets. When considered proficient they graduated to air-to-air firing and it was scores in this latter stage which counted towards a course assessment.

Marking for low-level bombing practice involved range staff taking bearings on the flash and smoke from explosions, from several observation towers. These bomb-plots were telephoned to the main range control tower where the fall of bombs was quickly co-ordinated. Each pilot's results were then telephoned to the airfield for discussion when he landed.

This aspect of a pilot's training drew acutely upon his perception of distance, height, angles, speed and in-flight attitude. Such factors were often influenced by the poor weather conditions for which The Wash area is notorious and at the prevailing operating heights there was little margin for error.

Former Leading Aircraftman J.L Goward was, from 1937, an airframe rigger at Sutton Bridge. Fifty years on he recalled: *"It was the custom for the engine fitter or rigger ground crew of a particular aeroplane to double-up as drogue operator on towing trips. Pay for that extra duty was the princely sum of one shilling (5p) per day as flight pay."*

Confirming implementation of the experiments

Fairey Gordon K1763 of 207 Sqn. Bricham Newton crashed at North Bank, one and a half miles north of Crowland on 12 July 1934. [via B. Baines]

mentioned in 1933 he went on:*"towing duty could occur at night as well as daytime, particularly as the war drew closer. Illuminated by searchlights at each landward end of the range, targets were held in the beams while aircraft made several firing passes."*

Fairey Gordons were in evidence at Sutton Bridge by mid-1934 and as LAC Goward observed: ".*"..we enjoyed many hours of day and night flying, interspersed with 'hairy' experiences which made that shilling-a-day flight pay well earned indeed."*

One such incident alarmed those on the ground just as much as those in the air.

Engaged in target towing on July 3, 1934, a Gordon suffered engine failure. Losing height rapidly its pilot pointed the nose inland, seeking a flat field near the range. It appeared to the villagers of Gedney Drove End though that he might drop into their school playground but the pilot - who may have had similar misgivings - lifted the nose a fraction more, reached the safety of Mr Slater's grass field next door, clipping a hedge with the starboard wingtip as he slid the big biplane in. Mechanics from Sutton Bridge could not restart the engine so the aeroplane was dismantled and carted ignominiously back to Camp.

A whole year passed by before another Gordon mishap which, in view of their high workload, is a very creditable record.

Perhaps it was the reporting of this sort of occurrance to HQ which brought up a proposal to acquire a field adjacent to the range as the site of a new emergency landing ground. Whatever the cause, it warranted a visit by AM Brooke-Popham and Wg. Cdr. De Crespigny to the Camp in May 1934, in connection with the project which subsequently came to fruition, contributing much to the future safety of pilots in trouble over the range.

Having joined the staff of 3 ATC in February Flg. Off. Cedric Williams was getting the hang of life as a tug pilot by the time he was briefed to tow targets over the range on July 3, 1935. Lifting the nose of K1766 when the engine suddenly spluttered to a halt. Dropping like a brick from thirty feet into a wheat field it turned somersault when the crop acted as a vicious brake. Williams emerged unhurt from underneath the wreckage.

OFFICERS COMMANDING
RAF SUTTON BRIDGE 1926 - 1935
No. 3 Armament Practice Camp
No. 3 Armament Training Camp

YEAR	NAME
1926	Flt. Lt. A. R. Mackenzie.
1927	Sdn. Ldr. A. R. Arnold DSC, DFC.
1928	Sqn. Ldr. W. Sowrey DFC, AFC.
1929	Sqn. Ldr. Cooke.
1930	Wg. Cdr. D. L. Allen AFC.
1931	Wg. Cdr. W. Sowrey DFC, AFC.
1932	Wg. Cdr. W. Sowrey DFC, AFC.
1933	Wg. Cdr. W. Sowrey DFC, AFC.
1934	Wg. Cdr. W. Sowrey DFC, AFC.
1935 (to Aug)	Sqn. Ldr. C. L. King MC, DFC.

This incident can be viewed as a benchmark in time, with Williams typifying that breed of pilot whose age and career situation destined them for front line service in the forthcoming war. Posted later in the 30's to 17 Sqn, Flg. Off. Williams made a return visit to Sutton Bridge this time as a fighter pilot on the other end of the target. On that occasion, October 28, 1938, he was returning to the airfield at night and misjudged his landing approach. Undershooting he flew Gloster Gauntlet K5345 into the ground some 200 yards short of the flare path. Once again he walked away unscathed.

Having survived these two mishaps and with many years flying experience under his belt, Williams went on to play a distinguished role in the Battle of Britain. Promoted Squadron Leader of 17 in July 1940, he

"...for an extra shilling a day". Ground crew often doubled as winch operators in aircraft such as Wallace K606-, one of Sutton Bridge Station Flight's target tugs.

[J. Goward]

Westland Wallace I K3562, a rebuilt airframe that was formerly Wapiti K1346

[Westland Ltd]

personally claimed a Dornier Do17 and a Junkers Ju88 before being killed in action on August 25, 1940 at the age of thirty years.

Returning from leave on December 13, 1933 all airmen were greeted by the news that the ground firing range was to be ready for action by end of January 1934. It must have been a cold, uncharitable job out there on the Marsh in the depth of winter but the seeds of war were being sown and the Air Force needed more live firing capacity. Firing therefore began much earlier than had been the practice in previous years - and on the date stipulated!

Five squadrons sent small detachments at two or three day intervals, flying into Sutton Bridge then returning to base daily. This was a departure from the usual practice but the Camp accomodation facilities and majority of staff were not yet in place for a full-scale programme under winter conditions, so there was nowhere for aircrew to bed down nor have their aeroplanes serviced. The Officer's Mess remained closed until March when the Main Party Staff arrived from Eastchurch. Until then Nos.19 (Duxford), 29 (North Weald), 41 (Northolt), 54 and 111 (Hornchurch) Sqns operated from their bases during the month of February.

From time to time new faces appeared over the range as time permitted. For the first time mighty Handley Page Hinaidi bombers from 503 Sqn. at Waddington trundled across the range to give their gunners a bit of practice, returning in ones and twos intermittantly. Similarly, Wapitis of 600 Sqn. from Hendon popped up on other days while 207 Sqn., just down the road at Bircham Newton despatched a single Wallace for gun tests every now and again. Good use seems to have been made of the extra month of toil.

Arriving on March 8, Wg. Cdr. J. Sowrey took command again and with the Officers mess open and Main Staff operational, two days later declared the Range fully open. By that time Station Flight aeroplanes, under the command of Flt. Lt. V. Q. Blackden, had also arrived.

Over the previous winter a new training syllabus had been prepared and it was decreed that Camp Armament Officers drawn from all three Armament Camps would test it at first hand. For this purpose Bulldog aircraft were sent to Sutton Bridge from AAS HQ Flight, Eastchurch and between March 9 and 16 these new operating procedures were tried out over Holbeach Range, under the watchful eye of Air Cdre. Pattinson DSO MC DFC, Commandant of AAS and many of his subordinates. Evidently it all worked well since AAS Staff and Camp Armament Officers dispersed to their bases and the firing programme got under way on March 23 with 13 (AC) Sqn. 3 ATC Camp Armament Officer at this time was Flt. Lt. Victor Beamish, whose brother was destined to return to Sutton Bridge several years later as Station Commander, Central Gunnery School in 1942.

23 Sqn. followed on and interspersed by VIP visits, the now familiar procession of fighter squadrons

Flg. Off. MacLachlan's Gauntlet K4083 chewed up the tail of 19 Sqn's CO's K4095 in a taxying mishap at Sutton Bridge.

A truly delightful air-to-air of a flight of Gauntlets of 19Sqn from Duxford en-route to practice on the range at Sutton Bridge. The picture shows the typical pre-war colour scheme and the closeness of flying! K4095, the leader with the chequered tail was damaged in a landing accident with K4083 on 11 September 1935 at RAF Sutton Bridge. [Business Press International]

graced the broad Fenland sky. Brightly decorated Bulldogs abounded when, in May, 41 and 54 Sqns. flew in, the former losing Sgt. F.Baker in K2194 in an accident referred to earlier. June brought 32 and 56 Squadrons and 3 in July accompanied by 800 Sqn. FAA. Navy blue was much in evidence on the ground when Rear Admiral Sir Alexander Ramsey, C-in-C Aircraft Carriers paid a visit to watch some of his charges at practice.

Annual Air Exercises interrupted 19 and 25 Sqn during mid-July 1934 but both returned to complete their practice at the month end. While these two were absent, 'B' Flight Bulldogs from AAS HQ brought a batch of potential Squadron Armament Officers under training to sample the joys of air firing at first hand for a week. August saw 43 Sqn. Furies sharing Wash airspace with aircraft of 802 Sqn. FAA, followed by Furies from 1 and Bulldogs of 'Treble-One' in September. The programme was brought to a close by 17 and 29 Sqn., both of whom departed on October 9.

Ten days later Air Marshal Brooke-Popham, accompanied by a veritable plethora of 'brass-hats', graced the annual air-firing competition, won for the second time by Flg. Off. E.M. Donaldson of 3 Sqn.

Autumn brought a repetition of the night flying trials of the previous year when 23 Sqn., no doubt to the dismay of the local villagers, flew between 18.00 and 02.00 hours firing off loads of tracer for a couple

600 Sqn. exchanged the aging Westland Wapiti for Hawker Harts. K2985, one of its new mounts was written off in a landing accident at Sutton Bridge on 18 July 1935.

of weeks. No attempt was made this year to keep the camp open through the winter so perhaps the logistical problems involved were deemed not worth the effort. Whatever the reason, on November 21 shortly after the Station Flight left for Eastchurch, the Camp gates were padlocked for the winter.

Early starts to the firing season were now an established pattern. In mid-January 1935 this meant target repairs were set in hand out on the bleak marsh, mains water turned on to the Camp and tested early in February and even the drains subjected to inspection by Command M.O.! By the time telephone service was connected towards the end of February all was ready for the 15-strong advance party.

Command was assumed this year by Sqn. Ldr. C.L. King MC DFC who declared the range open on March 4, coinciding with the arrival of 41 and 111 Sqns. Thereafter Nos. 2, 3, 25, 800 FAA (HMS *Courageous*), 802 FAA (HMS *Eagle*), 56, 54, 65, 29, 600, 32, 17, 1, 23 and finally 19 Sqn. in mid-September.

Mishaps still occured as, for example, when 600 Sqn. wrote off Hart K2985 on August 18 in a landing accident and Flg. Off. J.R.MacLachlan (19 Sqn) 'put up a black' by taxying a shiny new Gloster Gauntlet, K4083, into K4095 his CO's personal mount. James MacLachlan, another typical product of the mid-1930's RAF, redeemed himself later, not least as CO of 46 Sqn. during the majority of the Battle of Britain and retiring in the '50s as Group Captain.

1935 was, of course, the year of King George V's Silver Jubilee for which the RAF staged a flypast. Sutton Bridge played host to nine Hawker Harts from 15 Sqn. for a day on July 2, as part of the practice for this Royal event.

Playing host was also regarded as a necessary part of maintaining good relations between the Camp and the local community. It was in this context that a motley group of clergy and gentry, representing the Society for the Protection of Rural England, accompanied by two senior RAF officers visited Holbeach Range to observe the effect of Air Firing on local bird life. Taking place on July 11 it could not have been a particularly thorough examination as later the same day the two RAF officers also managed to find time to visit the schoolmaster at Gedney Drove End to investigate a complaint of annoyance caused by aircraft as they proceeded to and from the Range. The school visit seems to have been a more productive session since Station Standing Orders were amended to try to alleviate the problem.

The 1935 VIP visits at the Camp are quite well documented and while not an exceptional year, nevertheless no less than 54 separate visits by senior officers were recorded between the opening on March 5 and closure on November 21.

Sqn. Ldr. King's tenure as CO was shortlived when, in August, he was promoted to Wing Commander and posted, leaving the damp Fens for sunnier climes of HQ RAF Iraq. Wg. Cdr. Harry Smith MC took his place as OC, this popular man remaining in command for a number of years until posted in November 1938 to command 9 Sqn. at Stradishall, where, just a few months later, he met with a tragic death in an air crash.

The epitomy of 1930's pilots!

Flg. Off. James MacLachlan (left) with Flt. Lt. Harry Broadhurst (centre), twice winner of the Brooke-Popham Trophy for aerial gunnery. Also in the photograph is Plt. Off. B. G. Morris.

Among the comprehensive diary entries this year was noted a curious item on September 5, as follows:

"Flying Flea (+ M Mignet) for repair." This refers to one of the civilian home-built aeroplanes of a notorious French design but no explanation for the repair is recorded. Mignet was in the area on a sales tour and may have met with a mishap.

It fell to 19 Sqn. to stay on to conduct the night firing trials in September. A name already notable in the RAF as a marksman par excellence and soon to become even more prominent, Flt. Lt. Harry Broadhurst, established a record score for night firing during the trials. Furthermore when, for the first time, the Brooke-Popham trophy competition was cancelled, Broadhurst was adjudged the winner on his performance from the annual training programme results, in which 19 also emerged in first place.

Annual leave for ground staff, in 1935, began in October of that year. Another new innovation, Winter firing practice, began on a reduced scale, with what was called 1 Short Armament Training Course, on November 1.

Detachments of fighter aeroplanes from Nos. 4, 13, 16 (AC) and 18 followed by 57 (Bomber) Sqn arrived at Sutton Bridge, staying until November 21. Further small numbers flew in from Nos. 2, 4, 13, 16, 26 (AC), again swelled by bombers from 15 and 18 Sqns collectively forming 2 (Short) Armament Course which finished on December 16. With the end of these two short courses 3 Armament Training School, Sutton Bridge rapidly went to sleep for its regular winter hibernation. When it re-awoke in during the spring of 1936, life at the Camp would never be quite the same again. The country was heading inexorably towards war.

From 1936 Sutton Bridge, while continuing to do what it did best, would gradually cast off its summer camp image and take on the role of 'finishing school' in the run-up to conflict.

Chapter Two

False Peace - Phoney War!

Sqn. Ldr. Philip 'Dickie' Barwell was a fighter pilot, an outstanding leader of men and a true 'Fen Tiger'.

A native of Peterborough, he joined the RAF in 1925 and led 46 Squadron into combat from RAF Digby, on the northern boundary of the Fens. His gallantry in action on October 21, 1939 earned him a DFC for routing the first enemy air attack on a convoy off the Lincolnshire coast, during which Barwell displayed qualities of discipline, leadership and courage which were to become his hallmark. It is the early part of his all too short wartime flying career which will be outlined here, illustrating how men, places and events become interwoven in this story.

Responsible for providing convoy air protection along the Lincolnshire coast, 46 Sqn. was ordered on October 21 to fly to its forward base at North Coates Fitties. Early that afternoon six Hurricanes of 'A' Flight, lead by Sqn. Ldr. Barwell, were scrambled to patrol a convoy off Spurn Head. Sector Control then reported by radio: *"Twelve enemy floatplanes approaching convoy at 1000 feet - intercept!"*

Spotted by one of the Flight the enemy, quickly identified as Heinkel He115's, came under fire from Naval anti-aircraft guns and promptly turned away from the convoy.

Barwell manoeuvred to close with his quarry, easily overhauling the slow torpedo bombers straggling along at 4000 feet, heading south. Wheeling his Hurricanes up-sun, he called calmly for *"line astern"* and *"No.5 attack"* then, selecting the left-hand enemy aircraft, told his pilots to pick their own target and follow him down. Pushing throttle and stick forward, he bore down on the '115, opening fire at 400 yards.

Closing his target very fast he broke away at only 30 yards range, with the satisfaction of seeing flames trailing from the '115's starboard engine. This Heinkel dived to the water below, flopped onto the surface whereupon its starboard wing collapsed. In this first pass Plt. Off. Frost and Flt. Sgt. Shackley together brought down another '115 which crashed into the sea.

Keeping an overall watch on the attack after he broke away, Sqn. Ldr. Barwell spotted two enemy floatplanes beating a hasty retreat further south towards The Wash. Calling for support he set off in pursuit.

The Luftwaffe prepares for action against North Sea convoys with a Heinkel 115B, one of the war's principal maritime reconnaisance attack aircraft. A practice torpedo is winched into the bomb bay of an He115 from a simple but effective flat bottomed work boat, while other armourers load ammunition for the defensive weapons. [Heinkel Archiv, via J.Huggins.]

Heinkel He115B floatplane S4+LH of 1/Kfg406 was one of the convoy raiders put to flight by Dickie Barwell's 46 Sqn. Hurricanes. Powered by two 960hp BMW radials giving it a top speed of 105mph, with only two MG15 machine guns, this lightly armed torpedo bomber was no match for contemporary RAF fighters. [Don Hannah.]

Closing once more to 300 yards he fired off all his remaining ammunition at one e/a with no apparant result. Then Plt. Off. Cowles and Flt. Sgt. Shackley, joining the fray, fired at this target also without visible effect. With the CO urging them to get in closer, it fell to Plt. Off. Plummer to finish off the Heinkel and it plunged upside-down into The Wash below.

While this fight was in progress, Plt. Offs Lefevre and Frost were harrying yet another '115 which was flying in and out of cloud cover also in the direction of The Wash. Snapping at the e/a as it ran out of cover they forced it to 'pancake' onto the sea with both engines stopped.

Philip Reginald 'Dickie' Barwell DFC after his promotion to Group Captain.

The epitome of a pre-WW2 fighter squadron leader, he 'led from the front' inspiring all those under his command.

As station commander of Biggin Hill in 1942, although restricted by his rank, he still managed to fly occasional operational sorties and it was during one such flight that he died, shot down by a Spitfire in a tragic accident of mistaken aircraft identity.

[Crown copyright].

Re-assembled by Sqn. Ldr. Barwell into formation, the Flight returned to Digby in bouyant mood. Little opposition by way of return fire had been encountered and only a handful of bullet strikes were found among the six Hurricanes. According to the Air Ministry, only five from the original raiding force of nine Heinkel 115's managed to get back to Germany.

Recent research indicates these twin-engined enemy floatplanes brought down in the Wash area were from 1/Kustenfleigergruppe 406. The first was S4+DH, from which Oberleutnant-zur-see Peineman and his two crew were posted as missing. Second to fall in that area was S4+GH whose crew: Oblt-z-s G. Royman, Unteroffizier H.Schultze and Feldwebel R.Findersen were rescued and made POW.

A further example of how continuity and coincidence occurs throughout this story can be found when Plt. Off. P.W.Lefevre's name surfaces in a later chapter dealing with the Central Gunnery School at Sutton Bridge, to which he returned in 1942 as a Sqn. Ldr. and Battle of Britain veteran.

Like many of his contemporaries, having been with his squadron since January 1937 and having re-equipped with the high performance Hurricane, Sqn. Ldr. Barwell had patiently honed the squadron for battle. Heinkel 115's may not be considered a difficult target but in their keen-ness to get to grips with the enemy it would have been all too easy for these untried pilots to dash in less effectively. Considering that none had previously experienced combat, it is obvious that morale was high among the 46 Sqn. pilots under Barwell's command. Exemplifying pre-war professional aircrew, Barwell and his pilots carried out a disciplined textbook attack - just the sort of engagement to provide combat experience without wasting the opportunity. In retrospect, while providing that experience it showed up the limitations of rifle calibre armament and the need to get in close in order to achieve a telling effect. In his combat report, for example, Sqn. Ldr. Barwell wrote that he expended one third of his ammunition on his first target - equating to some 800 rounds and the remaining two-thirds on his second target - about 1600 rounds. Even then it required attacks from three other Hurricanes to bring that e/a down. This also suggests that incendiary ammunition may not have been used at this early stage of the air war.

Furthermore the successful use of a standard 'Fighting Area Attack' formation on this occasion might have given those pilots a false sense of its effectiveness. As the air war intensified, this subject became a cause of controversy between front line fighter pilots and some of their commanders. Fortunately experience, hard won, prevailed and such rigid attack formations became a relic of the past.

Perhaps it was this force of character which made Sqn. Ldr. Barwell a good choice to command Sutton Bridge where his task would be to oversee the gestation of several new and much needed, squadrons in quick succession.

In 1939 Sutton Bridge seemed to be drifting, somewhat, on the rising tide of war; going through a period of abrupt re-adjustment - as no doubt was the rest of the war machine - until a new sense of direction and purpose could be established.

This new direction was not too long in coming for, on November 1, 1939 Sutton Bridge was transferred from Training Command to Fighter Command (12 Group) and a few days later newly promoted Wg. Cdr. Philip Barwell DFC took command of the station.

A change of status.

In order to bring this story up to date, it is necessary to go back to 1936 when both the RAF and RAF Station Sutton Bridge underwent a significant change of structure. The RAF itself was re-organised in July 1936 into four new Commands: Bomber, Fighter, Coastal and Training.

Since March 1 1936 Sutton Bridge ceased to be a Summer Armament Training Camp, being given the status of a permanent RAF Station, while remaining under the control of Air Armament School (Eastchurch). The main function of the Station was as the home of 3 Armament Training School in which revised identity still resided the now well-established live firing role. With the advent of the new Command structure that July, RAF Sutton Bridge was transferred, for all technical and equipment matters, to direct control of the newly created HQ Training Command. In matters of personnel, discipline and training, it was controlled by HQ 25 Armament Group (AOC: AM L.A.Pattinson DSO,MC,DFC).

At this point in its life the Sutton Bridge Station '540' becomes decidedly sparse again, recording only Air Commodore Garrod OBE, MC, DFC taking over from Air Cdre. Pattinson in February 1937 and Wg. Cdr. F. O. Soden DFC taking over command of Sutton Bridge from Wg. Cdr. Smith in February 1938. It is however, recorded elsewhere that at long last, the station acquired the first of its married quarters, housing the permanent staff of 3 Armament Training School.

OFFICERS COMMANDING RAF SUTTON BRIDGE, 3 A.T.S.

From	To	Name
1935	Feb 1938	Wg. Cdr. H.A.Smith MC
Mar 1938	Jul 1939	Wg. Cdr. F.O.Soden DFC
Aug 1939		Wg. Cdr. J.M.Mason DSC DFC

Despite the paucity of official station diary entries, newspaper reports and the diaries of other squadrons show it was business as usual for at least another three years.

As already noted, 1936 saw no less than four Bulldogs lost at Holbeach Range; all from Treble-One Sqn. Setting the scene for the remaining years running up to the war it is possible through the medium of accident reports, both official and those carried by local newspapers, for some of the gaps in the station '540' to be filled.

In his excellent book *Fighter Command* (Dent 1980) Chaz Bowyer summarises the sea-change in RAF organisation after 1936. Hugh Dowding was appointed AOC Fighter Command that year and Bowyer states: *"Equally important to Dowding were his... reserves in both men and machines. In 1935...five fresh Flying Training Schools (FTS) were opened (Nos 7 to 11). In addition nine Armament Training Camps were to be opened as soon as suitable sites could be agreed and purchased by the Air Ministry."*

Established at Westwood, over on the opposite side of the Fens, 7 FTS now enters this narrative more prominently while a number of the earlier established FTS', notably 2 (Digby), 5 (Sealand) and 6 (Netheravon) will also feature.

Situated on the northern outskirts of Peterborough, Westwood aerodrome itself came to life as an idea in 1928. Informing readers on May 30, 1928, the *Peterborough Citizen* newspaper stated: *"At a meeting of the Council Allotments Committee the Town Clerk submitted a letter from the government Directorate of Lands together with a plan showing an area of the Westwood allotment estate. The 30 acre designated area was being bought by the Air Ministry from the owners, the Ecclesiastical Commissioners*

In the mid 1930's the mainstays of 7FTS were the Hawker Hart and Audax. In the foreground is Audax K4388 which remained with 7FTS until it was handed over to the South African Air Force in 1940. The other aircraft are Hart(T) of which second in the front row is K5875.

The Westwood district of Peterborough, circa 1935, showing Baker Perkins Factory after the construction of its multi story office block in the centre foreground. Behind the factory is a strip of land forming municipal allotment gardens and beyond these, are the arable fields which were transformed, from 1929, into RAF Peterborough, home to 7FTS. The cornfields went, replaced by a single permanent hangar and eight canvas 'H' hangars of the same type in use at Sutton Bridge, an RAF station on the opposite side of The Fens, with whom it would maintain strong links throughout the next twenty years.

and was required for occupation from September 1928". The article continued: *"Provided the level of compensation received for disturbance of the present tenants and Council was adequate, then the Clerk considered the proposed date could be met".*

During the following year, however, much discussion ensued before, in July 1929, the *Peterborough Advertiser* announced work on the project had actually begun, taking the form of drainage and foundation works. By this time the aerodrome project encompassed no less than 250 acres, being described now as The Great Peterborough Aircraft Park. In addiition to the allotments, other parcels of land were acquired mainly from G. C. W. Fitzwilliam, J. R. Horrell, W. Headding and the Peter Brotherhood Company as well as from the Ecclesiastical Commissioners.

According to the local MP, speaking on the subject in the House of Commons, work was scheduled to take two or three years to complete. It was indeed August 1932, some four years after inception, that the first stirrings of RAF occupancy could be detected at the aerodrome.

From late-1932 the aerodrome became home for No. 1 Aircraft Storage Depot, under RAF control but staffed mainly by civilians, charged with assembling aeroplanes for the RAF, storing and preparing them for issue to operating units as required. Little or no detailed information of the routine of life at the Depot has been found thus far. Its work continued, however, to be a source of steady employment for the workers of Peterborough until Dowding's scheme for the general expansion of the RAF in 1935 resulted in the creation of new Flying Training Schools.

By the New Year 1936, the atmosphere at Westwood had changed significantly. Gone was the civilian-oriented Aircraft Depot organisation, replaced now by RAF personnel operating 7 FTS.

Having received basic flying training at civilian flying schools - the RAF had not yet established its own fully integrated flying training system - the first batch of 45 pupils began training at 7 FTS on January 6, 1936 under the command of Gp. Capt. A.Shackleton and with the dulcet tones of an RAF Station Warrant Officer 'Dinger' Bell ringing in their ears.

Soon 7 FTS Hawker Hart and Audax aircraft became familiar sights across the region as the new training system gathered momentum. But it was not without a price, as both stations would discover.

Acquiring confidence through aerobatic flying is integral to any pupil pilot training programme and while results might appear polished to an air show audience, that skill does not come without exposure to some danger. This was brought home very forcibly for example at 7 FTS on April 16, 1936 when three Harts took off to practice formation aerobatics.

Wheeling above Westwood airfield they flattened out of a loop at 300 feet then dipped to begin another. Tragedy struck when the wheels of K4986 touched ground in front of the hangar area. Flt. Lt. E.Dawson could not keep the machine airborne and it careered forty yards directly into the gaping mouth of a hangar where it exploded in a ball of flame. The canvas structure was engulfed by a fire which destroyed two aircraft inside and spread to devour Tutor K3444 and Audax K5125 parked outside. Flt. Lt. Dawson, his passenger AC1 H.E. Smith-Langridge and two airmen working in the hangar, LAC P. Cuthbert and LAC S. A. R. King, died in the conflagration.

Whereas in past years, virtually only front-line fighter squadrons came to Sutton Bridge, 1936 saw the regular use of the range and airfield by FTS pupils, too. June saw pupils of No.1 course from 7 FTS arrive at Sutton Bridge while in August 1936, for example, three pilots from 6 FTS suffered accidents while attached for air firing. Clearly it had become policy to include live firing practice into the training programme, rather than leave it until a pilot was posted to a squadron. This may seem a perfectly sensible approach to adopt but it is one which does not seem to have been followed prior to 1936.

Back in 1935 it was deemed essential to have a landing ground immediately adjacent to Holbeach Range, for emergencies; easing movement of range staff to and from Sutton Bridge and aircraft or drogue servicing. A grass field was therefore purchased that year near the sea bank at Gedney Dawesmere.

Acting Plt. Off. G. B. Andrews (6 FTS) had mixed feelings for that small strip of grass when, on August 18, 1936 the engine of his Fury K3738 failed. Attempting a forced landing, he undershot his approach, stalled while trying to hop over a fence,

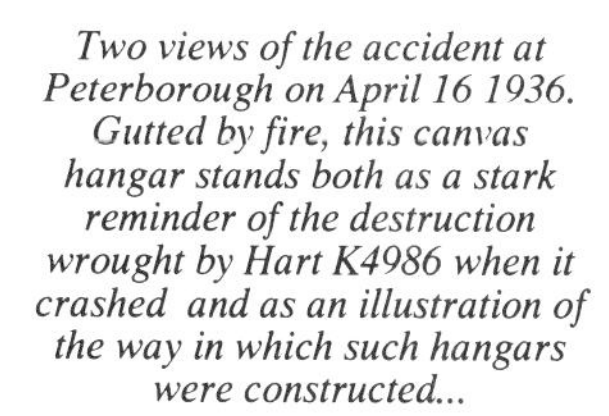

Two views of the accident at Peterborough on April 16 1936. Gutted by fire, this canvas hangar stands both as a stark reminder of the destruction wrought by Hart K4986 when it crashed and as an illustration of the way in which such hangars were constructed...

...the same could be said of the skeletal remains of the Tutor and Audax standing nearby.

[Peterborough Advertiser].

Right: Pupils not minding their P's and Q's! 6 FTS based at Netheravon was fortunate not to lose two of its pupils when Harts(T) K6428 'P' and K5842 'Q' collided at Sutton Bridge while on a detachment for armament training.

crashed and overturned. By now the sleek Fury was somewhat dated and being gradually relegated to training duties.

6 FTS also operated Hawker Hart Trainers at this time but two of these, K5842 and K6428, were reduced to matchwood at Sutton Bridge rather suddenly on August 21. Acting Plt. Off. N. M. Boffee, in one of three Harts making a formation landing, drifted into his leader's slipstream. The lower wing of K5842 dipped and hit the ground while the upper wing caught K6428 alongside, locking them together and causing both to crash to the ground.

Units of the Auxiliary Air Force augmented regular squadrons but only three AAF fighter squadrons, 600, 601 and 604 existed in 1936, operating Hawker Demons. Two-seat biplane fighters were much in vogue in the late 1930's but fortunately for their crews, were very soon rendered obsolete. Budding Battle of Britain pilot Flg. Off. Stanley Skinner (604 Sqn), brought Demon K4499 to Sutton Bridge where, in the cold evening air of January 24, 1937, out on a D/F Homing exercise, he failed to receive the radio signals and had to make a forced landing. Although he pulled off a reasonable landing in the gathering darkness, the aeroplane tipped onto its nose in boggy ground. An AAF pilot since 1934, Skinner was called up when war broke out and flew with 604 throughout the Battle. It is ironic therefore, having flown and survived in combat, that he should meet his death in 1942 as a sea-borne observer on the Dieppe raid. Another Demon, this time K4533 from 41 Sqn., met with a similar mishap on approach to Sutton Bridge on March 3.

Empire Air Days.

Both RAF Sutton Bridge and Peterborough became a focal point for air displays in the district and for the next three years assumed the mantle previously held by the civilian air-pageant operators, who had served the district exceedingly well in past years.

Providing light relief to both the participating stations and spectators alike, Empire Air Day air displays were the means by which the efforts of an expanding - and modernising - RAF were brought to the attention of the public. It was a way, too, for the government to show the taxpayer what they getting for their money. Proceeds from entrance fees were donated to the RAF Benevolent Fund, a worthy cause but was this not also just a thinly dressed-up ploy to ease the inevitability of war into the minds of the public? Whatever the motive, on Saturday May 23,1936, No.3 ATS, RAF Sutton Bridge and 7FTS Peterborough were two of 49 stations throwing their gates open for the public to come and enjoy themselves.

Attracting good coverage by local newspapers, according to the *Spalding Guardian: "... all roads in the district led to Sutton Bridge"* that afternoon. For the first time since Empire Air Days were instituted three years earlier, Sutton Bridge now with the status of a permanent RAF establishment, was included in the open day list.

Almost 3000 people visited the station, availing themselves of the opportunity to wander through hangars and even climb into aeroplane cockpits. Pilots and ground crew were on hand to answer patiently questions from a curious public.

Despite the far from ideal weather - occasional showers and blustery winds, relieved by the sight of the sun from time to time - it was possible to put on a varied, interesting and exciting programme. Promptly at 14.15 hours three Bulldogs from 56 Sqn. took to the air, giving a spirited aerobatics display to open the show. Fresh from their success at Hendon, three Fury aeroplanes of 25 Sqn. thrilled the crowd with precision formation aerobatics. In those days of relatively slow speeds, aeroplanes like these could be thrown around

'Two Six!' With its prominent alternate red and yellow triangles, an airman clutches the rear fuselage of 604 Sqn Hawker Demon K4499, while being buffeted in the fierce slipstream whipped up by its 485hp Kestrel engine being run up against the chocks.

Right: Curiously, most allocation listings of Hawker Hinds omit K4637 but it is photographed here at RAF Sutton Bridge 1936 Empire Air Day by the local news photographer. K4637 is the second production Hawker Hind and is believed to have been issued to 21 Sqn based at nearby Bircham Newton.

Captured on film at the same event is a brand new Gloster Gauntlet billed as "...the latest RAF fighter". It may have been brought to Sutton Bridge by 56 Sqn. which was attending for its annual air firing summer Camp and had also just begun the process of re-equipping with the Gauntlet. [Lincolnshire Free Press].

"on a sixpence" and low cloud was not a problem although the blustery wind would tax the pilot's skill during aerobatics. Then came individual displays by various single Bulldogs, including one from 56's CO, Sqn. Ldr. C. L. Lea-Cox.

Fighter attack techniques, the basis of everyday life at Sutton Bridge, were ably demonstrated by a flight of Bulldogs again from 56 Sqn., upon a drogue towed by a Station Flight Gordon. A comic interlude of 'crazy flying' was staged with a DH Moth displaying 'L' plates. The stiff wind enhanced these hair-raising stunts but in the hands of Flt. Lt. McGill the little Moth appeared perfectly safe.

Naturally everything stopped for tea; the first part of the programme being brought to a close by a sedate formation of three Station Flight Fairey Gordons flown by Flt. Lt. Palmer and Sgts. Drake and Roberts. Air drill controlled from the ground by radio, followed a screaming, ear-splitting dive-bombing routine by three Furies, opened the second half. Somewhat more gently a Hawker Hind from Bircham Newton was put through its paces by Sgt. Roberts, while the final item on the flying agenda was a 'mass' formation flypast by nine aeroplanes; three Gordons, Furies and Bulldogs.

Meanwhile at ground level, a Gloster Gauntlet was the focus of much interest as 'the latest RAF fighter'. Elsewhere the staccato rattle of machine gun fire rent the air as the twin Vickers of a Fury, propped up in front of the firing-butts, were made to turn streams of lead into fountains of sand, much to the delight of the watching crowd. Armourers demonstrated how to fill ammunition belts, assembled and dismantled machine guns, while aerial photographers showed pictures of local landmarks taken from the air. The intricacies of wireless telegraphy were explained by the signals section and aeroplane servicing workshops opened for closer inspection. All in all there was much indeed for the visitors to see and enjoy that year.

By contrast the weather for the 1937 Sutton Bridge Empire Day was ideal. Attracting 5000 people this year the four-hour programme included even more variety of aeroplanes.

Above: Bulldogs in the sun. 56 Sqn. Bristol Bulldogs drawn up in front of hangars at summer armament practice Camp, RAF Sutton Bridge May 1936. Its presence on the airfield enabled the squadron to provide aerobatic thrills for the Empire Air Day programme [Lincolnshire Free Press].

Left: Resplendent in its red/white chequerboard squadron markings and showing the excellent all round view afforded the pilot, this 56 Sqn. Bulldog, K2227 took part in Sutton Bridge's 1936 Empire Air Display.

[Lincolnshire Free Press.]

It was the turn of pupils from 5 FTS (Sealand) to bring their Hart and Audax aeroplanes to the Range for air firing practice in late May and early June 1937. They, too, supplied some of the thrills for the Empire Air Day held this year on May 29; pupils from that FTS opening the busy programme with a formation flypast of five Harts. All went without mishap today considering that during practice the previous day two Harts collided during landing, luckily each sustaining only minor damage and causing no crash. Four Bulldogs flown by Flt. Lt. H. Eales in company with Sgts. Smith, Wood and Stanford dived and wheeled repeatedly in simulated attacks upon a towed drogue target. Later, Sqn. Ldr. J. F. F. Paine displayed accurate low flying skill by dropping and picking up message bags using a hook attachment beneath his aircraft fuselage. Several solo aerobatic items were contributed by Flt. Lt.'s D. B. D. Field, N. H. Fresson, E. A. Springall and Plt. Off. J. D. Ronald; even the Station Commander, the irrepressable Wg. Cdr. Harry Smith got in on the act with his own solo aerobatic effort. The inevitable comic turn was provided by Flt. Lt. V.Q. Blackden, who made numerous flour-bomb attacks on an old car driven erratically at high speed across the airfield. His aim must have been pretty acceptable as Blackden rose to prominence in 1941 when, promoted Wg. Cdr., he commanded 12 Sqn. as they were re-equipping with Wellington MkII bombers. Sadly, however, Wg. Cdr. Blackden was lost on April 9/10 during his squadron's first raid using their new mount.

By mid-1937 the Westland Wallace had replaced the ageing Gordon and a splendid formation of these new target tugs, lead by Flt. Lt. F. A. A. Strath, flew sedately over the airfield. A delightful show of syncro-aerobatics by Flt. Lt.'s Springall and J. C. Evans, in a pair of Furies, followed before the day's proceedings closed with a grand formation flypast. Three Wallace's, three Fury's, one Boulton Paul Overstrand bomber and one Avro Anson provided this year's finale.

The final Air Show at Sutton Bridge was scheduled for Saturday 28 May 1938. In common with other aerodromes throughout the country that display suffered continuous rain all day causing practically all flying items to be 'scrubbed'. Nevertheless a substantial crowd gathered, despite inches of water on the grass and tarmac areas, particularly braving the weather to inspect what was described by the *Spalding Guardian* as *"the new type all-metal bombers in the aircraft park"*. These were un-named in the article but may have been Bristol Blenheims, some of which were based at nearby RAF Wyton at that time.

For most of the afternoon with poor visibility and a cloud base of 400 feet, only one aeroplane at a time was allowed into the air for restricted aerobatics when the rain eased off. By tea-time however it was brighter, the clouds having risen sufficiently for nine fighters to carry out squadron air-drill in the form of 'Fighting Area' set-piece manouevres of the sort mentioned elsewhere. A Hawker Audax flown by the CO of 5 FTS demonstrated the in-flight art of picking up messages from the ground. Despite the rain, visitors made the most of a similar range of ground attractions as in previous years with the addition this time of anti-aircraft searchlights, sound locating gear and the parachute packing shed. This was the end of an era in more ways than one for RAF Sutton Bridge never opened its gates to the public again.

Accidents and incidents

Following its performance at the 1937 air show it can be established that 5 FTS remained at Sutton Bridge until at least June 11, because MoD accident records show that on that date Acting Plt. Off. M.J.Earle in Audax K5161 undershot his approach, succeeding in turning over the machine onto its back when the nose dug into long grass just short of the field. Plt. Off. Earle walked away uninjured but the next unit to arrive for a stay in July and August, 6 FTS, was not so fortunate.

In rapidly deteriorating visibility Acting Plt. Off. Philip Bailey taxied out Audax K5253 with A/Plt. Off. Douglas Bagot-Gray in the rear cockpit. It was 08.00 on August 4 and one of the first air firing sorties of the day. Bailey took off but at only 200 feet altitude he entered early morning mist while still near the airfield. At this juncture he seemed, wisely, to decide to abort the flight and turned back towards the sanctuary of the airfield. There were only two civilian witnesses to what followed. Mr G. Kirk and Mr T. Tibbles were out hedge clipping on the banks of the river Nene. *"We are always interested in 'planes that fly past"*, said Mr Kirk, *"and as we looked up to see this one passing overhead it swung round. Flying lower it dipped behind some trees and a large glasshouse. Just before it disappeared from view I could plainly see...that the pilot was having difficulty in handling the aeroplane. I expected it to appear over the top of the glasshouse but instead I heard a most awful crash"*.

Both men rushed to the scene and faced the grim task of extricating the unfortunate airmen from the crumpled wreckage, which fell on Mr Sole's farm some 400 yards from the airfield.

The *Boston Guardian* newspaper of August 6 carried that story together with another accident only

Based at RAF Worthy Down, in October 1937 35 Sqn. was still re-equipping with the Vickers Wellesley bomber. The pilot of K7738, Sgt. T.E.Moon and his crew, Sgt. V.Hedley and AC1 G.J.M.Nunn were briefed to carry out a fuel consumption test to RAF North Coates and back. On the return leg they ran into thick fog and crashed near Boston with the loss of all on board [F.J.Adkin].

Below: No.1 Sqn. Hawker Furies at Tangmere in 1937. Sgt. R. A. Albonico is in the white flying overall in front of K8249 a Mark II similar to the aeroplane in which he crashed at Sutton Bridge. 1 Sqn. Fury II's were from the second batch of that model and were not fitted with the wheel spats more common to the first batch. While cleaning-up the already pleasing lines of the Fury, spats tended to clog up on grass airfields and 1 Sqn. chose not to use them

Above: Off to war!

A group of No.1 Sqn. NCO pilots at "...an airfield somewhere in France" on 8 September 1939. This was Octeville airfield near Le Havre and the pilots are, from left: Sgts. Hancock, Luckham, R.A.Albonico and Cuthbert. [R. A. Albonico].

two days earlier. A/Plt. Off. Albert Ferris, also believed to be from 6 FTS, lost his life when his aeroplane crashed onto the shore at Holbeach Range. Closing what was a sad catalogue of mishaps in so short a space of time, was yet a third crash, also on August 4, this time at Gedney Dyke. Flt. Lt. Stephenson, whose unit was not stated, sustained minor injuries in this incident.

After this period, a tragic illustration of the high price of flying training in human terms, there was a lull in the accident rate for a few months.

Evidence of the return to Sutton Bridge of front line fighter squadrons later that year, together with the 604 Sqn. crash, indicates that the airfield and range was now in constant use all the year round.

Having completed his air firing exercise over Holbeach Range, Sgt. R.A.Albonico of 1 Sqn., was returning for a well-earned rest, his being the last sortie on December 1. With twilight turning to dusk, a thick mist developed, obscuring the ground near the airfield. In his own words some fifty years later, Sgt. Albonico wrote: *"I misjudged my height in the mist. My approach was fine until I realised I was actually still some way up in the air. The aeroplane stalled and crashed heavily, ripping off the mainplanes, undercarriage and prop, in the process. I scrambled clear, unhurt, but the aeroplane was a complete write-off."* The aeroplane was Hawker Fury II, K8258.

Sgt. Albonico continued to serve with 1 Sqn., being posted to France with the squadron in 1940. He flew several operational sorties in a Hurricane during the Battle of France before being shot down by 'flak' on May 18, 1940 while escorting bombers near St. Quentin. He crash landed the Hurricane and was made POW for five long years.

Regular visitors to the range in 1938 were Audaxes and Furies from RAF College FTS, Cranwell (RAFC) and inevitably these students encountered a few mishaps, too.

With an engine de-rated for FTS use, the Audax, a

The double black bars of 25 Sqn. stand out clearly on this crumpled Hawker Fury II K7267 which crashed near March on 26 April 1937. Sgt. E. W. J. Monk was on a cross country training flight from Hawkinge when his aeroplane suffered engine failure. Most of the damage was caused when the aeroplane hit a tree during the forced landing. [Peterborough Advertiser].

Air Incidents in the Fenland Region - 1936 to 1940

Date	Aircraft type	Serial	Sqn/Unit	Incident location	Pilot	Fate
10/06/36	Hart	K3130	7 FTS	RAF Sutton Bridge		U
19/06/36	N/K	N/K	N/K	Peterborough		U
29/07/36	Gordon	K1773	3 ATS	RAF Sutton Bridge	Sgt. L.J.Brown	U
29/07/36	Audax	K7484	N/K	RAF Sutton Bridge	None	U
18/08/36	Fury I	K3738	6 FTS	Holbeach Range	A/PLt. Off. C.B.Andrews	U
21/08/36	Hart	K5842	6 FTS	RAF Sutton Bridge	A/Plt. Off. N.M.Boffee	I
21/08/36	Hart	K6428	6 FTS	RAF Sutton Bridge	N/K	U
23/10/36	Hart	K3072	7 FTS	RAF Peterborough	A/Plt. Off. W.D.Coppinger	K
23/10/36	Hart	K3128	7 FTS	RAF Peterborough	A/Plt. Off. P.Shaugnessy	U
01/12/36	Hart	N/K	7 FTS	RAF Peterborough	A/Plt. Off. T.G.Robertson	U
01/12/36	Hart	K3138	7 FTS	Corby Glen	LAC. J.Hogg	K
15/12/36	Hart	N/K	7 FTS	Whaplode Drove	LAC. H.A.V.Davies	K
24/01/37	Demon	K4499	604	RAF Sutton Bridge	Flg. Off. S.H.Skinner	U
04/03/37	Demon	K4533	41	RAF Sutton Bridge	Plt. Off. L.Maxwell-Muller	U
26/04/37	Fury II	K7267	25	March	Sgt. E.W.J.Monk	U
07/05/37	Gordon	K2728	3 ATS	Sutton Bridge	Sgt. J.T.Freeman	U
28/05/37	Hart	N/K	5 FTS	RAF Sutton Bridge	N/K	U
28/05/37	Hart	N/K	5 FTS	RAF Sutton Bridge	N/K	U
29/05/37	Gipsy Moth	K1825	3 ATS	RAF Sutton Bridge	Flt. Lt. V.Q.Blackden	U
04/06/37	Audax	K5241	5 FTS	RAF Sutton Bridge	LAC. L.H.Sawyer	U
10/06/37	Gordon	K1738	3 ATS	RAF Sutton Bridge	Plt. Off. S.M.Bird	I
11/06/37	Audax	K5161	5 FTS	RAF Sutton Bridge	A/Plt. Off. M.J.Earle	U
02/08/37	N/K	N/K	N/K	Holbeach Range	A/Plt. Off. A.E.R.Ferris	K
04/08/37	Audax	K5253	6 FTS	Sutton Bridge	A/Plt. Off. P.H.Bailey	K
04/08/37	N/K	N/K	N/K	Gedney Dyke	Flt. Lt. Stephenson	U
20/10/37	Wellesley	K7738	35	New Leake	Sgt. T.E.Moon	K
25/10/37	Hart	N/K	11 FTS	Deeping St James	Plt. Off. P.H.D.Broughton	U
25/10/37	Hart	N/K	11 FTS	Deeping St James	A/Plt. Off. H.A.Smith	U
01/12/37	Fury I	K8258	1	RAF Sutton Bridge	Sgt. R.A.Albonico	U
07/01/38	Audax	K5603	RAFC FTS	RAF Sutton Bridge	Flt. Cdt. C.W.Newman	U
31/01/38	Audax	K5210	11 FTS	Ufford	A/Plt. Off. T.K.G.Dudley	K
18/03/38	Hart	K2122	7 FTS	Peterborough	N/K	U
22/04/38	Blenheim I	K7146	110	Crowland	Plt. Off. H.D.Green	K
20/06/38	Fury I	K3730	2 FTS	HolbeachRange	N/K	
22/06/38	Audax	K7466	RAFC FTS	Holbeach Range	Flt Cdt. A.F.Halliwell	U
27/06/38	Fury II	K8302	RAFC FTS	Holbeach Range	Flt.Cdt. C.B.F.Kingcombe	U
05/09/38	Hart	K5797	7 FTS	Pinchbeck Marsh	A/Plt. Off. P.K.Bone	U
14/09/38	Audax	K7375	RAFC FTS	Ancaster	Flt. Cdt. G.K.R.Drimmie	I
14/09/38	Hurricane	L1620	87	Holbeach Range	Sgt. T.F.D.Dewdney	K
15/09/38	Gauntlet	K7840	213	Stamford	Plt. Off. B Van Mentz	U
15/09/38	Magister	L2863	213	Stamford	Plt. Off. J Sing	U
19/09/38	N/K	N/K	4 ERFTS	Dorrington Fen	A/Plt. Off. D.G.Baker	K
28/10/38	Gauntlet	K5345	17	RAF Sutton Bridge	Flg. Off. C.W.Williams	U
03/11/38	Demon	K5730	23	Barholm	Sgt. J Bullard	U
03/11/38	Demon	K5712	23	Barholm	Plt. Off. A.E.Slocombe	U
07/11/38	Blenheim I	L1160	61	The Wash	Plt. Off. A.D.Steele-Perkins	I
24/01/39	Wallace	K6067	3 ATS	RAF Sutton Bridge	Sgt. J.T.Wyse	K

Delicately balanced on its propeller, this Hawker Hart(T) K2122 emerged relatively unscathed when a 7FTS pupil pilot had to force land near Peterborough on 18 March 1938. [Peterborough Citizen].

10/02/39	Hind	N/K	22 ERFTS	Chatteris	Mr R.E.Wright (RAFVR)	K
17/03/39	Hart	N/K	7FTS	RAF Peterborough	Flt. Sgt. R.Amor	U
29/03/39	Hurricane	L1792	46	Corby Glen	Plt. Off. R.A.C.Kent	K
11/04/39	Battle	K9403	52	Wisbech	Sgt. A.M.Taylor	U
02/05/39	Hurricane	L1647	32	RAF Sutton Bridge	Plt. Off. J.W.Gillen	U
09/05/39	Tiger Moth	N6634	30 EFTS	Wiggenhall St Germans	I.A.Norris	U
09/05/39	Huricane	L1566	73	RAF Sutton Bridge	Plt. Off. N.Orton	I
26/05/39	Magister	L8338	3 ATS	Holbeach Range Ldg Grd	Plt. Off. M.T.Kirkwood	U
26/05/39	Blenheim I	L8367	23	RAF Sutton Bridge	Plt. Off. A.M.Cooper-Key	U
26/05/39	Blenheim I	L1458	23	RAF Sutton Bridge	None	
06/06/39	Blenheim I	L1460	23	RAF Sutton Bridge	Sgt. R.C.Young	U
06/06/39	Blenheim I	L8369	23	RAF Sutton Bridge	None	
07/06/39	Blenheim I	L1464	29	RAF Sutton Bridge	Flg. Off. J.S.Adams	U
10/06/39	Audax	K7461	19 EFTS	Stamford	Sgt. C.W.Farrow	U
20/07/39	Blenheim	L8368	23	Sacrewell Lodge	Sgt. J. Bullard	K
20/07/39	Blenheim	L1448	23	Did Not Crash	Plt. Off. A.T.Williams	U
15/08/39	Magister	P5945	3 ATS	Terrington	N/K	U
16/08/39	Blenheim If	L1436	25	RAF Sutton Bridge	Plt. Off. A.J.S.Pattinson	U
26/08/39	Hart	K3129	7 FTS	Bourne	A/Plt. Off. C.Marshall	U
24/09/39	Harvard	N7067	12 FTS	Folkingham	Flg. Off. W.S.Pryde	K
22/10/39	Heinkel He115b	S4+GH	1/KFG40	The Wash	Oblt-z-s G. Reymann	U
22/10/39	Heinkel He115b	S4+DH	1/KFG40	The Wash	Oblt-z-s Peinemann	K
19/11/39	Hart	K3762	7 FTS	Peakirk	Flt. Sgt. Biddulph	U
01/12/39	Blenheim	N6186	107	RAF Sutton Bridge	Sgt. Sarll	U
09/12/39	Battle	L5350	266	RAF Sutton Bridge	Flt. Lt. J.B.Coward *	U
12/12/39	Battle	P5246	266	RAF Sutton Bridge	Plt. Off. N.G.Bowen *	U
18/12/39	Wellington	N2873	9	RAF Sutton Bridge	Sgt. F.C.Petts	U
30/12/39	Battle	K9465	207	Guyhirne, Wisbech	Plt. Off. A.G.W.Hough	U
04/01/40	Blenheim	L1466	23	Helpston Hth,P'boro	Plt. Off. R.G.A.Barritt	K
14/01/40	Hampden	AE292	106	Butterwick, Boston	Sgt. D.Lawton	K
17/01/40	Battle	P5244	266	Sutton Bridge	Plt. Off. D.Armitage	U
17/01/40	Blenheim	K7150	254	RAF Sutton Bridge	Plt. Off. K.Illingworth	U
18/02/40	Spitfire	N3120	266	Littleport	Flt. Lt. I.R.Gleed	I
21/02/40	Wellington	P2919	99	Walsoken, Wisbech	Flt. Lt. J.F.Brough	U
26/02/40	Battle	P2260	6 OTU	Gosberton Risegate	Sgt. J Owen	K
01/03/40	Hampden	P4374	144	Wainfleet St Mary	Plt. Off. C.P.D.Price	U
01/03/40	Wellington	N2907	38	Wisbech	Sgt. F.Lupton	U
02/03/40	Hart	K5886	7 FTS	Deeping St James	Flt. Lt. V.A.H.Tuck	U
02/03/40	Wellington	N2984	149	Burnt Fen, Downham	Flg. Off. L.R.Field	K

Right: The classic lines of Hawker Audax K5210 are shown off by the pristine condition of this 11FTS example. It all went wrong on 31 January 1938, during a training flight from Wittering.

Left: Plt. Off. T.K.G.Dudley had difficulty in changing to the gravity petrol tank when the main ran dry. When the engine cut out, he had to force land at Ufford but stalled on approach and crashed with fatal consequences for himself. His Observer Plt. Off Burton Gyles escaped with injuries.

[Stamford Mercury]

By 1938 Hawker Furies were in widespread use with training units. Fury K3730 was operated by 2FTS when it visited Sutton Bridge for air gunnery practice but became another casualty out on Holbeach Range on 20 June 1938.

general-purpose variant of the ubiquitous Hart, was used mainly by trainees destined for Army Co-operation or Day Bomber squadrons, while single-seat Fury II's were allocated to those pupils displaying fighter pilot qualities.

Fortunately none of the RAFC accidents were fatal but one incident is noteworthy because it involved a cadet who, having survived it, carved out a reputation second to none in the Battle of Britain and its aftermath. Under training since early 1936, Flight Cadet C. B. F. (Brian) Kingcombe flew to Holbeach range on June 27 1938 in Fury II, K8302. As he did so he made an elementary error of forgetting to change over his fuel supply from gravity to main tank en route and ran the tank dry. His engine stopped abruptly and unable to make it to the range landing ground, he was obliged to force land. During his approach he stalled and the Fury fell heavily into a sugar beet field, smashing the undercarriage. Flt. Cdt. Kingcombe fortunately lived to fight another day.

One month later Kingcombe had completed his two and a half year period of training - a lengthy process for an RAFC cadet in those days - and was posted to 65 Sqn. When war came he saw action over Dunkirk then, posted to 92 Sqn., fought all through the Battle of Britain. He held a number of senior operational appointments for the remainder of the war, finally leaving the RAF in 1954 as a Group Captain with the DSO and DFC.

As a member of 87 Sqn's. aerobatic team, Sgt T. F. D. Dewdney was acknowledged as a skilful pilot. On June 18, 1938, for example, in company with Flg. Off. Feeny and Plt. Off. Lorimer, their 'tied-together' aerobatics display in three Gloster Gladiators dazzled spectators at Brooklands Flying Club, a performance repeated on July 10 before a French audience at the Paris Air Show. Just two months later, on September 14, Sgt. Dewdney was dead, killed at the controls of Hawker Hurricane L1620 when it dived headlong into Holbeach Marsh mudflats.

While Sgt. Dewdney was engaged in air to air firing practice thick clouds rolled in across the range

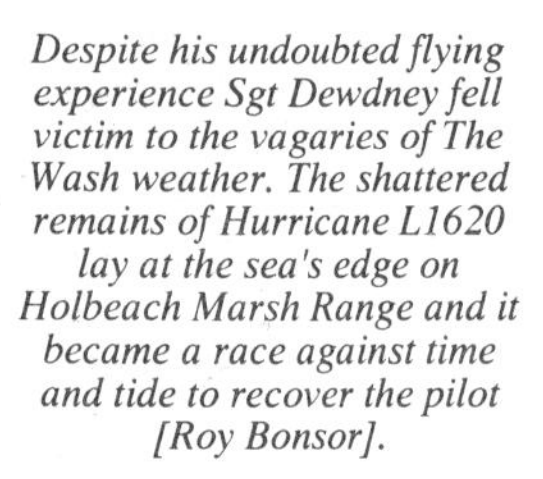

Despite his undoubted flying experience Sgt Dewdney fell victim to the vagaries of The Wash weather. The shattered remains of Hurricane L1620 lay at the sea's edge on Holbeach Marsh Range and it became a race against time and tide to recover the pilot [Roy Bonsor].

RAF Hendon was renowned for its Air Pageants and a particular crowd thriller was the 'tied together' aerobatics performed by a 'vic' of three aircraft, attached to each others wing tips by rubber ropes. 87 Sqn. provided one of these precision flying teams for the 1937 show. Sgt. T.F.D.Dewdney (right) was a member of that team and is seen here with the other members, Plt. Off. Lorimer (centre) and Flg. Off. Feeny (left), in front of their Gloster Gladiators.

with a swiftness for which the Wash is noted. Strange to relate, in view of his undeniable flying skill, the MoD record card for Dewdney's accident seems to suggest he had done little blind flying.

With the Munich crisis emerging into the light of day, the race was on to re-equip the RAF with modern monoplane, multi-gun fighters. Among the first to convert to Hurricanes, 87 Sqn. was anxious to become fully operational and for all pilots this included firing the battery of eight Browning machine guns.

Exactly what happened will never be known but perhaps being unfamiliar with the Hurricane - 87 had only re-equipped between July 12 and August 4 - Dewdney may have stalled in that low cloud and was unable to recover in time. His thus became the first accident at Holbeach Range to involve one of the new generation of monoplane fighters.

As Europe slid downhill to war, the year 1939 would bring many changes to RAF Sutton Bridge, too. First of these occurred on February 6 when the station diary recorded: *"The Station commenced to be re-equipped with Hawker Henley aircraft."*

Underpinning this terse statement is a little-appreciated effect of the significant technological advance heralded by the latest monoplane fighters. Elderly Wallace and Gordon target-towing aeroplanes,

First introduced to the RAF in 1932, by 1939 the DH Tiger Moth was used mainly by Elementary and Reserve Flying Training Schools (E&RFTS) for ab initio training. Civilians as well as RAF personnel were trained to fly at these units pre war. N6634 was operated by 30 E&RFTS from Marshalls Airfield, Cambridge and was involved in a forced landing at Wiggenhall St.Germans, south of Kings Lynn, when the pilot, Mr L. A. Norris became lost on the return leg of a cross country from Derby to Cambridge.

"Can't you see I'm a target tug?" The broad black diagonal stripes on yellow fuselage and wings are the distinctive markings of a target towing aircraft. The four Hawker Henleys of 3 ATS Sutton Bridge Towing Flight were always hard worked. [J. Flint]

in use for example over the years at Sutton Bridge, were by 1939 incapable of providing realistic air to air firing training conditions for Hurricanes, Spitfires and Blenheims now visiting the range.

Hawker's attempt to produce a monoplane light bomber was met with little enthusiasm by the Air Ministry and although production went ahead, it was converted for target-towing work. Fitted with a windmill-driven winding device mounted on the port side of the rear cockpit, the Henley TT III was limited in RAF service to a cruise speed of 220 mph in its target-towing role. In the transition period from peace to war and even on into the early war years, this speed restriction - apparantly officialdom's attempt to reduce engine wear - was not the problem it was to become later. With Hurricane and Spitfire engines and airframes being developed to raise speeds ever higher, together with the advent of the next generation of fighters, even the Henley's performance was found wanting.

Thus Wallaces were phased out; but not before one of their number, K6067, came to grief with tragic consequences. Air firing continued apace and Sutton Bridge Station Flight target-tug crews, flying flat out day and night, must have been very weary under the continual pressure.

Returning from a night sortie to the range, Sgt. J. T. Wyse undershot his approach and K6067 hit King John Bank, the raised road on the airfield's eastern boundary, overturned and burst into flames. Sgt. Wyse died although his Observer escaped with injuries. Although by no means the last accident, it was the last fatality to befall the station before the outbreak of war some seven months later.

Dark clouds of war...

Events began to rush one after another now. On August 8, 1939 Wg. Cdr. Mason took over command from Gp. Capt. Soden (posted to command RAF Finningley) but no sooner had this occurred than, with the declaration of war and mobilisation no more than three hours away, 3 Armament Training School was transferred from Sutton Bridge to West Freugh. In the opinion of the Air Ministry the East Anglian coast was going to be no fit place for aeroplanes to be caught "stooging around" a firing range.

In view of this, on September 2, 1939, Sutton Bridge was placed on a Care and Maintenance (C & M) basis, under the temporary command of Flt. Lt. R.P.Smillie and a small group of airmen. What a sudden come-down!

On September 3 - that fateful day - with only the C & M party remaining, war was declared and at 03.00 the first air raid warning to be experienced by the

At the RAF Sutton Bridge 1937 Empire Air Day 3 ATS put up an impressive flypast of five Westland Wallace Target Tug aircraft. Holding tight formation off the leader's port wing is Wallace K6067 which was later destroyed in a fatal crash at the station on 24 January 1939 [J. L. Goward].

station was sounded.

One week later it was all change again when Flt. Lt. H.N. Hawker arrived together with another small group of airmen, to form the nucleus of No.3 Recruits Sub-Depot.

In common with several similar establishments hurriedly set up at the outbreak of hostilities (e.g at Catfoss and Finningley), this unit was created: *"...for the purpose of accomodating and training recruits as per the War Syllabus."*

Administered initially by 24 (Training) Group, 3 Sub-Depot, Sutton Bridge was affiliated to 2 Recruiting Centre, Cardington. Its aim was to train airman recruits in the essentials of Air Force discipline, kit them out, give them time to mark such kit issued, undergo medicals and variously integrate those raw recruits rapidly into the wierd and wonderful ways of the Service - including, it seems, digging pits and trenches for many obscure reasons!

Originally, in the case of Sutton Bridge, 336 recruits were to be accomodated for a 4-week sojourn and the first, no doubt bewildered, batch of 144 arrived on September 11 from Cardington. Ten days later the unit was re-named No.3 Recruits Training Pool and transferred to the jurisdiction of 25 (Armament) Group. A further 176 embryo airmen turned up on September 30, bringing the total at the station to 320.

In rapid succession new orders were received from Group to prepare to accomodate a total of 576 men, who were to be organised into a 'Squadron' of four 'Flights' each with 144 recruits and overseen by an Headquarters staff.

The initial intake completed its training by October 27 and during the next two days, with the exception of 68 airmen, were all posted away. Having been deemed to have done its job, the unit was officially closed down on October 29 when the remaining recruits were posted. All, that is, except one solitary soul who according to the unit diary remained behind for reasons which were never recorded. As the final entry dated November 16 so eloquently puts it: *"With one exception, all recruits have been disposed of."!*

Officers and airmen from both the C & M party and HQ No.3 Recruits Pool were posted into and out of Sutton Bridge Station HQ (SHQ) in quick order during November.

It soon became evident that the reason for this flurry of activity was to re-arrange enough manpower in such a manner to produce an organisation capable of forming three twin-engined fighter squadrons at the station. Now THIS was the real thing!

Postings to and from SHQ were designed to create a Station establishment to support the formation and operations of 264 Sqn., under the command of Sqn. Ldr. S. H. Hardy and 266 Sqn. under Sqn. Ldr. J. W. A. Hunnard.

As a result of all this change, Flt. Lt. Smillie was promoted Acting Sqn. Ldr. (Admin) and the SHQ strength at the end of the month stabilised at 12 officers, 129 airmen and 46 civilian staff.

264 Sqn. officially came into existance on November 1, 1939 with the arrival at Sutton Bridge of Sqn. Ldr. Hardy. During the next week a number of pilots were posted in from 12 FTS Grantham and 14 FTS Kinloss, to be joined later by two flight commanders, Flt. Lt. W. A. Toyne from 213 Sqn, Wittering and Flt. Lt. N. G. Cooke, 611 Sqn, Digby.

As yet, no aircraft were allocated to 264 but three Miles Magisters - N3857, N3867, N3868 - were collected from Hullavington in order to enable the new boys to keep their hand in until their 'proper' aircraft turned up. Fighter Command, on November 14, declared the squadron was to be equipped with Boulton-Paul Defiant fighters and a week later announced 264 would move to RAF Martlesham Heath. This prompted Sqn. Ldr. Hardy, his two flight commanders and the ground crew SNCO, Flt. Sgt. Lines, to visit Martlesham to inspect the facilities preparatory to the move. That same day, November 25, Sqn. Ldr. Hardy travelled on to RAF Northolt to scrounge a flight in a Defiant - for none had yet reached Sutton Bridge! Organisation....!!

Finding something to keep these aircraft-less fellows occupied was difficult, resulting in numerous visits to Sector Ops at RAF Wittering and further individual visits by squadron pilots to RAF Northolt to get the feel of a Defiant. This air experience was augmented by ground personnel being sent off to attend Boulton and Paul's Wolverhampton factory for a four-day Defiant servicing course. All in all Sutton Bridge seemed to resemble no more than an 'hotel' for transient 264 Sqn. personnel.

While eagerly awaiting delivery of their alloted aircraft, pilots of the embryo fighter squadrons forming at RAF Sutton Bridge at the end of 1939 had to settle for more mundane mounts in the shape of the Miles Magister. [J Cheney collection]

Although it had a single engine and a single seater like pilot position, the Fairey Battle could hardly be mistaken for a fighter. But it was all that was available for 266 Sqn. to work up to operational readiness until it took delivery of its long-awaited Spitfires. This Battle is seen visiting RAF Peterborough in late 1939 [Peterborough Museum].

This period of relative inactivity, however, came to an end on December 7, 1939 when all air and ground elements of 264 'upped sticks' and left Sutton Bridge bound for a new home at Martlesham Heath, where, within days, Defiants began arriving from depots such as Brize Norton and Little Rissington.

Meanwhile, across the airfield 266 Sqn., too, had been stirring since October 30 when it began the process of forming under the command of Sqn. Ldr. Hunnard.

The established size of this (proposed) two-seater squadron, in manpower terms, was declared as 13 officers, of whom 11 were pilots and 204 airmen, of whom 10 were NCO pilots and 20 aircrew (air gunners). One of the most notable names to arrive at Sutton Bridge for flight commander duty with 266, was one of Wg. Cdr. Barwell's old squadron colleagues, the diminutive Flt. Lt. Ian (Widge) Gleed, posted in from 46 Sqn, Digby. Experience and leadership were obviously the qualities most required to bring a squadron to an effective state quickly and it was for this reason that Gleed was selected for this job, together with another 'old hand' Flt. Lt. James Coward formerly of 19 Sqn., Duxford.

Any aircraft, let alone a 'real' fighter, were hard to come by in those days of rapid expansion so 266 also had to settle for three Magisters, collected from 10 MU Hullavington, on which to begin their work-up. With the arrival of the 'Maggies' on October 11, local flying got under way, while the Link Trainer was also put to good use. The inevitable stand-by activity, those visits to Sector Ops Wittering, still continued.

On November 18 word came down from on high that 266 Sqn. was to be equipped with Battles, instead of Blenheims as originally intended. At a guess, neither would have inspired these hopeful fighter 'tyros' but it seemed to point to an intention to turn 266 into a single-engined - most likely Spitfire - unit eventually, once the production lines moved into top gear. Accordingly the squadron personnel establishment was quickly scaled down as the air gunners were shipped out to pastures new.

It was not until December 4, however, that the first three Fairey Battle I's : L5348, L5350 and L5374, materialised at Sutton Bridge, flown in from 24 MU Ternhill by Hunnard, Gleed and Coward. Within a couple of days, training began with these three which were joined shortly after by a further batch comprising L5343, L5365 and P5244.

Practice and more practice

A spell of fog, rain and low cloud hampered flying but soon the sky around Sutton Bridge echoed to the roar of six Battles doing everything from circuits and bumps to formation practice. It was not long therefore to the first 'prang'.

Finding the undercarriage of L5350 refused to lock in the 'down' position Flt. Lt. Coward, with Plt. Off. J.L.Wilkie in the back seat, had to belly-land on the airfield on December 9. Both emerged unhurt.

Next day five more Battles (L5375, L5442, P5248, P5368 and P5369) were collected from 24 MU Ternhill by other squadron pilots: Plt. Off.'s Wilkie, Williams and Bowen and Sgts. Eade and Jones.

Being December, the weather was a constant hazard and flying subject to continual interruption. Plt. Off. Bowen bent the tailwheel of L5246 in a heavy landing on the 12th but by now the flow of aeroplanes and pilots was sufficient to cope with a few minor mishaps like this.

And so the cold, misty, damp month wore on. There was even formation flying practice on Christmas Day and by the turn of the year, the training programme included fighter attacks and longer cross-country flights.

Although on December 31 the flying strength stood at 20 pilots and 15 Battles, the ground echelon was desperately short of servicing equipment for their charges. In fact if it had not been for the co-operation of RAF Upwood, 266 might well have been grounded as most of its aircraft were due for 30-hour inspections. To overcome the difficulty, Battles were flown one by one to Upwood for vital servicing and repair until the arrival of ground equipment; yet another bottleneck in the system.

Despite day after day of severe frost in January 1940, 266 pressed on with its task, even raising the daily totals of hours flown compared to previous months. In the end it all seemed worthwhile for, on January 10, Fighter Command ordered the squadron to be re-equipped with Spitfires "...forthwith". With renewed vigour the pilots continued to practice in all weathers, severe frosts, ground fog, snow and even blizzard conditions (during which Plt. Off.'s Wilkie and Mitchell in P5244 were forced down near East Kirkby without being hurt) until, finally on January 19, the great day arrived. The first three Spitfire I's were flown to Sutton Bridge by Sqn. Ldr. Hunnard and his two flight commanders, with a fourth arriving a day later.

The weather, though, did not relent. More snow fell daily until in the last week of the month, with more than six inches laying on top of the already frost-hardened grass airfield and the temperature below zero day after day, flying was abandoned. It was no better when February arrived either. A thaw set in and the rains came, turning the airfield into a quagmire. Not until February10 was the grass surface sufficiently water-free for flying training to re-commence.

On this date training with the new Spitfires began.

Within days most of the Battles had been exchanged for Spitfires, the former being flown to or collected by other squadrons, such as 234 and 245. By mid-February, 266 was upto strength with 19 Spitfires on charge but on February 18 one of these, N3120, was written off by Flt. Lt. Gleed.

Part of the work-up process involved taking the Spitfires up to its rated altitude, in this case 18,000 feet. It was a test like this that, on December 18, very nearly brought to a premature and abrupt end the promising flying career of Flt. Lt. Ian Gleed.

Airborne from Sutton Bridge, Flt. Lt. Gleed eased N3120 ever higher into the cold afternoon air, climbing in circles through one cloud layer after another until he broke out into bright sunshine. The official version of subsequent events states that the Spitfire was being air tested at 18,000 feet and all was going well until the pilot throttled back into a gentle turn towards base. There is no suggestion in the report of any high speed manouevre which might have led to over-stressing. Suddenly, there was a loud bang; Gleed found himself torn out of his harness and thrown clean through the cockpit canopy as the aeroplane began to disintegrate around him.

For a personal account of those events there is no better place to turn to, however, than Ian Gleed's autobiography *Arise to Conquer* (Gollancz, 1942.).

"As soon as I reached 18,000 feet I levelled out ... checked all instruments and opened up to full throttle. Boost was OK, revs steady at 2850, speed just right. She seemed to be flying a bit right wing low but we could put that right later. It was a bit nippy up there so I decided to go home.

I nosed down into a gentle dive; the speed rose and I began a gentle left-hand turn, closing the radiator as I did so. CRACK! Christ! what was that?

I was thrown forward, my harness just stopping me from hitting the dashboard. I tried to lift my head, but could not. BANG! Blackness! Everything was black. Where am I? Christ! I must still be in the air! Oh God, where's the ripcord? Fumbling, at last, I found the metal square and tugged hard. Felt a jerk; then nothing."

After recovering from his brush with death in Spiffire N3120, Flt. Lt. Ian Gleed was posted to 87 Sqn. in France. He was soon in the thick of the air battles as 'A'Flight leader and began to build up his tally of 'kills' flying the Hawker Hurricane.

Knocked semi-conscious when he went through the canopy, Gleed fell through the rarified air and was fortunate indeed to recover his senses just sufficiently to pull his parachute ripcord with height to spare. In a

Mounted on a wall in Kent Battle of Britain Museum, on the former RAF Hawkinge airfield, is the port wing from Spitfire N3120. This remarkably intact relic was discovered during the 1970's at Woolwich Arsenal and is part of the 266 Sqn. aircraft from which Flt. Lt. Ian Gleed baled out on 18 February 1940, while based at RAF Sutton Bridge.

daze he managed to release his 'chute as he was dragged along the snow covered ground. He could not see for coagulated blood from cuts about his head, a shoe was missing, his left arm and right leg were hurting like hell, possibly broken.

He lay shivering in a biting wind before hearing voices approaching.

"Gawd, don't 'ee look a bloody mess," said one voice. *"doctor's comin' soon, mate. Yor 'plane be orl in pieces."*

After what seemed a nightmare of being carried and bumped on foot and in vehicles, Ian Gleed finally arrived at hospital. He was operated upon and woke later to find himself flat on his back, weak, his left arm in plaster and his head and right leg swathed in bandages.

Spitfire N3120 had fallen to earth at Little Ouse, near Littleport and as his first rescuer had remarked, it was in little pieces. Ordinarily that would mean just another load of scrap to be melted down but an odd coincidence, concerning N3120 came to light in 1989 almost fifty years on from that fateful day. During that year this writer visited Kent Aviation Museum on the former Hawkinge airfield, near Folkestone. There, mounted on a wall, was the virtually intact starboard mainplane of N3120. Its route to Hawkinge was said to be via Woolwich Arsenal but no reason was offered for it being deposited with the latter. It can only be assumed that Air Ministry investigators, in view of the disturbing circumstances of this accident to a relatively early Spitfire, may have gathered up wreckage and sent it to Woolwich Arsenal for technical examination. Perhaps only this major component survived and by way of some personal contact was scrounged by or donated to the embryo museum.

It was fully three months before Ian Gleed was passed fit to fly single-seat fighters again, by which time 266 had moved on and he was posted to 46 Sqn. to fly Hurricanes in France. He was lucky that day but recovered to carve out a reputation for aggressive leadership in the Battles of France and Britain and beyond, before being killed on active service in North Africa in April 1943. Flt. Lt. Gleed's story is one more from the stream of personalities to pass through the portals of RAF Sutton Bridge.

In spite of the setback of the loss of one of its flight commanders, 266 Sqn pressed on apace with war practice. Daily now the programme tested engine boost at rated altitude - fortunately without further mishap - formation flying, cross country's, cloud penetration, battle climbs, fighter attacks and rapid re-fuel and re-arm exercises. This intense activity culminated in Fighter Command's acceptance, on February 26, of 266's readiness to join the fray. On February 29 the squadron moved out of Sutton Bridge for a new home at RAF Martlesham Heath.

On that day too another piece of fate dropped into place when Flt. Lt. Sydney Bazley was posted in from 611 Sqn as replacement for Ian Gleed. Eventually 266 relocated to RAF Wittering from where it played its part in the Battle of Britain. There was little daytime enemy air activity in that sector, which included the Fens and the north Norfolk coast, although from time to time the monotony was relieved by a scramble. It is in this context, then, that Flt. Lt. Bazley enters the story.

Now firmly established as 'B' flight commander, Sydney Bazley was 'scrambled' at 07.00 on March 3, 1941 to investigate an unidentified enemy aeroplane approaching the coast. Ordered to patrol Wells-next-the-Sea at 10,000 feet he made one radio call to base on route to the patrol area and was never heard from again. Wreckage from his Spitfire I, X4613, was discovered in a field at Gedney Hill about ten miles south of Spalding, roughly a third of the way along his anticipated track to the patrol area. The cause of his crash was never established.

The third flying unit to find its feet at RAF Sutton Bridge in these opening months of the war was 254 Sqn. It had been re-formed at RAF Stradishall but in need of time to become effective, it was relocated from that operational station to quieter climes at Sutton Bridge to undergo that process. Thus on December 9, 1939, 254 arrived with just nine Blenheim Mk I's, which were intended to be converted to Mk If nightfighter standard. Only one of these was fitted out for dual control and all were sorely under-equipped, lacking essentials such as R/T, oxygen apparatus and guns.

Pilot training begun at Stradishall now ground to a halt through a combination of lack of the afore-mentioned equipment with which to continue the next stages of training plus an acute shortage of aeroplanes themselves. Didn't anyone know there was a war on!

By mid-December two Blenheims were grounded awaiting 360 hour engine inspections, three others would reach a similar position imminently and a further two were grounded for lack of spares. A sorry state indeed and only slightly relieved by a plea for the engine overhaul limit to be extended to 420 hours being accepted by Fighter Command.

Even so, serviceability continued to be a 'bind' to such an extent that on January 10 the only alternative was for the ground crews to work longer hours trying to cobble together sufficient aeroplanes to put just a few into the air each day.

HQ Fighter Command must have been equally exasperated for in mid-January 1940 it announced a change of heart. 254 was to be re-equipped with 'long-nosed' Blenheim Mk IV *"...for employment in trade defence."* This coincided with the return of ten RAFVR air gunners to the station from a gunnery course at RAF Evanton.

The squadron diary lamented the fact that three months had elapsed since re-forming and it was still far from being declared operational. Blame was laid squarely on the appalling present equipment and that there seemed no chance of the squadron crews reaching effectiveness until the unit was fully equipped with the new aeroplanes. In the meantime the Mk I's were still going u/s through lack of spares or plain mishaps.

Among the latter was K7130 which on January 17 had been landed by Plt. Off. Illingworth who then inadvertantly selected the wrong lever and neatly raised the undercarriage instead of the flaps.

Sgt. T.K.Rees had a lucky escape from death on January 23. Carrying out local flying practice in a Blenheim, for reasons best known to himself, he

While 264 Sqn. was starved of its Defiants and 266 Sqn. made do with Battles instead of Spitfires, at least 254 Sqn. arrived at Sutton Bridge with half a squadron of Bristol Blenheim I's to begin its work up. K7037 is representative of a basic 'short nose' Mark I, without the underbelly .303" calibre 4 gun tray normally associated with the Mark If to which 254 Sqn aspired.

attempted a half-roll. Being at 7000 feet he may well have had sufficient altitude but at 200 mph his speed was too high. When he came to ease the Blenheim out of the inverted position it would not respond. By this time he was diving vertically towards Mother earth with the speed rapidly increasing while the altimeter equally rapidly unwound.

Frantically winding the tail trimmer back and heaving on the control column, Rees finally regained control at just 200 feet altitude and with 320 mph on the clock. His troubles were not yet over as further difficulty was encountered when he found he could not maintain that control during landing at less than 110 mph.

Having brought the machine to rest on Sutton Bridge airfield an inspection showed the damage to comprise: starboard tailplane tip lost; rivets securing the stiffening flange to the main tailplane had sheared; port tailplane tip bent to a right angle; part of the starboard cowling was missing and during the landing the port undercarriage axle gave way causing each propeller blade to be bent backwards as it touched the ground. No doubt Sgt. Rees discovered the colour of fear that day!

254 Sqn. was being reduced inexorably to a standstill by this attrition rate and in fact never became operational at Sutton Bridge. On January 27, 1940 the luckless squadron was ordered to transfer to Coastal Command and move immediately to Bircham Newton, where it did eventually receive its MkIV's, maintaining an anti-shipping role for the rest of the war.

While all these new boys were striving to become operational under all sorts of trying conditions, the 'regular trade' of range firing practice continued to be provided by the Station.

One of the last squadrons to arrive before war broke out, for example, was 25 Sqn., at this time operating the Blenheim If. Arriving on August 14 and leaving on August 22, indicates that annual firing practice had been reduced from two to one week, probably to enable more units to squeeze in time to squeeze the trigger.

Another Blenheim casualty involved L1436 on August 16, when Plt. Off. Aberconway Pattinson returned from a camera gun sortie for the benefit of his rear gunner. He forgot to lower the undercarriage and the cockpit horn failed to operate to warn him of this omission. In consequence he belly-landed the Blenheim, without injury to those on board. Posted later to 92 Sqn., Pattinson flew in the Battle of Britain, sadly being killed in combat in October 1940.

By early 1939 the Fairey Gordon Target Tugs had gone, replaced by the Hawker Henley described earlier. Sutton Bridge Station Flight, comprising the Henley contingent and known locally as the Henley Towing Flight (HTF), was integrated with 254 Sqn. when the latter arrived as space was at a premium on the airfield with the influx of those three fighter units in the process of working-up. From December 16, 1939 therefore the HTF, comprising Plt. Off. N. L. Banks, Sgts. (pilots) R. F. Worsdell, M. U. Wilkin and J. M. Cockburn with four Henley aeroplanes L3310, L3320, L3335 and L3375, was attached to 254 Sqn. for matters of maintenance and discipline.

Foul weather prevented customers from visiting the range so there was little for the Henley Boys to get worked up about. In fact during the whole of January 1940 only two towing sorties, on behalf of 254, were flown. For the remainder of the time tug pilots used the station 'Maggie' for local flying practice.

In common with the other units at Sutton Bridge at that time, the Henley's also arrived minus certain essential equipment. R/T sets in particular were missing and made early towing sorties fraught with problems due to the inability to communicate effectively in the air. That in itself made range control difficult and not a little dangerous to say the least. However, the situation was resolved in early January when R/T sets were finally installed. At the end of that month the officer i/c, Plt. Off. Banks, was posted away

The transition from peace to war only served to increase the quantity and frequency of visiting aircraft from all types of unit to the range facility at RAF Sutton Bridge. In the last months of peace 19 Sqn. brought Spitfire I, K9851 (below)...

...while (above) this Blenheim I, L1468 flew in with 64 Squadron.

Below: Blackburn Skua L2879, a two seat, carrier borne fighter/dive bomber was a rarity...

... from the Fleet Air Arm whose crews put their range practice to very effective use against the Luftwaffe and German Navy in the Norwegian Campaign of April 1940.

Below: 46 Sqn. Gauntlet dropped in from RAF Digby whilst with No.3 ATS.

to Aston Down and Sgt. Worsdell had to assume command temporarily.

With adverse weather conditions persisting into February, again only two hours local flying practice could be completed. By March the weather had perked up so that an hour or two towing over the range could be achieved most days but it was more a case of lack of customers than problems within the HTF. Initially the Flight worked for the squadrons based at Sutton Bridge itself - 254 and 264 - but with the poor servicablility encountered by these units gradually other relatively local squadrons seem to have been invited along. For example, 29 (Debden) and 213 (Wittering).

At the beginning of April 1940 Henley L3335 was reallocated to RAF Aklington for towing duty at that station, while L3375 came in as a replacement. In this month, too, Plt. Off. S. C. Sutton took up residence as the new CO for Station Flight. Perceptably now, there was an increase in the towing hours flown, while more squadrons, such as 23 (Wittering) and 66 (Duxford), called upon HTF services in addition to 213 and 264, the latter having now moved out to Martlesham Heath.

Time now for events at RAF Sutton Bridge to take another significant, historic, twist. This latest change of direction allowed the station to retain its niche as a vital component of that chain - begun before the war - which enabled the Royal Air Force to engage the enemy with growing confidence.

On March 3, 1940 an advance party from No.11 Group Pilot Pool arrived from far-off RAF St. Athan in S Wales. This was the forerunner of what, one week later, became known as 6 Operational Training Unit (6 OTU), which was to remain at Sutton Bridge for the next two years - training Hurricane pilots for battle.

Chapter Three

HURRICANE HARVEST.

For Sgt. Peter Montgomery the summer of 1941 was a halcyon one. Four and a half months of blazing Canadian prairie sunshine had provided him with 60 hours of Tiger Moth flying, 100 hours on the Harvard and his RAF pilot wings. By train across Canada, two weeks in a troopship and a week's leave had barely taken the shine off his brevet when he reported to 6 OTU RAF Sutton Bridge in mid-October 1941 to learn to fly the Hawker Hurricane fighter.

Sgt. Montgomery joined No.38 Course with 44 other pilots, a quarter of whom were officers and the remainder sergeants. It was also a mixed bunch of nationalities - but highly typical of the time - American, Canadian, New Zealanders, Australian and one Dane, as well as British airmen - who stepped onto the platform at the tiny railway station.

For an in depth, pupil's-eye view of life at RAF Sutton Bridge, some years ago Peter Montgomery wrote an account of his experiences at No.6 OTU which, with his permission, is drawn upon here.

Before tackling the mighty Hurricane, new boys were first given a dual check flight in a two-seat Miles Master. In Peter Montgomery's case his log book shows 35 minutes dual with Sgt. Staniforth in Master I, N7567 on October 12, followed next day with an hour's solo in Master N8022.

Confrontation with a Hurricane (P3039) came the day after, first just for fifty minutes to get the feel of her then for a few local area flights each lasting about an hour and a half during the days which followed. One flight per day seems painfully slow but the combination of two overlapping courses, less than 100% aircraft serviceability as a norm, the notorious English weather and being kept busy in the classroom, tends to sum up the situation quite well. Visits to sample the sparse amenities of the village were few in

With a wooden structure covered by plywood, the tandem two-seat Miles Master I trainer was powered by a 715hp Rolls-Royce Kestrel in-line engine and capable of 226mph. From the first production batch, Master I, N7547 seen here, was the stable-mate of N7567 in which Sgt. Peter Montgomery had his first check flight at 56 OTU, prior to being let loose in a Hurricane.

Hawker Hurricane P3039 had seen service with 55 OTU before reaching 56 OTU at Sutton Bridge. P3039 is seen here, with its code letters PA-J somewhat crudely applied, leading two other Hurricanes from 55 OTU. At 56 OTU, Peter Montgomery had his first taste of a Hurricane when he took P3039 into the air for 50 minutes on 13/10/41. This aeroplane managed to survive until 30/10/41 before it was involved in a landing accident at RAF Sutton Bridge in the hands of Canadian Sgt. Zadworthy.

number and usually meant going to one of the pubs but only after a long day and at that time of year, in darkness. Occasionally a bus would run these boys to Kings Lynn for a Saturday night out.

Hard beds.

Food and accomodation at the camp itself was *"...reasonable in the prevailing circumstances but we gave it little thought as we were all keen to get the course over and go on to a squadron."* Conditions at the Camp must have improved somewhat in the year since a raw New Zealand pilot, Sgt. Desmond Scott, sampled the delights of 6 OTU in late 1940. In the second volume of his memoirs: *One More Hour,* (Hutchinson 1989); Gp. Capt. Desmond Scott DSO,OBE,DFC wrote: *"We were packed off from Uxbridge like a bunch of schoolboys, each with a rail warrant that would take us to RAF Sutton Bridge, a grass airfield and hutted camp a few miles west of Kings Lynn. It was to prove one of the most uninteresting parts of England I was ever to serve in. Not only was the surrounding countryside cold, low and wet, but the station's domestic complex resembled aircraft crates all camouflaged in black and green and designed to sleep about 20 pilots to each hut. This accomodation was both ridiculous and austere. Our beds were iron stretchers that concertina-ed into a third of their length when not in use. On each bed were three square canvas-covered squabs filled with sawdust, instead of a mattress. As we were not issued with sheets it was virtually impossible to keep them in line or together. It was hardly compatible with a Lincolnshire winter. We usually woke up with our backsides filling a gap between the squabs and resting on the cold iron slats that took the place of springs. This discomfort was partly overcome by placing thick layers of newspaper beneath the squabs and sleeping in our overcoats. I have often wondered how many young lives were lost through lack of sleep."* Apart from this jaundiced view, Sgt. Scott appears to have followed a similar training pattern to that of Sgt. Montgomery.

Masters and Hurricanes.

For the latter, it was back to the Master in week two for a spell 'under the hood' practicing instrument flying. Again, once checked out, at this stage it was quite usual for one pupil to fly 'under the hood' while another acted as safety pilot keeping a lookout for other aircraft. Sgt. Montgomery accumulated four hours in Master N8342 during this phase before graduating to cloud-flying and map-reading exercises in various Hurricanes.

Peter recalled that when taking off dual in the Master, the rear seat was raised and the top of the canopy angled up to form a windshield. The pilot in the back seat could then see over the head of the man in front and correct any swing that might develop during a 'blind' take off.

Once airborne, stress on the canopy mechanism became excessive at speeds above 120mph so it was necessary to lower the rear seat and close the canopy. Apparently it was as well to remember to carry out both actions in the right order otherwise one's forgetfulness was rewarded by a severe blow on the head, proportional to the airspeed!

For those trained on the Harvard the change to a British design also brought the need to remember that wheelbrakes were operated by a hand lever rather than toe-brakes. More than one pupil taxying for take off had to be pulled up by the Duty Pilot who spotted smoke curling from the brake drums. Another significant difficulty for pilots such as Peter, trained in the Canadian prairies in high summer, was getting used to the cloud and poor visibility of England in early winter, factors which could lead to dire consequences for the unwary.

Week three saw pupils gaining in confidence; doing everything from battle climbs to 25,000 feet, aerobatics, low flying (authorised!), formations and

Piles of new-mown grass surround a forlorn-looking tennis court. Even in summer it is hard to escape the feeling of bleakness engendered by RAF Sutton Bridge domestic site in the 1930's. It was these wooden huts which soldiered on into WW2 and made such a lasting impression on New Zealander Desmond Scott, who while an embryo Hurricane pilot at 6 OTU, likened them to living in an aircraft packing crate! [Wisbech Museum].

pin-point navigation exercises, rounding off the week by air to ground firing at Holbeach Range and a few air attack manoeuvres.

After relatively sedate training aeroplanes these new Hurricane pilots found the 'kick in the back', as the throttle was pushed forward, most impressive and the ground dropped rapidly away. On the Mark I though, it was an awkward task then to get the wheels up as it was necessary to change hands on the stick to be able to reach the undercarriage selector lever located on the right-hand side wall of the cockpit. This lever also operated the flaps, working through an 'H' type gate so in order to avoid the embarrassing situation of lowering the flaps just after take-off it was usual for a new boy to look down to make sure the lever went into the right position. Unfortunately the combination of changing hands and taking an eye off the horizon usually resulted in the nose dropping followed by a sudden over-correction as earth seemed to replace sky through the windscreen. This sequence might well be repeated if 'wheels up' was not quite selected the first time. In consequence many first time solos on the Hurricane began with the aeroplane disappearing from the view of those on the ground in the manner of a Big Dipper!

Once airborne and 'clean' Peter considered the performance and handling characteristics were excellent, although the early Marks had only a fixed rudder trim tab rather than an adjustable one. This was bent manually by the ground crew to compensate for torque at cruising power but it was a bit of a strain on the right leg after an hour or so in the air trying to counteract with rudder the additional torque encountered at higher speeds.

After the long tarmac runways of Canada, landing a Hurricane on Sutton Bridge's small undulating grass field was quite exacting and despite the robustness of its undercarriage, it could not absorb as much rough handling as the Harvard.

There is some evidence that Pierced Steel Mat was laid some time in 1941 or shortly after in an effort to stabilise the grass surface. Air Ministry Directorate of Works drawings show it was laid over an area of 1150yds by 50yds on the NE/SW run, together with another 800yds of Sommerfeld Track running at right-angles from the northern end.

Watching other pupils landing, Peter saw many Hurricanes bounce rather too high, hit harder the second time and descend a third time with their undercarriage legs swinging free because the locking strut joints had broken on impact. On such occasions naturally the wheels folded on final touchdown and the aeroplane skidded along on its belly showering wooden propeller splinters in all directions. There was usually no injury to the pilot - except perhaps his pride and he had more to fear from the subsequent sticky interview with the Sqn. Ldr. (Flying). The incident listing contains statistical evidence to the litany of bent undercarriages and worse, sustained by 6 OTU Hurri's at the hands of erstwhile fighter pilots.

It was November now and poor weather made it difficult to get time in the air. During the next two weeks Peter Montgomery managed only six hours in Hurricanes, most on aerobatics and formation flying and two hours instrument practice in a Master.

One week of the course was spent attached to the Gunnery Flight. With just over an hour on air to ground gunnery and a mere fifteen minutes air to air firing at a drogue, Sgt. Montgomery's limited experience included using a Hurricane fitted with an early experimental gyro gun sight. Whether the shortcomings of this instrument were responsible, or whether the entry reflects the standard of air to air firing at the time, he did not know but in his recollection he scored no hits at all on the drogue although his gunnery efforts were still assessed as 'average' in his log book!

During one lecture on combat tactics it was pointed out to the students that German fighters had fuel injection systems enabling them to be nosed over from level flight into a dive without any loss of power or speed. Our own engines, on the other hand, had normal float carburettors which, when subjected to the same negative 'G' manouevre, would interrupt the fuel supply and the engine would cut. Pupils were told that the way to deal with this situation was to half-roll the aeroplane, then pull the stick back to maintain positive 'G' and keep the fuel flowing in the ensuing dive.

Curiosity about this technique got the better of Peter one day. After firing practice he climbed to 15,000 feet and with 350mph on the clock he rolled the Hurricane over and pulled through into a dive. With the aeroplane in a vertical dive and 500mph indicated airspeed, the control column became solid and immoveable. He realised many years later that he had experienced the onset of compressibility but little was known of such things in those days, least of all by curious trainees.

Hauling with both hands on the stick for all he was worth and with Mother Earth gaining rapidly in clarity, gradually it moved and the nose came up. At this point he blacked out and when the blackness turned red then pink then blue, he found the aeroplane travelling vertically but this time upwards. A hasty glance at the ASI showed the needle dropping past the 100mph mark so in order to avoid a stall which seemed imminent, Peter kicked on rudder to get the nose down onto the horizon. Much to his consternation the ASI needle continued to rotate rapidly anti-clockwise and it was only as the zero figure was left behind that he realised he had mis-read the wretched instrument and it had another complete circuit of the dial to go before flying speed would have become critical. Much enlightened and sobered he returned to Sutton Bridge and kept quiet about his little escapade but it said much for the inherant strength of the Hurricane and the reliability of the Merlin engine.

The Human Cost.

Many and varied were the mishaps to befall these OTU pupils; four of Sgt. Montgomerey's course were killed in separate incidents, one was seriously injured and numerous others suffered forced landings or undercarriage collapses of the type mentioned earlier. In human terms his No.38 Course would become the costliest ever for 56 OTU.

Plt. Off. N.J.Choppen was first to go on October 20. He was flying a formation practice in V6690 when its engine began to lose power. Pulling away from the

FRONT GUN QUARTER ATTACK

a) FIRE BETWEEN 60° AND 20° ANGLE OFF

b) RED FIRES ON RED PORT ATTACK, GREEN ON GREEN STARBOARD ATTACK.

NOT TO SCALE

S E A

SIGHTING

POSITIONING

600 YARDS

CURVE OF PURSUIT

SIGHTING

600 YARDS

CURVE OF PURSUIT

POSITIONING

L A N D

A diagram from instruction material used in Pilot Gunnery Instructor course at Central Gunnery School while located at RAF Sutton Bridge. The 'Land' represents the bank at Gedney Drove End and the 'Sea' in this case would be The Wash. During this quarter attack excercise, Towing aircraft travel parallel to the land and attacking fighters fire out to sea.

Above: Resplendent in factory-fresh paint, this Fairey Battle TT1, L5598 shows off the standard Target-Tug broad black and yellow stripes to great advantage. Also visible is the horizontal wind-driven cable winching gear mounted on an arm attached to the rear cockpit.

Right: Stable-mate to the Battle Target-tugs was the Hawker Henley, whose portly lines can be seen in this example, L3276

formation he approached the ground in a shallow dive but was seen to crash when the Hurricane went into a steep turn close to the ground south of Reffley Wood near Kings Lynn. Plt. Off. Choppen was killed and he remains forever at Sutton Bridge, being laid to rest in the village churchyard.

October 30 was a particularly unfortunate day for Canadians Plt. Off. McKillop and Sgt. Zadworthy who, together with Sgt. G.A.Johnstone each wiped the undercarriage off P3888, P3039 and P2992 respectively. Three in a day, however, was not at all unusual at the airfield. Plt. Off. Hosking did the same to R4076 on November 3 while later that day American Plt. Off. James. A. Gray took the undercarriage off Master T8286 on his first solo on the type. On November 6, Sgt. D.C.Goudie, a Canadian, force landed on Carter's Farm, Burtoft when the engine of P2814 failed while he was on a map-reading exercise. One of the few Danes in the RAF, Sgt. Jens Ipsen, was badly injured the same day when his Hurricane, V7004, broke up after hitting a tree in a steep turn during low flying practice. Sgt. D.Meisner was killed on November 7, followed four days later by Sgt. M.Willson, both Canadian pilots who crashed outside the district.

There were few days without incident but the worst during Peter Montgomery's course occurred on November 24.

It was a dull morning with a grey stratus layer covering most of The Wash area. A close friend of Peter Montgomery, Sgt. G.A.Johnstone, had been sent off in V6864 on what was intended to be one of the last exercises of No.38 Course. Sadly, for Sgt. Johnstone, it would be very final indeed.

During the morning a flight of Avro Manchester bombers from 97 Sqn. (Coningsby) was cruising in formation, just below the cloud base, near the Sutton Bridge circuit. Flying above the unbroken cloud layer was Sgt. Johnstone being homed back to base by R/T. Nearing the airfield he was instructed to descend through the cloud and on breaking out below flew bang into the centre of the bomber formation, colliding with R5792 flown by Flg. Off. H.T.Hill. From the tangled mass of wreckage there were no survivors. Flg. Off. Hill's crew which perished with him was: Flt. Sgt. A.Smith (2nd pilot), Sgt. J.Newton (Obs), Sgt. F.E.Martin (WOp/AG), Sgt. F.Holt (WOp/AG), Sgt. E.C.Hutton (AG)(Aus), Sgt. J.Few (AG).

Both aeroplanes fell to earth near the village of Walpole St. Andrew and Sgt. Johnstone, too, was laid to rest in Sutton Bridge churchyard.

By the end of Peter Montgomery's six-week course at 56 OTU no less than four of his fellow pupils had been killed without ever reaching a squadron, a loss rate by no means untypical of the time at training units.

Last sortie of Peter's OTU course was 45 minutes of night flying in V7645 and then graduation day - November 24, 1941, arrived. To its collective surprise, on November 14, No.38 Course had already had the honour of being inspected by no less a person than AOC Fighter Command, ACM Sholto Douglas, who happened to be visiting the station at the time - much 'bull' that day!.

Finally came the postings. These were avidly scrutinised before the mad dash to go on ten days leave. Sgt. Montgomery found himself posted to a Defiant nightfighter squadron but returned to Hurricanes with an AA Co-operation Unit later in the war.

11 Group Pilot Pool.

This, then, was the basic pattern into which life at 56 OTU had settled in the eighteen months since it had moved from St Athan to Sutton Bridge. But how did it all begin?

Formed originally at RAF Andover in January 1939, the purpose of what was then known as 11 Group Pilot Pool was twofold:

a) to bring pilots posted from FTS to 11 (Fighter) Group up to the standard of fully trained fighter pilots before their posting to service squadrons.

b) to train RAF Volunteer Reserve (VR) pilots who had completed 120 hours flying solo and who were willing to devote from two to six months to learn the

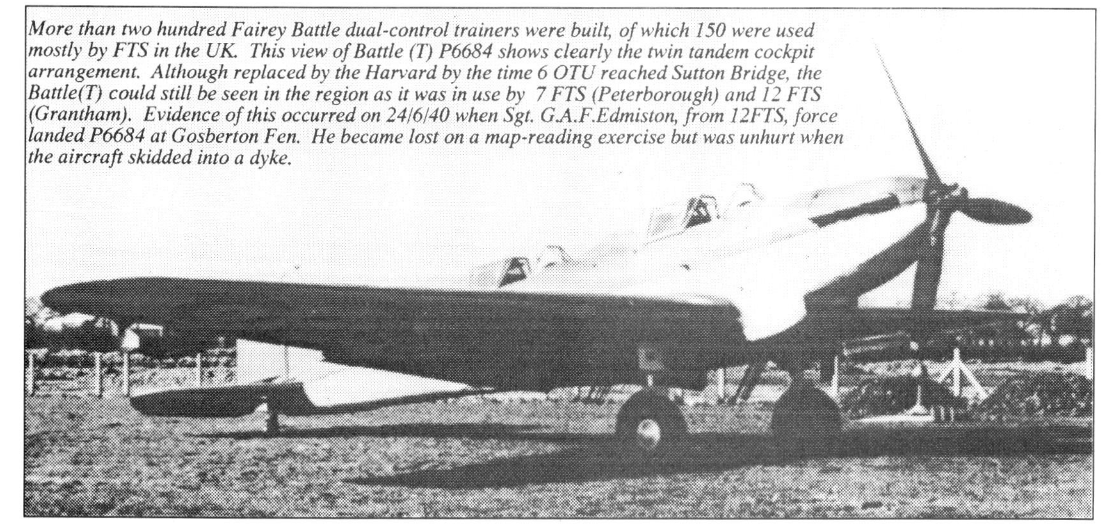

More than two hundred Fairey Battle dual-control trainers were built, of which 150 were used mostly by FTS in the UK. This view of Battle (T) P6684 shows clearly the twin tandem cockpit arrangement. Although replaced by the Harvard by the time 6 OTU reached Sutton Bridge, the Battle(T) could still be seen in the region as it was in use by 7 FTS (Peterborough) and 12 FTS (Grantham). Evidence of this occurred on 24/6/40 when Sgt. G.A.F.Edmiston, from 12FTS, force landed P6684 at Gosberton Fen. He became lost on a map-reading exercise but was unhurt when the aircraft skidded into a dyke.

North American Harvard I, N7008 seen visiting RAF Sutton Bridge in late-1938, probably while attached to 3 FTS at Grantham, which was one of the first units receive this two-seat trainer. Harvards were operated at RAF Sutton Bridge by 6 OTU in 1940 which, together with other units in the region, meant their distinctive 'buzz-saw' propeller noise would be a regular sound in Fenland skies throughout WW2 and beyond.

operational side of work as a fighter pilot. This latter referred to a pre-war situation.

Equipment was to be the Hawker Hurricane for operational training, and the Fairey Battle (T) for dual flying instruction. Establishment in men and machines was to be equivalent to that of a front-line, single-seat, fighter squadron. After six months the Pool moved to St.Athan in South Wales where North American Harvards replaced Battles and it remained there until the move to Sutton Bridge whereupon it also transferred to 12 Group.

Fenland climes may seem an odd choice to locate a fighter training unit, particularly in view of the vagaries of the weather around The Wash - already mentioned on many occasions in this narrative - and the decision, just six months earlier, to banish 3 Armament Training School to the far north. In fact RAF Speke (Liverpool) and Hucknall (Nottingham) were both considered as potential homes for the Pool but the former suffered from a surfeit of balloon barrages and bad weather(!) while the latter had too many night-flying restrictions, so both were discarded.

Thus on March 10, 6 OTU, with a complement of 7 Hurricanes, 3 Harvards, 5 Miles Mentors and 1 Gladiator was created and its aeroplanes and team of instructors, under the command of Sqn. Ldr. R. Pinkham arrived at Sutton Bridge. The following day the first course to be run at the station, No.5, got under way.

Springtime, too, arrived in Fenland and with it the rain, fog, frost and snow, which be-devilled previous months, faded into the past.

Each training course was scheduled to last six weeks, although this of necessity was much reduced as that fateful year progressed. In that length of time it was intended to teach pupils how to fly a Hurricane, hopefully without bending it too much; something of what to expect in an operational squadron situation and perhaps how to stay alive in battle. Sadly, though, many young men trained here were yet to lose their lives in combat, while others never even made it that far. The importance of their task, however, was emphasised during a visit, on April 22, by the AOC Fighter Command himself, ACM Sir Hugh Dowding.

Fourteen students made up the first fighter pilot course to graduate from RAF Sutton Bridge on April 27, 1940. It was followed the next day by the start of No. 6 Course, but before long batches of trainees became less defined, at least until the foriegn pilots began to arrive.

Action in France.

Air fighting, sporadic upto now, was about to erupt over the Franco-German border area, culminating in the Wehrmacht invading France and the Low Countries on May 10, backed up by the Luftwaffe. With one exception, the whole of No.5 Course was pitched headlong into the thick of the Blitzkreig in France.

6 OTU, No.5 Course	Posted to	Notes
Plt. Off. R.H.Dibnah	1 Sqn.	Survived war
Plt. Off. G.E.Goodman	1 Sqn.	Killed 1941
Plt. Off. C.M.Stavart	1 Sqn.	Survived war
Plt. Off. H.W.Eliot	73 Sqn.	Killed 1945
Sgt. Friend	73 Sqn.	
Plt. Off. A. McFadden	73 Sqn.	Killed 1942
Plt. Off. Roe	73 Sqn.	
Plt. Off. R.D.Rutter	73 Sqn.	Survived war
Plt. Off. D.H.Wissler	85 Sqn.	Killed 1940
Plt. Off. Jarvis	87 Sqn	
Plt. Off. LeBreuilly	87 Sqn.	
Sgt. Penikett	87 Sqn.	
Sgt. Townsend	607 Sqn.	

Sgt. Wright: Injured in training accident 22/4/40.

Such was the mounting loss rate in 1 Sqn., for example, that by May 20, less than a month after leaving Sutton Bridge, Stavart and Goodman were leading sections of aircraft several times daily on

Powered by a 200hp DH Gipsy Six engine, forty-five Miles M.16 Mentors were supplied to the RAF just before the outbreak of WW2. This three-seat aircraft was used by 6 OTU to train fighter pilots in the use of radio equipment and radio procedures. At least five were brought to RAF Sutton Bridge in 1940 and L4400 is known to have been one of those. [P.H.T. Green Collection]

combat sorties in French skies while Dibnah, equally committed, had been put out of the fight for three months with a thigh wound.

Relations between 1 Sqn. and 6 OTU were further cemented when the squadron was forced to re-organise in France in late-May. Two worrying factors brought about this situation and was the point at which members of Sutton Bridge's ex-No.5 Course 'won their spurs'.

Exhausted by incessant - though successful - air combat, mounting losses and a nomadic existance, 1 Sqn's CO, Sqn. Ldr. P.J.H.Halahan pleaded with authority to replace his dwindling pool of experienced pilots and return them to England before they all succumbed to the inexorable attrition rate. Not only were combat losses among the pre-war trained pilots and early products of 11 Group Pool robbing Dowding of his hard core of experienced men but he was also short of replacements and equally short of men capable of teaching them how to stay alive in the air. RAF Sutton Bridge was now going to play a vital role in dealing with this situation.

In the cold light of reality there was no other choice - if Fighter Command was to have any chance of growing sufficiently to defend mainland Britain - but to send the 'new-boys' into the fray, thus releasing what was left of the weary 'old-hands' to inject backbone into new units and pass on their combat experience. The new boys, too, acquitted themselves with honour and those who survived also went on to play a key role in the next big battle - the Battle of Britain.

Halahan's recommendation was accepted and on May 28 the following pilots from 1 Sqn., all distinguished Battle of France veterans, each with many 'kills' to his credit, reported to 6 OTU Sutton Bridge for duty as flying instructors:-

Flg. Off. J.I.Kilmartin DFC
Plt. Off. R.G.Lewis
Plt. Off. P.W.O.Mould DFC
Flg. Off. C.D.Palmer DFC
Flt. Sgt. F.J.Soper DFM
Flg. Off. W.H.Stratton DFC
Flg. Off. Billy Drake
Flt. Lt. Prosser Hanks DFC

The last two were original 1 Sqn. pilots, both wounded in combat in mid-May and hospitalised in England where, on recovery, they too were posted to Sutton Bridge as instructors:

Sqn. Ldr. Halahan with his remaining original members of No.1 were posted to the other Hurricane OTU (5 OTU) at RAF Aston Down.

Pitched into battle.

The pattern of training at 6 OTU was therefore established and while the next few of courses of ex-FTS pupils, becoming ever shorter in duration, provided more replacements for the final weeks of the campaign in France, subsequent ones helped rebuild depleted squadrons for the imminent Battle of Britain. Number 5 course had a duration of six weeks but number 6 lasted less than three weeks. During that hectic summer some pilots were posted to squadrons with less than a week at OTU. These tended to be those pilots processed by 6 OTU in parallel to the intakes from FTS, who were drawn from a variety of units and selected for rapid conversion to Hurricanes in a desperate attempt to top up the flow of fighter pilots to the front line.

Much has been written about young replacement pilots - in both Wars - being pitched into the cauldron of battle with woefully little experience. Some lived, some died but all were indeed brave young men. 6 OTU can provide the contrasting stories of two such men from this band.

Commissioned on May 26, 1940, Plt. Off. Kenneth Carver was posted to 29 Sqn. RAF Digby, to fly the twin-engined Blenheim If. His subsequent posting can be seen as an example of the policy of trawling for potential single-seat fighter pilot material as the Battle of Britain gathered momentum and highlighted gaps in manpower. Sutton Bridge was to play a key role in this process, too.

Plt. Off. Carver with Plt. Off. Neville Solomon and Sgt. R. F. Bumstead were three 29 Sqn. pilots detailed to report to 6 OTU on July 16 for what was termed "...a flying refresher course". Interviewed for Lincolnshire Life magazine in 1990, Ken Carver recalled turning up at Sutton Bridge and being billetted in the local doctor's house. That same day he was confronted by his first Hurricane and swiftly shown over the controls. Climbing into the cockpit he took off gingerly only to be alarmed to find the windscreen gradually becoming obscured by leaking glycol (engine coolant fluid). Landing safely after "... a hairy flight" he was blithely informed he should not have been allocated that particular aeroplane as it had been declared unserviceable! The very next day, now considered capable of flying a Hurricane, he was posted out to join 229 Sqn. at RAF Wittering!

Fortunately perhaps for Plt. Off. Carver, Wittering sector was pretty quiet and he had time to find his feet before 229 moved to Kent to take a more active part in the Battle. Plt. Off. Carver finally got to grips with the enemy but was shot up and badly burned on September 11. He baled out and survived his ordeal, returning to 229 Sqn. after many months of hospitalisation and retired after the war as a Sqn. Ldr. with the DFC.

Plt. Off. Solomon was less fortunate. He left Sutton Bridge bound for 17 Sqn. at Debden after just three days on the Hurricane. Debden, being closer to the action, offered no gentle breaking-in period but fortunately for him, Plt. Off. Solomon's woeful lack of experience was quickly recognised and he was packed off for more Hurricane training, this time to 5 OTU Aston Down. It was August 15 before he returned to 17 Sqn. where he took his place in action with his hard pressed comrades. Plt. Off. Solomon lasted just three days before he was shot down and killed.

Pressure such as this at OTU level brought accidents with it. The extent varied from one course to another, with no discernable pattern except that of inevitable errors of judgement or mechanical failures. For example, during the first course six mishaps were recorded, all without fatal result but the second course was completed with a clean record - although the latter was to become a rarity as we shall see later.

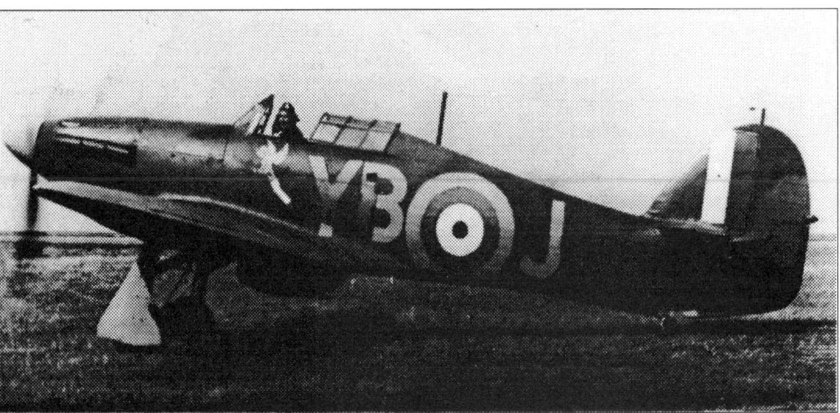

In July 1940 the time taken to convert pilots onto Hurricanes was sometimes just a few days. Plt. Off Neville Solomon was posted to 17 Sqn., one of whose Hurricanes N2359 is seen here at Debden coded YB-J and with a 'Flying Popeye' motif beneath the cockpit. After active service with 17 Sqn., N2359 was relegated to 6/56 OTU for training duty, where it met with a minor landing accident at Sutton Bridge on 11/6/41.

Having arrived in March with a handful of Hurricanes, by June the quantity of serviceable aeroplanes available to 6 OTU rose to a more practical 24 Hurricanes, 4 Harvards, 5 Mentors and 3 Gladiators.

With effect from June 9, therefore, to get the supply of pilots flowing more effectively, flying training was organised on a 'Flight' basis; 'A' commanded by Flt. Lt. Greaves, 'B': Flg. Off. Palmer and 'C': Flg. Off. Dawbarn. Sqn. Ldr. G.C.Tomlinson was officer i/c Flying and Wg. Cdr. J.H.Edwardes-Jones was OC 6 OTU.

Escape from France.

At about this time the RAF was pulling out of France, being harried from airfield to airfield by the advancing German army. The plight of 1 Sqn. comes yet again to the fore bringing with it a stirring tale of determination and resourcefulness, recorded in detail by Michael Shaw in his book *No.1 Squadron,* (Ian Allen 1986.)

During its sojourn in France, Sous-Lieutenant Jean Demozay, a French Air Force pilot, was attached to the squadron as official interpreter. In the closing days of the campaign the squadron ended up on Nantes airfield from which all its remaining aeroplanes were flown back to England. When the last Hurricanes disappeared over the horizon Demozay and a group of 18 RAF ground crew were left to fend for themselves. The idea was for them to drive another 100 miles south to La Rochelle for evacuation by sea.

Demozay was not enamoured of this proposal and spotted an old Bristol Bombay transport out on the field. A quick inspection established it was topped up with fuel but due to a broken tail wheel assembly it had been left behind as useless. Some of the ground crew had other ideas and set to work to put this defect to rights, whereupon Demozay offered to fly them all back to England.

Assisted by the senior NCO, Demozay took off and set course for the South Coast, intending to land at Tangmere. During a singularly uneventful flight the NCO told Jean that most of his group lived in East Anglia and would he mind flying on to RAF Sutton Bridge? Readily agreeing he carried on and duly delivered them to their preferred destination.

Now an exile and determined to return to operational flying, the redoubtable Jean Demozay subsequently entered the RAF, was posted to 5 OTU Aston Down later rejoining 1 Sqn. with which he enjoyed an illustrious flying career as a fighter pilot, using the *nom-de-guerre* of 'Moses' Morlaix. Surviving the war, Demozay returned to France where, about to embark on a promising political career, he lost his life in an air accident in late-1945.

With his cap set at a jaunty angle is Sous-Lieutenant Jean Demozay, a French Air Force pilot who was attached to 1 Sqn. as interpreter. He remained with 1 Sqn. as it was harried across France and refused to be left behind when the time came to retreat to England. He fought on under the nom de guerre of Moses Morlaix in order to protect his family in occupied France.

Tools of the Trade.

Having looked at those teachers who were to mould fighter pilots destined for the Battle of Britain; RAF Sutton Bridge was the school but what of the tools of the trade?

Principal aeroplane at Sutton Bridge was the Hawker Hurricane, supported by Harvards for dual instruction and three-seat Miles Mentors for radio training. Most of the Hurricanes on 6 OTU inventory were Mark I's with fixed-pitch, two-blade, wooden propellers; either issued pre-war to squadrons which then upgraded to newer models and passed on the old or, later, war-weary aeroplanes again relegated to training duty as new models arrived. A full listing of Hurricanes involved in accidents while based at Sutton Bridge can be found in this chapter and reference to their serial numbers presents a random cross-section of aircraft on charge at various times.

First of the accidents to result in a fatality for the OTU was that involving Sgt. C. F. Cotton, who lost his life in L1897 on June 25,1940, near the village of Upwell.

Tony Steer of Norwich was 10 years old at the

Treble-One ready for action. An impressive line-up of Hurricane I's of 111 Sqn. at Northolt aerodrome in July 1938. Sqn. Ldr. J.Gillan briefs his pilots in this highly posed publicity photograph taken shortly after the squadron took delivery of its new aircraft. Many of the Hurricanes in this photo found their way to 6/56 OTU. Accident records confirm, for example, that L1552, L1548 and L1555 were at Sutton Bridge in 1940.

time of the accident and recalling the event in 1991 he said: *"The crash remains very vivid in my mind, happening at that impressionable age and living in an area much frequented by the aeroplanes from Sutton Bridge. My cousin and I were standing near a large metal-framed bridge spanning Middle Level Drain. We watched this Hurricane following the drain, flying towards the bridge at about 60 feet. I could see the pilot quite clearly, waving at us and we waved back. Approaching the bridge, which is about 40 feet high, the aeroplane suddenly climbed steeply. At a guess, when it reached between 1000 and 1500 feet it appeared to stop in mid-air then plunged nose down to crash into a wheat field at the side of the drain."*

"Running like mad to the field, at first sight there was no sign of the aeroplane. Everything was below the level of the wheat crop and all that marked the passage of the Hurricane was a relatively small crater with a little wisp of smoke rising from it. Hereabouts the soil is very soft, with a lot of peat and I think this would account for the Hurricane going in so far."

"I remember being frightened by the thought of perhaps seeing a dead man so I held back from going any closer. That night, too, I overheard talk of removing the remains of the pilot to our farmhouse and had a nightmare about it. I never discovered if the pilot was found or what happened to him. Next day a long RAF recovery lorry arrived and tried to get close to the crash site but it was unable to do so because of the gateways from the river bank being too narrow."

"During 1980 my cousin and I re-visited that field and found a few small fragments from all those years ago. We even found some pieces with blue and red paint on, probably from the roundels."

According to the MOD (Air) accident record card, Sgt. Cotton was authorised to carry out aerobatics in a low flying area but for unknown reasons appeared to have gone below the recommended height of 10,000 feet. It was considered that when he pulled up to avoid a bridge the aeroplane stalled and hit the ground before he had time to recover.

Exiled Patriots.
In its time RAF Sutton Bridge saw aircrew of all Allied nationalities pass through its gates. Poles, the first of many batches of exiles destined for active service in the summer of 1940, arrived on June 23 complete with an interpreter. The latter was a highly necessary role in a potentially hazardous situation. Some of these fellows, in most cases trained pilots (to varying degrees) already, had little command of the English language, high performance aeroplanes in which all the knobs, levers and dials were labelled in a foreign tongue, or RAF radio procedures. 6 OTU was eventually to train with great success these men and a stream of foreign pilots many of whom carved out distinguished war records.

It is not intended here to record in detail the wealth of individual careers and feats as these are far more adequately handled in books such as Kenneth Wynn's *Men of the Battle of Britain* (Glidden 1989). Instead, a few examples will be outlined to illustrate the richness of activity at Sutton Bridge and some of the more prominent incidents which occured.

To say that these exiled patriots, be they Poles, Czechs, Belgians, French, Danes, Norwegian and many others, simply 'arrived' at Sutton Bridge is to understate the tortuous lengths to which these individuals fought their way across Europe and even North Africa to first fight the Germans in the air with their respective Air Forces then, when that failed, they undertook lengthy and hazardous journies to reach England in order to carry on that fight.

The next Polish course, comprising 12 pupils, began on July 14 and it was from this batch that the next fatality occured.

Plt. Off. K.Olewinski was airborne at 07.00 on July 29 in Hurricane L1714, authorised to practice air combat and aerobatic manoeuvres above 5000 feet altitude. His aeroplane was last seen by one of his comrades to begin a dive at 10,000 feet altitude from which it never pulled out, crashing deep into the earth at Walsoken, near Wisbech. Olewinski thus became the first of the long lines of wartime graves in Sutton Bridge village churchyard.

Composition of first Polish pilot course at 6 OTU
Posted In: 23 June 1940. Posted Out: 16 July 1940.

Name	Posted To	Notes
Plt. Off. S. Lapka	302 Sqn.	* Survived the war
Plt. Off. T. Nowak	253 Sqn.	* KIA Sep 1941
Flg. Off. A. Ostowicz	145 Sqn.	* KIA Aug 1940
Flt. Lt. W. Pankratz	145 Sqn.	* KIA Aug 1940
Plt. Off. E.R.Pilch	302 Sqn.	* KIA Feb 1941
Plt. Off. W.M.C. Samolinski	253 Sqn.	* KIA Sep 1940
Plt. Off. Virpsha	Retained as interpreter	

* Fought in Battle of Britain

Central to the co-ordination of this embryo training system was SHQ RAF Sutton Bridge. It will be remembered from an earlier chapter that Wg. Cdr. Barwell was at the helm initially. Having got the three embryo fighter squadrons 'off the ground', leaving the way open for 6 OTU to take up residence, Dickie Barwell saw that safely established then on June 13 handed over command of the Station to Gp. Capt. H. D. O'Neill AFC. Barwell subsequently took command of RAF Coltishall until June 1941 when he was appointed Station Commander of RAF Biggin Hill. Having made a practice of flying occasional operational sorties, consistant with his policy of leading from the front, it was on one such patrol, July 1 1942, that Wg. Cdr. Philip Barwell lost his life, shot down by mistake by a 'rookie' Spitfire pilot who made a tragic error of identification.

On July 20 it was the turn of the Free French to arrive, followed ten days later by three Belgians, more

Multi-national No.1 Sqn. at RAF Wittering in November 1940. A fine example of how 'old boys' of Sutton Bridge were absorbed by front-line fighter squadrons during1940. Sitting on Hurricane wing, from left: Plt. Off. Clowes; Sgts. A. Zavoral and J. Prihoda (Czech); Plt. Off. Elkington. Middle row: Sous/Lt. J Demozay (Fr); Sgts. Kuttelwascher, Novak and Stefan (Czech). Front: Plt. Off. Hancock; Flt. Lt. M.H.Brown (Can); Plt. Off. Chetham; Sgt. Plasil (Czech). Prihoda, Plasil and Chetham were ex-6 OTU; Hancock served with 266 Sqn at Sutton Bridge and Demozay arrived at 6 OTU after his escape from France. (Sqn Archives.)

Tucked away among Hurricanes awaiting repair, is Hurricane L1714 seen below the nose of a Spitfire at No1 Crash Repair Unit (1CRU) in Morris Motors works, Cowley. Photographed in May 1940, L1714 is still marked in the distinctive half black/half white undersurfaces with the serial marked under the starboard wing. This Hurricane was allocated to 6 OTU but crashed and was destroyed near Wisbech on 29/7/40, killing Plt. Off. K. Olewinski (Pole). (P H T Green Collection)

Inset: The grave of Plt. Off. K. Olewinski in the Commonwealth War Graves section of Sutton Bridge village churchyard.

Poles and on August 17 the first group of twenty Czechs. Of course, interspersed between all these was a steady flow of English and Commonwealth pilots too, a further illustration of overlapping the courses among the three Flights to keep the momentum going. For example on the day of the Czech's arrival a group of 13 English pilots also appeared, 3 from 9FTS and 10 from 10FTS. Among their number was one, Sgt. F.J.Howarth, whose name would be for ever linked with the Czechs due to a mid-air collision near the station.

This accident, which occurred at 08.30 in the bright sunlight of September 3, 1940, seems to have been due simply to an error of judgement by one or both pilots during an authorised combat flying exercise. Perhaps in that sunlight - mentioned by an eyewitness - they momentarily lost sight of each other with fatal consequences. In the opinion of that same eyewitness, *"... both aircraft seemed to be stunting... in an effort to gain an advantage one over the other... and collided at about 700 feet altitude."*

Composition of first French pilot course at 6 OTU

Posted In: 20 July 1940. Posted out date not known.

Warr. Off. J. Denis	Warr. Off. R. Speich
Warr. Off. L. Ferrant	Warr. Off. A. Littalf
Warr. Off. G. Grasset	Flt. Sgt. A. Moulenes
Flt. Sgt. R. Grasset	Sgt. J. Joire
Sgt. N. Castelain	Sgt. R. Guedon
Sgt. E.M. de Scitivaux	Sgt. C.A.D.Deport *

* This pilot is noted on staff of 6 OTU later in 1940.

At this stage of the airwar - it was the height of the Battle of Britain - there were not enough instructors to accompany pupils on a regular or individual basis, therefore trainees were sent off in pairs to practice combat tactics amongst themselves. Training course lengths were being cut to the bone and once a pupil could be trusted with a Hurricane he was shown the ropes then left to get as much air experience as the time permitted.

Frederick Howarth in L1654 fell about half a mile from Czech Sgt. Karel Stibor in L1833, near the village of Wiggenhall St Germans. At the time a minimum of site clearance was carried out - just enough to recover the bodies of the unfortunate airmen and clear farmers property of ordnance and surface debris. It was not until the early 1970's that the site of L1833 was excavated by the landowner to remove the engine and other major components. The site of L1654 was left undisturbed until 1985 when FAPS undertook an extensive and successful excavation in the course of which the Merlin III was recovered. That project and its aftermath are covered in detail in their excellent booklet *The Saddlebow Hurricanes* (Ketley, FAPS 1990).

These two Hurricanes were neither the first nor the last collision to be experienced by 6/56 OTU. In fact

Left: *Karel Stibor is believed to have arrived in England in June 1940 and like many Czech compatriots he was initially attached to 310 Sqn. at Duxford as potential fighter pilot material. He was posted to 6 OTU RAF Sutton Bridge where he met with a tragic end in the mid-air collision of 3/9/40.*

Right: Sgt. F.J.Howarth aged 20 years, victim of a mid-air collision on 3/9/40. A native of Burbage, Frederick Howarth was a pre-war RAFVR trainee. Joining up immediately war was declared, his training between Sept.1939 and May 1940 followed a conventional route via 1 ITW and 7 EFTS. In May 1940 Sgt. Howarth was posted to 10 SFTS and thence to 6 OTU Sutton Bridge for advanced training on the Hawker Hurricane.

(both via Andy Ketley)

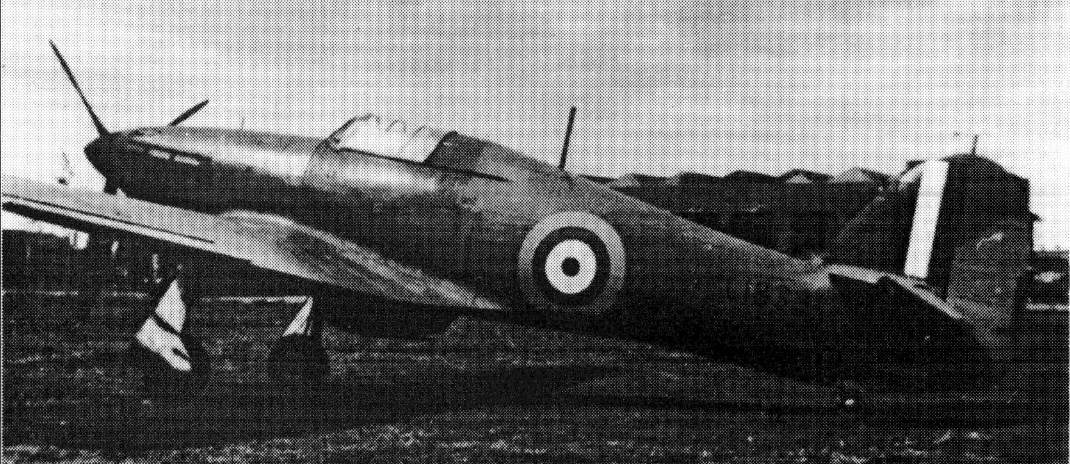

Hurricane I, L1833 was initially allocated to 85 Sqn. in February 1939. After about a year it was withdrawn from squadron service and stored by 19 MU. L1833 was then issued very briefly to 7 OTU in July 1940 but on August 1, moved on to 6 OTU. One month later it was destroyed in a mid-air collision with L1654 near Kings Lynn.

the first collision at 6 OTU occurred on August 8, only two weeks prior to the Howarth/Stibor incident. Fatalities on that occasion were Sgt. D. McGee in L2082 and Maj. K. Niedswiecki, a Polish pilot in 324, one of the ex-Canadian Hurricanes mentioned elsewhere.

Fortunately many more months were to elapse before the next collision.

The flying career of Flt. Sgt. John Craig is a typical example of a pre-war NCO pilot who had to share the burden of the early air battles. Craig joined 111 Sqn. in 1938 and went into action over Dunkirk in May 1940. He fought gallantly in the Battle of Britain until August 31 when he was injured in combat and forced to bale out of his aircraft. Credited with eight enemy aircraft by that time, Craig was awarded the DFM and after a spell in hospital he was posted to 56 OTU, RAF Sutton Bridge, as an instructor.

Having survived all the enemy could throw at him, on June 6, 1941 Flt. Sgt. Craig met a tragic end when his Hurricane W9114 collided with P3162 flown by an OTU pupil, Sgt. Bisgood, who also died in the accident. Both aircraft fell in the Walpole/Terrington district and Craig's site was excavated thoroughly by FAPS in 1976.

The last collision suffered by 56 OTU, before it moved north to RAF Tealing in March 1942, occured near Walpole St. Peter on 7/1/42 and involved two more Czech trainees practicing combat manoeuvres. Plt. Off. J.F.Zerovnicky died when V7469 dived into the ground but Sgt. F.Pokorny by some stroke of good fortune managed to crash land W9180, although he sustained severe head injuries in the process.

Composition of first Belgian pilot course at 6 OTU

Posted In: 30 July 1940. Posted Out: 17 August 1940

Name	Posted To	Notes
Plt. Off B.M.G. de Hemptinne	145 Sqn.	* KIA May 1942
Plt. Off. A.R.I.G. Jottard	145 Sqn.	* MIA Oct 1940
Plt. Off. J.H.M. Offenberg	145 Sqn.	* Killed Jan 1942

* = Fought in Battle of Britain

Two pictures - same person.

Left: With boots polished and forage cap at the regulation angle, Sgt. John T.Craig is on parade, immaculate in smart white flying coverall and leather gauntlets. The occasion is an inspection of 111 Sqn. at RAF Northolt by visiting MP's in April 1938.

Above Right: Standing on the wing of his Hurricane, named Weaver V, more than two years later is an older, more confident Sgt. John Craig DFM, Battle of Britain ace with eight enemy aircraft to his name. Craig was to lose his life in a mid-air collision on 2/6/41 while serving as an instructor with 56 OTU (via Bill Welbourne)

The composition of these first foreign courses is set out in the following tables. Needless to say the influx of this tide of foreign airmen had a profound effect on the local population who took many into their homes and quickly became used to meeting them in pubs and on other social occasions in that small community

Composition of first Czech pilot course at 6 OTU.

Posted In: 17 Aug 1940 Posted Out: 17 Sep 1940

Name	Posted To	Notes
Sqn. Ldr. J Ambrus	312 Sqn.	*Survived the war
Plt. Off. J. Bryks	310 Sqn.	*Survived the war
Plt. Off. F. Fajtl	310 Sqn.	*Survived the war
Plt. Off. S. Fejfar	310 Sqn.	* KIA 1942
Plt. Off. J Himr	79 Sqn.	* KIA 1943
Plt. Off. F Kordula	1 Sqn.	*Survived the war
Plt. Off. J. Machacek	310 Sqn.	* KIA 1941
Plt. Off. K. Mrazek	43 Sqn.	*Survived the war
Plt. Off. R. Rohacek	238 Sqn.	* KIA 1942
Plt. Off. K. Vykoukal	111 Sqn.	* KIA 1942
Plt. Off. F. Weber	145 Sqn.	*Survived the war
Sgt. F. Bernard	238 Sqn.	*Survived the war
Sgt. V.Cukr	43 Sqn.	*Survived the war
Sgt. J. Hlavac	79 Sqn.	* KIA Oct 1940
Sgt. V. Horsky	238 Sqn.	* KIA Sep 1940
Sgt. V. Jicha	1 Sqn.	*Killed in accident 1945
Sgt. T. Kucera	111 Sqn.	*Survived the war
Sgt. V. Kopecky	111 Sqn.	*Survived the war
Sgt. J. Postolka	Not known	
Sgt. K. Stibor	Killed in training accident at 6 OTU, 3/9/40.	

* = Fought in Battle of Britain

Readiness Section.

To cope with the rising tide of pupils, 33 for example arrived to begin training on August 17, the inventory of 6 OTU was increased. Serviceable aircraft on that date included 34 Hurricanes, 4 Harvards, 8 Masters, 4 Battles and 4 Mentors. In addition to a few remaining Fairey Battle Trainers, four Battle Target Tugs also appeared in the OTU inventory during July 1940. This seems to reflect the increased work load on Sutton Bridge Station Flight - which operated the Henley Tugs primarily for 'visitors'. Up to July, the Henleys provided a service for OTU trainees when required as well as towing Sleeve or Cone targets for any squadron wishing to book air-to-air firing time over Holbeach Marsh range - much as their predecessors had done pre-war. Squadrons served regularly between April and June, for example, were 19, 23, 29, 32, 66, 213, 254, 264 and 611. It should be remembered, too, that air-to-ground firing continued apace on the Range and it was even recorded, on 15/18/19 and 27 October, that a cannon-armed Hurricane and Spitfire used Holbeach Range for that purpose. The Battle (TT) aircraft therefore were operated by the OTU which allowed Station Flight to concentrate on operational units while the OTU dealt with its own requirements.

Similarly the influx of so many aeroplanes caused another problem; how to accomodate upwards of fifty machines both for protection against the elements and for servicing purposes. To this end Wg. Cdr. Barwell had pressed for more hangarage and on May 1 work began to erect a new Bellman Hangar.

It did not escape the Station Commander's notice that, situated as it was, close to the east coast and

151 Sqn. at RAF Wittering operated a mixed bag of Hurricane and Boulton Paul Defiant aeroplanes on night-fighter duties in 1941. Being close to The Wash ranges, they were one of the frequent visiting squadrons served by the Henley Target tugs of RAF Sutton Bridge Station Flight. Defiant I, N3328 coded DZ-Z, here sporting a most uncharacteristic shark's-mouth nose-art, suffered a broken tailwheel when Sgt. J.A.Denys landed heavily at Sutton Bridge after one such air-to-air firing sortie on 18/8/41.

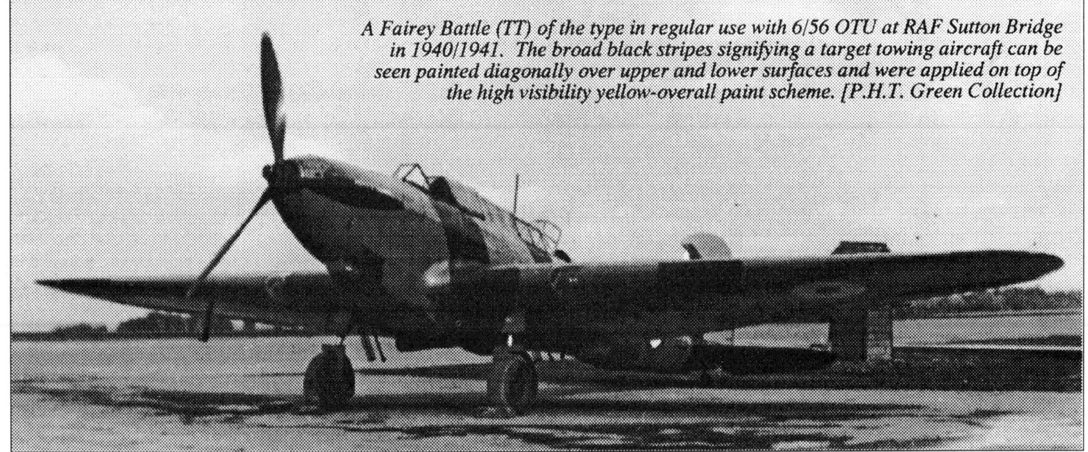

A Fairey Battle (TT) of the type in regular use with 6/56 OTU at RAF Sutton Bridge in 1940/1941. The broad black stripes signifying a target towing aircraft can be seen painted diagonally over upper and lower surfaces and were applied on top of the high visibility yellow-overall paint scheme. [P.H.T. Green Collection]

within the potential invasion area, his airfield might attract hostile attention from the Luftwaffe. He surmised that the enemy might attempt to carry out attacks on the aerodrome either by dropping bombs or parachute troops. Under certain circumstances they might arrive over or in the vicinity of the aerodrome without having been intercepted by fighter squadrons. Being a man of action therefore he drew up on May 12 his Operational Order No.1, the stated intention of which was: *"To provide from Station resources air opposition to an attack on this Station."*

Wg. Cdr. Barwell ordered the OC 6 OTU to detail one section of three Hurricanes to be brought to readiness:-

a) whenever air raid warning 'yellow' was received in daylight hours.

b) from half an hour before sunrise to half an hour after sunrise.

c) at other times as ordered by the Station Commander.

The readiness section, callsign 'Domino Green', must always be lead by an instructor but the other members could be either pupils or instructors. Pilots were to be strapped in, ready for take-off with aircraft positioned on the leeward side of the airfield, fully armed and with starter batteries connected. As might be imagined there was no shortage of volunteers!

Wary of trigger-happy ground defences and for the well-being of his men, Barwell also took care to warn the section to be particularly careful how they returned to the airfield after a sortie. There was to be no high spirited stuff - *"... a wide circuit at 1000 - 1500 feet must be made, at a speed of 140 mph so that ground defences may have time to recognise friendly aircraft. Pilots must NOT approach at low altitude, high speed or by diving on the airfield."* It was made pretty clear that if they did so they risked getting their heads shot off!

Ground defence at that time was composed of light AA weapons - Bofors and MG's - manned by 66 officers and men of 'D' Company, 1st Battalion Cambridgeshire Regiment, supported by a searchlight battery operated by 10 men of the Royal Engineers. The composition of these units changed from time to time as the war progressed, while in August 1940, at the height of the Battle of Britain, in additon to its transient pupils, RAF Sutton Bridge permanent staff numbered 386 Officers and Airmen and 54 Civilians.

Air-raids and Decoys.

Little opportunity for the readiness section presented itself for although there were plenty of air raid warnings, even 'red' ones, with very few exceptions these occurred in the hours of darkness. From mid-June 1940 for example, there was an air-raid warning at Sutton Bridge every night until the month end. A similar situation continued throughout July and August with alerts sounding at intervals of every two or three nights. Anticipating attacks by the Luftwaffe against RAF stations, the Air Ministry in 1940 implemented its plan for decoy airfields and other deception devices. Among these were 'Q' sites, an arrangement of night flare-path lights or Drem-type circuit lights erected

Officers Commanding RAF Sutton Bridge
Sep 1939 to Apr 1942.

Period	Name	Unit
Sep 1939	Flt. Lt. R.P. Smillie	Care & Maintenance
Sep 1939 to Nov 1939	Flt. Lt. N. Hawker	3 Recruit Training Pool
Nov 1939 to Jun 1940	Wg. Cdr. P.R. Barwell DFC	254/264/266 Sqns. & 6 OTU.
Jun 1940 to Aug 1940	Gp. Capt. H.D.O'Neill AFC	6 OTU
Aug 1940 to Jun 1941	Gp. Capt. B.B. Caswell	6/56 OTU
Jun 1941 to Sep 1941	Gp. Capt. F.O. Soden DFC	56 OTU
Sep 1941 to Apr 1942	Gp. Capt. I.A. Bertram	56 OTU

some distance, perhaps four or five miles, from a parent airfield. In the case of RAF Sutton Bridge a 'Q' site was established on farmland at the edge of Terrington Marsh and comprising electric night landing lights and obstruction lights, the intensity of which could be adjusted to simulate, for example, an oil-burning 'gooseneck' flare-path as well as more substantial runway lighting schemes.

The Luftwaffe took its first crack at RAF Sutton Bridge on the night of August 30/31, 1940 and proved the effectiveness of the Terrington 'Q' site. In the early hours of the 31st. farms in the vicinity reverberated to the crump! of four HE bombs exploding about 1000 yards NW of the glimmering 'flarepath'. A few minutes later 15 explosions heralded the arrival of more bombs, this time falling in a line 1000 yards to the SE of the site. Casualties were limited to one farm horse killed and a greenhouse damaged but the raid would not have done much for the nerves of the good farmers of the district.

Three weeks later the Luftwaffe tried again; equally unsuccessfully. At ten o'clock in the evening of September 22 those tempting lights at Terrington did their job again by persuading a single raider to unload seven HE bombs near the 'Q' site. The lights were doused when the first bomb exploded and the remainder landed a thousand yards SW. Five minutes after the enemy aeroplane departed the lights were turned on again but attracted no more customers. Once more it was the horse population which suffered with the loss of another and two more injured by shrapnel. A number of windows in Bentinck Farm house were broken by the blast. Perhaps it was this latter occurrance which finally prompted residents of Terrington district to send a petition on October 4 to RAF Sutton Bridge, pleading for the removal of the 'Q' site from their locality.

By now Gp. Capt. O'Neill had been posted away to HQ Fighter Command after only a few months as Station Commander and his place was taken on August 17 by Wg. Cdr. B.B. Caswell, formerly of RAF Acklington. How Wg. Cdr. Caswell dealt with the petition is not recorded but one might guess that while being sympathetic he would hardly be keen to give up such obviously effective protection - nor could he anyway. No doubt he would also consider two horses and a few broken windows in so sparsely a populated area a small price to pay.

As if to back up such a view 'Jerry' paid two more visits during the night of October 28 when the 'Q' site collected more bombs. At 19.40 hours 13 HE bombs whistled down at the lights and half an hour later another five dropped a quarter mile from the site. Fragments found later suggested these were of 100kg size and all fell into open fields. The residents would not be amused though, as one house had a ceiling damaged by blast.

There was a little respite for a time at night while the Luftwaffe directed its Blitz efforts elsewhere but occasionally daylight brought trade for the local fighter squadrons, much to the chagrin of the 6 OTU Readiness Flight.

One such foray by the Luftwaffe into the Fens, however, resulted in Sutton Bridge getting the closest possible sight of enemy aircrew.

Based at RAF Wittering, 1 Sqn. engaged the enemy on a number of occasions in late October 1940 when raiders entered its territory. For example, at dusk on October 29 three Spitfires, scrambled to investigate a hostile raid believed heading for Sutton Bridge or one of the other airfields in the vicinity, intercepted Dornier Do17's near Sutton Bridge. In the melee which followed, Blue section leader Sgt. W.T.Page claimed to have damaged one of the Dorniers before his own aeroplane, P3318, was hit by return fire. Glycol fumes forced him to return to base but he had to force land at Orton near Peterborough.

Re-emphasising once more that invisible bond between Sutton Bridge and 1 Sqn., came a most interesting engagement the next afternoon. Another section of three Spitfires caught a Ju88 - later found to have been making its way inland for an armed recce of the Metro-Vickers plant in Salford. Plt. Off. G.E. Goodman (in P2877) - a graduate of the very first 6 OTU course at RAF Sutton Bridge - Plt. Off. R.G. Lewis (P3229) - back with No.1 after his spell of instructing at 6 OTU - and Sgt. V. Jicha - a graduate of the first Czech course at Sutton Bridge - were directed onto a raider heading in from The Wash.

Coming at it head-on, Goodman mistook the aeroplane for a Blenheim and did not open fire. Recognising it as a Ju88, the other two half-rolled and pulled up to attack from the rear. Lewis opened fire from 200 yards, broke away and then Sgt. Jicha put in a short burst before it disappeared in cloud. The Ju88 had turned south before the attack and now heading towards Sutton Bridge, two of the enemy crew baled out. They landed at Lovell's Hall, Terrington

St.Clements where, slightly hurt on landing, they were captured by soldiers from 374 AA Battery, taken to RAF Sutton Bridge and thence to a POW camp in Dunstable.

Post war research shows this enemy aeroplane to be Junkers Ju88A-1, Werk Nr 5008, L1+GS from 8/LG1. The pilot was Uffz. W. Arndt who, with Uffz. A. Bronner, stayed in the aircraft to crash-land it at Middle Fen, Stuntney near Ely while the two who baled out were Ogefr. P. Flieger and Gefr. W. Kellner.

On November 1 1940, officialdom decreed that all OTU's were to be re-numbered by having '50' added to their Unit numbers and thus 6 OTU now became 56 OTU, still under the command of newly promoted Gp. Capt. Caswell.

Back came the Luftwaffe in strength on the evening of February 14, 1941. It had been a fine day for flying, after a spell of changeable weather and limited activity. Between the staff, pupils and 50 aeroplanes on the Station at that time, 122 hours of flying had been crammed in. A juicy target indeed!

By dusk the Station was in darkness but with the 'Q' site at Terrington Marsh lit up ready. At 19.50 hours the first of an estimated twelve enemy aeroplanes unloaded the first of 47 HE bombs, one oil bomb and about 1000 incendiaries in a concerted attack directed at the Terrington decoy. Many fell among farm buildings but only one house was hit and no casualties were reported. The only other damage was to yet another greenhouse and a minor road.

It would be quite reasonable by now for the Germans to believe they had dealt Sutton Bridge a serious blow and that it might no longer constitute a worthwhile target. A reconnaissance sortie would no doubt provide confirmation. With a daylight recce likely to be repulsed, just such a raid was mounted the very next night - February 15/16 - when an estimated six E/A dropped numerous flares around the 'Q' site. Photographic evidence would quickly confirm that RAF Sutton Bridge had been far from 'plastered' and the Luftwaffe response was swift but fortunately just as ineffective.

Low cloud and drizzle greeted the dawn of the 16th, curtailing flying training until later in the day. By mid-afternoon cloud base had lifted to 900 feet when, without warning, a single Heinkel He111 appeared out of the murk. It made a half circuit of the airfield, dropping a stick of nine bombs and spraying the area with bursts of machine gun fire, before disappearing back into the cloud as quickly as it came. The whole attack lasted less than two minutes. All bombs fell on open ground, none of which came within a hundred yards of the hangars and there were no casualties.

Evidently the returning crew reported a satisfactory attack, as only one more raid was made on the 'Q' site; two E/A dropped eight HE bombs just after midnight 17/18 February then there were no more attacks for three months. Since the 'Q' site was clearly very successful and obviously not going to be moved, the local inhabitants decided to make the best of things and submitted another petition to the Station, this time to have an air raid warning siren installed!

During the next three months though, the aeroplane population of the station almost doubled. At the beginning of May 1941, Sutton Bridge could now muster at least 80 aeroplanes, 70 of which were Hurricanes.

In a momentous weekend, London took its worst hammering of the Blitz on May 10/11; Rudolf Hess chose that night to fly to Scotland; while during the early hours of Sunday, May 12 Sutton Bridge was re-visited by the Luftwaffe, part of a series of country-wide raids directed at airfields and carried out by Luftflotte 3. The raid also coincided with the arrival of a new OTU course intake, at this time numbering 11

A fallen eagle. Junkers Ju88A-5 from KG30 being inspected by curious members of the public. The unit badge is a black diving eagle on a white background. A Ju88 from this unit came under fierce light anti-aircraft fire during a daylight attack on the British MARCO armament factory in Grantham on 27/1/41. It was severely damaged by several hits from 30mm cannon made in that very factory and staggering off homeward, was eventually forced to crash-land in Pilleys Lane, Boston, one of 15 German aircraft brought down in the district in 1941.

Thumbs up from Sgt. Josef Dygryn! A newspaper photo of this Czech pilot, who fought under the nom-de-guerre of Ligoticky to protect his family, published in May 1941. On the night of 10/11 May 1941, Dygryn flew his Hurricane on three separate freelance patrols over London during a particularly heavy air-raid, claiming to have shot down a bomber on each sortie. Sgt. Dygryn had been a pupil at 6OTU in Sept/Oct 1940 and managed to get his name recorded for posterity by 'bending' Hurricane N2367. Posted to 1 Sqn. just in time to participate in the Battle of Britain, he was k.i.a. while flying a Hurricane on an intruder sortie in September 1941.

Officers and 25 Sergeants. Instead of a quiet training station they would be greeted by the sight of bomb craters and smouldering aeroplanes. That night, between 01.00 and 02.00, three separate attacks, believed by a single E/A each time, were made on the airfield. Sixteen bombs fell among Hurricanes parked outside the hangars, setting two on fire, seriously damaging seven others and peppering many more with shrapnel. Luckily, apart from bomb splinter damage to roofs and broken windows, few buildings were affected. There was only one casualty; a soldier seriously injured by bomb fragments.

The Luftwaffe did not have things all their own way, however. One of the aircraft which attacked Sutton Bridge, Junkers Ju88A-5, V4+DM, Werk Nr 7170 of 4/KG1, was shot down by AA fire while passing over RAF Watton. Crashing at Scoulton in Norfolk, three crew were killed and the fourth made POW. Another 4/KG1 Ju88, detailed to attack Sutton Bridge, failed to return from the sortie and was reported to have crashed into the North Sea, although it is quite possible these two losses may in fact refer to the same aeroplane.

This was not the last time RAF Sutton Bridge was raided but later attacks were directed against the Central Gunnery School during 1942 and thus will be covered in a later chapter dealing with that period.

Enemy Air Raids directed at 6/56 OTU.
1940/1941

Date	Location
30/31 August 1940	Terrington 'Q' Site
22 September 1940	Terrington 'Q' Site
28 October 1940	Terrington 'Q' Site
14 February 1941	Terrington 'Q' Site
14/15 February 194	Terrington 'Q' Site
16 February 1941	RAF Sutton Bridge
18 February 1941	Terrington 'Q' Site
12 May 1941	RAF Sutton Bridge

It was a very long time before a 56 OTU pupil actually came anywhere near being able to have a crack at the enemy in this region.

During a cross-country flight on March 10, 1942, only a few days before the OTU moved out of Sutton Bridge, Sgt. C. Weaver flying along at 12,000 feet five miles north of Spalding spotted an E/A a little below his level. Identifying it as a Messerschmitt Bf.110 Weaver dived on his target, closed to 300 yards and let fly with two long bursts. No hits were seen and the E/A disappeared into cloud cover so the disappointed Weaver had to return to base empty-handed. It was unusual for a Bf.110 to be reported during daylight hours in this area but an aeroplane of that type had also been spotted at low level, early one morning, by a newspaper boy, in the vicinity of Crowland, near Spalding. No date was given for the latter incident and perhaps the two items are connected. It could have been a Luftwaffe photo-recce machine, perhaps with its range extended by drop-tanks, but on the other hand, there was also a Bf.110 on the strength of 1426 Enemy Aircraft Flight which was based at Duxford at that time, less than ten minutes flying time away...?

A taste of Instructing.

Despite all these interruptions, life at the OTU carried on apace and next day another batch of 33 officers and sergeants were posted out to join operational fighter squadrons.

So what was life really like at Sutton Bridge? Here is another version, this time from an instructor's viewpoint.

"With effect from November 8, 1940 Flg. Off. W. H. R. Whitty is posted to 56 OTU for Flying Instructor duties." So ran the order transferring Bill Whitty from 607 Sqn. (Turnhouse, Edinburgh) to RAF Sutton Bridge.

From his retirement home in Canada, Bill outlined his RAF service leading up to the posting and believed it to be typical of many of his contemporaries at the OTU. Joining 607 (County of Durham) Sqn. of the Auxiliary Air Force in 1937 he received his flying training via Avro 504N, Avro Tutor, Hawker Hart and Demon. Mobilised first after Munich then again in August 1939, Whitty went into action during the French campaign flying Hurricanes for up to four sorties a day.

Back in England on May 20, 1940 with just five pilots left, 607 Sqn. was sent to RAF Usworth for re-building. It was here that he had a taste of instructing as it was necessary for a dozen new pilots to be trained by the five 'old hands' because the OTU system was not yet fully in place.

Flg. Off. Whitty recalled the squadron was ready just in time for the Luftwaffe's attempted raid on Tyneside from bases in Norway. *"The Hun aircraft were off course when they reached the English coast and we were ready for them; it was good training for our new pilots,"* - echoing a sentiment expressed by Sqn. Ldr. Barwell in the previous chapter.

Flg. Off. Whitty took part in the Battle of Britain when 607 moved to Tangmere in September 1940 from where, after taking more losses it was sent north again to Turnhouse in November.

Arriving at Sutton Bridge, Bill found himself in the company of many ex-Battle of Britain veterans: Flt. Lt. George Greaves (ex-504 Sqn) was 'A' Flight commander; the Hon. Derek Dowding (ex-74) 'Stuffy's' son; Flt. Lt. Beardon 'B' Flight commander, Herbert Hallowes (ex-43); Peter Down (ex-56) and Flt. Lt. D.P.D.G.Kelly (ex-74) i/c the recently formed 'D' Flight. Flt. Lt. George Plinston was in charge of the target towing flight at that time. The list of instructors at Sutton Bridge in December 1940, contains a number of famous names. There was a constant turnover of Squadron pilots being posted in as Instructors for short periods. Not least amongst these were ex-17 Sqn, Battles of France and Britain veteran Flg. Off. Harold Bird-Wilson, a post-war Air Vice-Marshal with a CBE, DSO, DFC and Bar, AFC and Bar to his name, but a lowly member of 'B' Flight between November 7 1940 and January 16 1941.

Flg. Off. H. A. C. Bird-Wilson on the right and another airman in his Battle of Britain days with 17 Sqn. Debden.

The Commanding Officer and Officers wish you all Happy Christmas.
ROYAL AIR FORCE.
SUTTON BRIDGE.
XMAS, 1940
MENU
CREME OF TOMATO SOUP
JOINTS
ROAST TURKEY
ROAST PORK
ROAST GOOSE
VEGETABLES
ROAST AND BOILED POTATOES
BRUSSELS SPROUTS PEAS
STUFFING BREAD SAUCE GRAVY
SWEETS
XMAS. PUDDING
BRANDY SAUCE
MINCE PIES
DESSERT
APPLES NUTS
BEER MINERALS

Officers and airmen of 56 OTU still found time for traditional celebration at Christmas 1940. Despite the austerity of wartime this menu for the airmens mess Christmas dinner shows a range of dishes which would find favour even in modern times. Officers, including the CO Gp. Capt. B. Caswell carried out the traditional RAF role of serving dinner to the other ranks. Flight Mechanic (engines) AC1 Bill Law was busy collecting autographs on his menu. Beneath Caswell's signature can be seen that of the now-famous Flg. Off. Harold Bird-Wilson, an instructor at the OTU.

Flying Instructors on staff of 56 OTU Nov 1940.

Sqn. Ldr. D.P.D.G. Kelly (CFI)
Flt. Lt. F.J.L. Duus
Flt. Lt. G. Greaves
Flt. Lt. G. Harris
Flt. Lt. O. Hellyer
Flt. Lt. C.D. Palmer
Flt. Lt. G.H.F. Plinston
Flt. Lt. C.L.H. Roberts
Flt. Lt. J.E.J. Sing
Flt. Lt. W.A.Toyne
Flt. Lt. W.H.R. Whitty
Flg. Off. H.A.C Bird-Wilson
Flg. Off. D.H.D. Dowding
Flg. Off. P.D.M. Down
Flg. Off. K.C. Jackman
Flg. Off. R.F. Martin
Flg. Off. D.G. Smallwood
Flg. Off. W.H.M. Walker
Plt. Off. G.R. Bennette
Plt. Off. C.N. Birch
Plt. Off. F.J. Soper
Plt. Off. W.A. Waterton
Warr. Off. E. Mayne
Flt. Sgt. C.A. Deport (French)

On the question of a training programme, Bill Whitty observed: *"OTU's did not come under Training Command and we were not trained instructors so ideas about step by step training, with tests two or three times while the pupil was on the course, were generally lacking. You could only watch him while he was in formation with you in the air and talk to him on the ground afterwards."*

"Numbered flying exercises, for each pupil to carry out, were first described on the ground then practised in the air, often by the pupil flying alone. These seem to be recorded somewhat haphazardly in their logbooks and I cannot recall what each exercise number referred to. Generally pupils were given dual on the Harvard or Master then sent off solo on the Hurricane. This might be followed by cross-country's, formation flights, aerobatics and simulated 'dog-fights'. Occasionally we worked with a nearby Wellington squadron to give their gunners practice in defending against fighter attacks.

Late in the course pupils would be sent over to Flt. Lt. George Plinston's Aerial Gunnery Flight, for air firing experience but George's aircraft serviceability was poor at Sutton Bridge and Gedney Drove End - where some of the towing aircraft were located. We complained bitterly about this situation as it meant pupils did not get enough - if any - live ammo time. In those days things were not well organised and no-one bothered to check on the effectiveness of one's particular training method. I had my own routine worked out, which basically was to try to ensure all my pupils were happy with their aeroplane when airborne and learned to spend plenty of time practicing watching for Huns - or they wouldn't know what hit them when they went on ops!"

"In February 1941 I was sent on an instructor's course for a couple of months to Central Flying School (CFS) Upavon and upon my return to Sutton Bridge in April I took command of 'D' Flight.

Of all the many pupils I came across in my ten months at 6 OTU, Plt. Off. Richard Playne Stevens sticks in my mind most vividly. He was at the OTU in December 1940 and was desperate for a posting to nightfighters. Over thirty years of age, rather older than most trainees, it was said his wife and children were killed in the Blitz and he was thirsting for revenge."

Indeed, Stevens had considerable pre-war flying experience as a commercial pilot and was used to night flying, particularly on the London-Paris route, a skill he put to deadly use in 1941. Richard Stevens achieved his aim on both counts. Becoming a legend as a 'lone wolf' flying night intruder sorties in a Hurricane he rose rapidly to the rank of Sqn. Ldr., claiming 14 'kills' and earning a DSO and DFC in the short time before he himself was killed in action in January 1942.

During research, prior to building up a picture of life at this OTU, not only was correspondence exchanged with Bill Whitty but, by an enormous coincidence, on one occasion letters were received simultaneously from Bill in Canada and from one of his former 'D' Flight pupils now living in Cornwall.

Fifty years ago Eric Raybould was a newly qualified Plt. Off. who found himself attached to 6 OTU in the care of Bill Whitty and who can now put an alternative view of life at Sutton Bridge just prior to that period described earlier by Peter Montgomery. By way of contrast, Eric received his basic flying training in England and wrote:

"My elementary training was on Tiger Moths at Staverton where I did about 50 hours flying in ten weeks. This was followed by three months at 5 Service Flying Training School (SFTS), RAF Tern Hill, mainly on Masters. SFTS was probably the most perilous period of my RAF service since, out of a complement of 42 pupils a mere 20 survived the course. I think everyone who survived was given an "above average" assessment as a consolation!"

"Even at EFTS I had found aerobatics made me sick. I asked to go onto bombers so what did they do? - in true service tradition the opposite happened and I found myself on a fighter SFTS then was later posted to the fighter OTU at Sutton Bridge."

"It was June 5, 1941 and with about 140 hours flying time in my log book, including a grand total of two hours at night, I walked the short distance from the station across the swing bridge to the camp. My recollection of the course was that it was short, just five weeks and more than one course ran at the same time."

"The course content comprised aerobatics, formation flying, simulated dog-fights, gunnery, navigation and ground lectures on tactics and aircraft recognition. It was around this time that I realised I'd sooner be shot down than indulge in prolonged aerobatics - death would be a pleasant relief to the intense nausea I felt. Among my fellow students there was also a general terror of night flying but I found it a positive pleasure compared to aerobatics. Consequently, when nearing the end of the course, I volunteered for nightfighters, spending most of the final week practicing night flying on the Hurri."

"My compatriots were a mixed bunch and included American, French, Dutch, South African and Norwegian pilots and I recall one of our Instructors was the ex-No.1 Sqn. veteran Flg. Off. Prosser Hanks. There was only one fatality (Sgt. A.M. Duthie killed when L2055 spun in at West Walton 11/6/41) during my time at Sutton Bridge but numerous lesser 'prangs'.

Apart from the glorious weather that summer, another vivid memory is of a boxing match against a Midland Area ABA team, who made mincemeat of the Station team. When the show was over volunteers were called for to participate in exhibition bouts. I was a fairly hefty bloke with no pretensions as a boxer but I resented the behaviour of quite a good middleweight on the ABA team and asked to take him on. It was a helluva fight for an 'exhibition' and although I was not knocked about much, I was so utterly exhausted by taking on this chap in my completely unfit condition that I took to my bed for a day to recover."

The coincidence mentioned earlier, came to light when close inspection of Eric Raybould's log book showed it to have been signed for that period by none other than Bill Whitty. Furthermore an entry on June 11, 1941, recorded a two-hour flight in DH Rapide X7342 with Flt. Lt. Whitty as pilot and Plt. Off. Raybould as navigator.

Bill Whitty remembered that trip clearly: *"What a coincidence,"* he wrote, *"to hear from Eric Raybould at the same time. I remember that Rapide trip because we landed at RAF Halton first. It was a*

End of course photo for 35 officer and NCO trainees taken outside the officers mess of 56 OTU, RAF Sutton Bridge in July 1941. Plt. Off. Eric Raybould is in middle row, second from right. Eric Raybould and Plt. Off. Jack Sharpe, standing next to him on the end of the row, were the only (willing) volunteers for a night-flying posting. Jack went to 256 Sqn. at Squires Gate, Blackpool but was killed in a flying accident only a month later. (E.Raybould)

terrible landing on rough grass which seemed never to have been rolled for years. Then we went on to Portreath, near Newquay to drop off pilots who were to collect used Hurricanes for the OTU. It was a lovely flight across England, quiet and peaceful, reminding me of the days when I flew on summer evenings pre-war as an Auxiliary."

In July 1941, assessed as "average", Plt. Off. Eric Raybould got his wish, too, and was posted to a nightfighter unit. However, it was 256 Sqn. which at that time operated the Defiant and a few Hurricanes from Squires Gate, Blackpool. He was not keen on that arrangement and after a few months responded to a call (ever the volunteer!) for volunteers to join new Beaufighter squadrons being formed. He was posted to 68 Sqn. (High Ercall) never having flown a twin-engined aeroplane in his life. *"It didn't seem to matter,"* he said, *"as I was given an old Blenheim to play about with first."* After a nightflying career involving postings to North Africa, Tunis, Malta, Sicily, Salerno and Anzio, Eric Raybould finished his operational flying in December 1943.

Ground Crews and 'prangs'.

It was not all 'beer and skittles' for the ground crews at Sutton Bridge either. Always struggling against the elements and aircraft unserviceability, what was the view like from ground level?

Bill Law of Northampton was a Flight Mechanic at 6 OTU in 1940. What he remembered most clearly were the times of great camaraderie and the almost constant loss of pilots and aeroplanes in a variety of accidents. One incident of particular sadness for him was when, on October 13, 1940, his pal AC1. Edwards was killed. *"He was my opposite number on the servicing flight; in those days we did 24 hours on duty followed by 24 hours off. Edwards had just finished his spell of duty and was offered a trip in one of the Masters, N7962, with Plt. Off. S.J.Thompson. He jumped at the chance but when the pilot made a dummy landing approach out Wisbech way, the aeroplane stalled and dived into the ground killing both men."*

"The Master was not our favourite kite; they had no self starters fitted to their Kestrel engine. Consequently we had to use winding handles to start them up and this was a miserable job on a cold and frosty morning."

"Almost every day, during my time at 6 OTU, we suffered quite a few accidents, not just to the Hurricanes. These ranged from heavy-handed landings, which made even their sturdy undercarriages collapse, to full blown mid-air collisions or aeroplanes diving in from a great height."

During its two-year stay at Sutton Bridge nearly 300 of 6/56OTU's Hurricanes met with a variety of accidents referred to by Aircraftman Law.

"At one time there were quite a lot of ex-Canadian Hurricanes among those written off or damaged, distinguishable by their 3-digit serial numbers."

On this latter subject Mr. Law is referring to a batch of Hurricane I's shipped to Canada for use by the RCAF. Produced originally in England for the RAF, these had serials in the 'L' range. When 1 (RCAF) Sqn. arrived in England for active service in June 1940, seventeen of this batch came with it. In the same way that OTU's received other RAF 'hand-me-downs' so too did 6 OTU receive some of the RCAF cast-offs as they were gradually replaced by later models - which in this case must have been quite quickly as these serials began to feature in accident reports at Sutton Bridge as early as July 1940. Some seem to have soldiered on at 6 OTU until about April 1941.

Another of Mr. Law's pals, AC1. Arthur Watkins earned a place in the annals of RAF Sutton Bridge

Ex-RCAF Hurricanes used at 6 OTU, RAF Sutton Bridge.

Canadian Serial	Original RAF Serial	Notes
310	L1759	15/11/40 Tyre burst, u/c collapsed.
313	L1762	10/2/41 u/c collapsed, Plt. Off. J Briggs. 26/2/41 Heavy landing, Flt. Lt. Beardon testing variable pitch propeller.
314	L1763	19/7/40 Engine failure, f/l near Sutton Bridge, Flg. Off. H.C. Mayers (Aus).
315	L1878	7/11/40 Forced landing, Sgt. H.H.Jennings.
316	L1879	
318	L1881	21/3/41Forced landing, Leiston, Plt. Off. P.A.Grace.
319	L1882	4/10/40 Forced landing, Plt. Off. P.S. Merritt.
320	L1883	27/3/41, e/f, Fosdyke, Plt. Off. F. Raw.
321	L1884	
322	L1885	10/12/40, e/f, f/l, Wiggenhall St. Mary, Sgt. E.H. Burton.
324	L1887	18/8/40 Mid-air collision with L2082, Maj. K. Niedswieki killed.
325	L1888	
326	L1890	
328	L2022	7/8/40 Heavy landing, Flt. Sgt. R. Grasset (Fr). 21/8/40 Heavy landing, Sgt. C. Saward.

history by displaying great courage and presence of mind in an emergency.

It was December 17,1940 when, in deteriorating weather conditions, Plt. Off. J.D. Wright was recalled by radio from a pinpointing and homing exercise in Hurricane L1820. On reaching Sutton Bridge however, the pilot undershot his approach, striking the boundary fence a fearsome blow. Gunning the engine, Plt. Off. Wright managed to complete a tight circuit with L1820 in a semi-stalled condition before it crashed and burst into flames. It was completely burned out but not before the pilot had been extricated by prompt and selfless action on the part of AC1. Watkins.

For his bravery that day Arthur Watkins received the British Empire Medal (Military Division). The official citation reads:

"... without hesitation AC1 Watkins jumped onto the blazing aeroplane, assisted the pilot clear of the wreckage and put out his burning clothing. The presence of mind and courage of this airman undoubtedly saved the pilot from being severely burned and possibly from being killed. The aircraft contained ammunition which started to explode shortly after the pilot was clear of the wreckage."

Arthur Watkins had the honour of receiving his medal from HM The King at Buckingham Palace on June 17, 1941.

So much for the Men, now what about their Machines?

Aircraft unservicability.

It has been mentioned at several points that the aircraft serviceability at 56 OTU fluctuated daily quite considerably. Bearing in mind the size and condition of the airfield, the relatively small number of hangars and the use by heavy-handed trainees, this situation is not surprising. As an example at random the quantity of serviceable aeroplanes on the station in mid-1941 is shown below. The quantity of aeroplanes actually on charge was not recorded in the '540.

Serviceable Aircraft in Mid-1941.

Type	Minimum	Maximum
Hurricane	30	67
Master	5	14
Battle TT	3	5
Henley	2	3
Dominie	1	1
Tiger Moth	1	1
Leopard Moth	1	1
Harvard	1	1
Mentor	1	1
Magister	1	1

A Special Hurricane.

From among the thousands of Hawker Hurricanes built - or indeed destroyed - during the war and even among the hundreds which bore the brunt of back-, undercarriage- and engine-breaking duty at establishments like (5)6 OTU, one particular Hurricane epitomises the breed. It made a worthy name for both itself and its pilot, yet even though this aeroplane became just another 'hack' at Sutton Bridge it surely deserves a special mention.

Built at Hawker's Brooklands factory Hurricane I, L1555 became known unofficially as State Express - after a popular brand of cigarettes of the day called State Express 555 - and was, on January 31, 1938, first issued to 111 Sqn.

The Hurricane represented a vast increase in fighter technology and seemed to be viewed with some trepidation when it reached squadrons. In an effort to promote confidence in this brand-new aeroplane Treble-One's CO, Sqn. Ldr. John Gillan, undertook on February 20 a high speed flight from RAF Northolt to RAF Turnhouse (Edinburgh) and the Hurricane he chose to use was L1555.

Encountering strong headwinds on the journey north, he landed at Edinburgh, refuelled and decided to return to Northolt immediately. Sqn. Ldr. Gillan completed the return leg in a remarkable 48 minutes having covered the 327 miles at an average speed of 408mph. What was equally impressive was that

Hurricane I, L1555 dubbed by the newspapers State Express, being almost reverently pushed back into its hangar at Northolt after its epic high-speed flight in 1938. L1555 did much to boost confidence in the soundness of the Hurricane for squadron service. Full credit should go to Sqn. Ldr. John Gillan (inset), however, who typical of the breed of squadron commanders of his times, was a man with the foresight to recognise a problem and the strength of character to take uncompromising action.

L1555's engine had been running at full throttle, 2950rpm, for the whole trip without any sign of overheating and never missing a beat. It was this flight which did more than any other to convince those pilots that in the Hurricane they had a potent but utterly reliable machine.

An 80mph tailwind, a hinderance obviously on the northerly leg, had naturally the opposite effect on the return flight. But thus are reputations made and forever afterwards this pilot was known throughout the RAF as 'Downwind' Gillan.

However, even L1555 was to find its way - as did most of its compatriots from 111 Sqn.'s first batch - to 6 OTU on June 7, 1940. Here her proud past meant little and she simply became one of the many, eventually succumbing just like any other 'hack' to the heavy-handedness of budding 'tyros'.

On February 2, 1941, L1555 suffered an undercarriage collapse at the hands of Sgt. F.E. Earnshaw when he landed after a cross-country flight. Next Sgt. J.N. Yates was briefed on April 17 to carry out an aerobatics exercise in L1555. Burning up fuel prodigiously as he cavorted about the sky, he ran out of petrol and could not make it back to Sutton Bridge. To put the aeroplane down in a reasonable field Yates was obliged to land down wind with wheels and flaps up and L1555 was extensively damaged. A couple of days later it was shipped off to the Taylorcraft Company for repair but on inspection it was decided the 'old girl' could give no further useful service and L1555 was scrapped in June 1941.

Yanks in the RAF.

As has been clearly illustrated already, Sutton Bridge played host to virtually every nationality of pilot who joined the RAF. To this long catalogue of nations can now be added the USA.

America officially entered the war in December 1941 and it was not until mid-1942 that the US Army Air Corps sent men and machines to England. However, it is not so widely known that long before the US Eighth Air Force arrived 'Yanks' were serving and dying, in the RAF, alongside British, Commonwealth and other Allied pilots. Just a handful of Americans even flew in the Battle of Britain but with publicity about the air war in Europe gathering momentum within the United States - helped by such men as the American socialite Charles Sweeny - other pilots clamoured to join the RAF. Finding their way to England, usually via Canada posing as 'Canadians' in the RCAF, many of these American volunteers selected for fighters found themselves posted to 56 OTU (renumbered by this time) and soon the North American drawl joined Continental accents in the pubs and homes of rural Lincolnshire.

It was with the tacit approval of the US government that an organisation known as the Clayton Knight Committee recruited civilian pilots in the US ostensibly for service with the Canadian Air Force. Typical among those first Americans to arrive at Sutton Bridge was 25 years old Plt. Off. William L. Davis, a native of St Louis. Bill Davis had been an aviation enthusiast since childhood and by December 1940 had accumulated 325 private flying hours and held a commercial licence.

After a four-week training course in Dallas, Texas, roughly designed to take the place of the RAF Service Flying Training School stage, he departed St Louis on February 13, 1941, was commissioned in Ottawa and arrived in England on March 5.

Interviewed by the *St Louis Post-Dispatch* newspaper as he was about to leave Union Railroad Station for the last time, he said: *"I consider joining the RAF is a matter of sentiment and heritage as my grandfather was an English Army officer who fought in the Boer War."* Within a few short weeks Bill Davis was in England learning his trade at 56 OTU.

In his only cablegram to the folks back home, Davis told his fiancee, Marian Gall, *"Everything fine, England very beautiful, love you and miss you, Wish you were here."* Having solo'd on the Hurricane and already with a minor landing mishap in P5192 to his name on March 17, Bill was sent off next day for a routine map-reading flight in P5195. Becoming lost beneath a grey overcast, to Plt. Off. Davis the flat

6 WEEKS LATER HE WAS KILLED

William Lee Davis, 25-year-old St. Louisan and a member of a combat unit of the RAF, who was killed Tuesday in an aircraft accident over England, is shown here with his fiancee, Miss Marian Gall, 4537 West Papin street. This photo was taken less than six weeks ago at Union Station, when Davis stopped here for 25 minutes on his way from a Dallas training field to Canada.

With the notable exception of Billy Fiske who died in the Battle of Britain, Plt. Off. William L. Davis is believed to be only the second American national to die as a fighter pilot in the RAF in WW2. He lost his life in an air accident on 18/3/41 while flying with 56 OTU from RAF Sutton Bridge on a routine training flight. Fresh flowers from Springtime Fenland fields near the old airfield were placed on his grave by a childhood friend during a visit in 1994. As the first St. Louis casualty of the war he received extensive newspaper coverage in his home city.

No Jimmy Cagneys in here; these are the real-life Captains of the Clouds. The first batch of American nationals commissioned as VR Officers to undergo fighter pilot training for the RAF at 56 OTU Sutton Bridge. Photo taken between 5th and 17th March, 1941 outside the Officers Mess at RAF Sutton Bridge.
Back row from left: Plt. Off. Hillard Fenlaw - KIA. 7/9/41, 71 Sqn. Plt. Off. Reed. Plt. Off. Pendleton- Transferred to ATA then returned to USA. Plt. Off. Bill Davis - Killed in aero-accident at 56 OTU. 18/3/41. Plt. Off. Joe Durham - Transferred to Coastal Command. Plt. Off. Virgil Olson - KIA. 19/8/4, 71 Sqn. Plt. Off. Bill Hall- Shot down, POW, 71 Sqn. Plt. Off. Tom Wallace. Plt. Off. Warren McColpin RAF DFC.- Survived the war. Front row from left: Plt. Off. Ward - Returned to USA. Plt. Off. Hill- Killed in aero-accident with 111 Sqn. Plt. Off. Collier Mize - Survived the war. Plt. Off. Fred Scudday- KIA. India 14/6/44. Plt. Off. Loran Laughlin - Killed in aero-accident, 121 Sqn. Kirton Lindsey. Plt. Off. Oscar Coen - Shot down over France, 21/6/41. Plt. Off. Tom McGerty - KIA. 7/9/41, 71 Sqn. Not present for this photo: Plt. Off. Eddie Miluck.
[Collier Mize via Eagle Sqn. Assn.]

featureless Fenscape must have seemed miserable, uninviting and a million miles from home. Unable to determine his whereabouts he decided to land, electing to do so with the wheels down. He chose a suitable field, near New Leake Fen, Boston but his luck ran out. Soft ground made the wheels dig in as the Hurricane touched down and in an instant it flipped over onto its back. Bill Davis died from a broken neck, the first American fatality at Sutton Bridge and the first St Louis son to be killed in the war. He is buried in Sutton Bridge churchyard as a pilot of the RAF but the headstone gives no hint of his US nationality.

Plt. Off. Davis had the distinction of being one of the first carefree band of US citizens to undergo training at 56 OTU, Sutton Bridge. One of his buddies, Carroll 'Red' McColpin, survived the rigours of OTU, RAF, USAAF and USAF service, rose to the rank of Brigadier General in command of the US Fourth Air Force in post-war years, finally retiring in 1968. Of his entry into the RAF and his time prior to becoming an Eagle Sqn. 'ace', 'Red' McColpin remembers: *"...sailing with ten other Yankees...having been provided with one-way ship tickets (from Canada) to England."* (*The Eagle Squadrons,* Vern Haugland, pub:David & Charles).

The group of pilots of which Carroll McColpin spoke, actually numbered twelve in all. Sailing from Halifax, Nova Scotia on February 24,1941 aboard the SS *Georgic* as Batch No.8, were:

J.E. Durham, H.S. Fenlaw, J.M.Hill, L.L. Laughlin, C.W. McColpin, T.P.McGerty, E.T.Miluck, C.C.Mize, W. Pendleton, L.F.Reed, F.Scudday and T.M.Wallace

By careful examination of little known American documents called 'Boat Lists', it is possible to untangle the web of names and arrivals in England, of American volunteer products of US flying training courses.

In the second half of 1940 three flying schools were established in the US to train pilots for the RAF from those applicants who had around 100 hours or more, flying time. These courses were known in the US as the 'British Refresher Courses' and the schools located in Dallas, Texas; Tulsa, Oklahoma and Glendale, California (the latter was also called 'Polaris'). Later a fourth school was established at Bakersfield, California.

Although it is a fact of history that eleven American fighter pilots fought in the Battle of Britain and others joined fighter squadrons immediately after the Battle, there is no evidence to suggest that there were any US arrivals at RAF Sutton Bridge prior to March 1941. Equally though, it is not being suggested that the Boat Lists contain the names of the only American airmen to arrive at Sutton Bridge. For example, Virgil Olson is not recorded on any of the Boat Lists but he is in the photograph taken at Sutton

Budding US fighter pilot Red McColpin had a mishap while with 56 OTU at RAF Sutton Bridge. He 'pranged' Hurricane L2006 - seen here as 'Y' of 11 Group Pilot Pool in 1939 - on 2/4/41 but without injury to himself. L2006 led a quite charmed life since it acquired the dubious honour of becoming the 56 OTU Hurricane with the most accidents to its name.

Bridge of that first American course. By the same token, Bill Davis - photographed with Olson - is also not on the Boat Lists.

The other side of the coin can then be illustrated by Sgt. Hubert 'Bert' Stewart's story. In Haugland's book Bert recounted the tale of his own highly dubious journey to England in the company of Plt. Offs. Ward, Coen and Hall, with neither official knowledge, sanction nor ticket.

At his training station Bert had asked to be posted to fighters but was continually told he was likely to go to bombers or become an instructor. He would not accept this fate and skipped off to Canada, meeting Coen and Hall en route. They explained how it was done legally but he just decided to tag along and bluff his way to England - and it worked, too. Upon arrival at the London reception centre, however, Bert was 'rumbled' and detained while the authorities checked him out. Ward, Coen and Hall meantime were sent off to Sutton Bridge, leaving Bert to plead his case to be a fighter pilot once again. So determined was he with his pleading that the RAF authorities were convinced and on March 7 he claimed he was too was packed off to 56 OTU - to become a fighter pilot. Ward, Hall and Coen are also in the 1st. course photo but Bert is not, so this may mean either that the photo was actually taken on the 5th or 6th March before Bert's arrival, or that he was left out of the group because he was an NCO - which would seem a little unjust.

Several of that first batch of volunteers had narrow escapes during this vulnerable training period.

Plt. Off. 'Red' McColpin clearly marked his stay at Sutton Bridge as he is recorded in the '540' as having a minor mishap in Hurricane L2006 on April 2. Its engine failed and caught fire and he was obliged to force land at Peterspoint, west of the airfield. He claimed to have remained at 56 OTU for at least five weeks before being posted to 607 Sqn.

On his first solo, in Hurricane P1935, Plt. Off. Oscar Coen escaped unhurt on March 14 when it bounced on landing, dropped hard onto the port wing and caused the undercarriage to collapse. Oscar was posted to 71(Eagle) Sqn. but on October 20 was shot down over France. Evading capture, he was passed down the resistance chain, reached Gibralter and returned to England on December 28, 1941 for operations once more. He retired from the USAF in 1962.

On March 14 also, Plt. Off. Virgil Olson 'bent' Hurricane N2341 in a landing accident at RAF Sutton Bridge. Virgil followed Coen into 71 Sqn. but lost his life in action on August 19, 1941 while on a bomber escort sortie.

This apparent inevitability of most OTU pupils to have 'close shaves' put another of this first American batch, Plt. Off. Hillard S. Fenlaw into the mishaps listings. Probably mixing up u/c with flap, he neatly folded up the undercarriage of N8021 on April 4, while taxying out for take-off. Yet another member of 71 Sqn. he, too, was killed in action on September 7,

Ships carrying American Volunteer airmen to England, 1940-1941.

Sailing Number	Depart Canada	Ship Name	Qty of Airmen
1	30/7/40	Duchess of Bedford	3
2	13/8/40	Duchess of Richmond	6
3	27/8/40	Not Known	4
4	6/9/40	Erin	5
5	27/9/40	Duchess of Atholl	3
6	2/11/40	Duchess of Atholl	1
7	6/2/41	Johannes Barnevelt	4*
8	24/2/41	Georgic	12*
9	25/3/41	Jean Jarteau	11
10	20/4/41	Alania / Royal Ulsterman	4
11	30/4/41	Not Known	2
12	23/5/41	Not Known	10
13	5/6/41	Bayano	26
14	19/6/41	Not Known	14
15	27/6/41	Olaf Fostenes	8
16	6/7/41	Not Known	2
17	10/7/41	Mosdale	9
18	22/7/41	Not Known	9
19	4/8/41	Madura	6
20	15/8/41	Not Known	4
21	25/8/41	Richepense (sunk 3/9/41)	11**
22	26/8/41	Not Known	4
23	26/8/41	Manchester Division	8
24	27/9/41	Bayano	19
		Total	185

Notes:
1. * =These two batches made up the first distinct American course at 56 OTU RAF Sutton Bridge.
2. **= Four airmen from this batch were drowned when the ship sank.
3. Not all these American volunteers were posted to the three RAF 'Eagle' Squadrons (Nos. 71,121,133) and thus did not qualify to be classed as 'Eagles'
4 Most of the pilots on Boats 1 to 5 attended 5ATS in England and those on Boats 6 to 16 and 18 to 24 went to 56 OTU RAF Sutton Bridge.
4. Boat 17 went to 52OTU at Debden.
5. It is believed that Boats subsequent to 24 attended OTUs numbered 53 to 60.

"Held off too high on approach...bounced heavily...undercarriage collapsed..." This phrase was to appear in accident records time and again at Sutton Bridge while 6/56 OTU was in residence. Hurricane R2680 became one of those statistics when US trainee Sgt. F.H.Halvorsen made his first solo in this aircraft on 20/6/41.

1941. Sgt. Bert Stewart didn't get off scot-free either, since 56 OTU 'Form 540' records his Hurricane W9114 as suffering an undercarriage collapse while landing on May 8. Bert was posted to 121 Sqn., which formed that May.

It can only be wondered at what all these brave men must have been thinking when they stepped off the train at Sutton Bridge; British, Canadian, American, Polish, Czech, French, Belgian, Norwegian, Danish, Indian, South African, Dutch, Australian, New Zealanders - all were there, in that remote corner of England. In most cases they had, at least, the companionship of a few of their countrymen as it was customary - and more effective in view of language and culture difficulties - to send each nationality in groups to the OTU. Equally, in view of the multi-racial structure of RAF Sqns. in WW2, a key factor underpinning its long term cohesiveness, the value of mixed nationality courses such as those at Sutton Bridge can now be seen.

In summary then, the Hurricane OTU at RAF Sutton Bridge began life as 6 OTU in March 1940. As was stated earlier, during the summer of 1940 'courses' were difficult to identify, but the course numbering system re-appeared after the battle. Between then and the date 56 OTU moved out to RAF Tealing, at the end of March 1942, some 40 courses of aspiring fighter pilots had passed through its gates. That first intake, No.5 Course, comprised just 14 pilots but it has been noted that courses in late 1941 accomodated around 45 students while, for example, in March 1942 33 graduates are mentioned. The rates at which the intake fluctuated is not known precisely but it is reasonable to consider 25 students as representing an average course intake over the two years the OTU remained at Sutton Bridge. It can be estimated, therefore, that 6/56 Operational Training Unit, while located at RAF Sutton Bridge, processed at least 1000 pilots for fighter operations, of whom possibly as many as 200 Hurricane pilots were sent into battle at a most crucial period of the air war during the spring and summer of 1940. Sadly not all those who arrived were able to leave, for 30 of their number were killed during training (3% of the total).

In RAF Sutton Bridge can be found an excellent example of contemporary wartime training for fighter operations. Without doubt the contribution made by 6/56 OTU to the air war was one of the utmost value both to the RAF and to the nation and as such, deserves its place in recorded history.

Air Incidents in the Fenland region 1940 to 1942

Date	Aircraft Type	Serial	Sqn/Unit	Incident Location	Pilot	Fate
14/03/40	Hurricane	L2011	6 OTU	RAF Sutton Bridge	Plt. Off. A.McFadden *	U
22/03/40	Hurricane	L2072	6 OTU	RAF Sutton Bridge	Sgt. H.D.B.Jones *	U
23/03/40	Hurricane	L1896	6 OTU	RAF Sutton Bridge	Plt. Off. O.E.Lamb *	U
25/04/40	Hurricane	L2006	6 OTU	5miles N of Wisbech	Sgt. G Tock	U
25/04/40	Junkers Ju88	N/K	N/K	N/K		
03/05/40	Hart	K5897	7 FTS	RAF Peterborough	Mid. B.Sinclair RN.	U
06/05/40	Hart	K3133	7 FTS	RAF Peterborough	N/K	N/K
06/05/40	Hart	K3131	7 FTS	RAF Peterborough	N/K	N/K
06/05/40	Hart	K3131	7 FTS	RAF Peterborough	Sub.Lt. W.S.Ewing RN.	I
06/05/40	Hart	K3133	7 FTS	RAF Peterborough	Sub.Lt. D.H.Angel RN.	I
07/05/40	Hart	K4947	7 FTS	RAF Peterborough	A/Sub.Lt. E.D.Child RN.	U
07/05/40	Hurricane	V6860	6 OTU	Upwell	Sgt. A.A.Robinson	U
08/05/40	Magister	P2505	23	Thorney, Peterborough	Sgt. J.S.Rose *	U
23/05/40	Hurricane	L2011	6 OTU	RAF Sutton Bridge	Plt. Off. D.C.Leary *	U
29/05/40	Hurricane	N2617	6 OTU	N/K	Sgt. R.V.Ellis *	U
29/05/40	Hurricane	N2070	6 OTU	RAF Sutton Bridge	Sgt. A.D.Meredith *	U
31/05/40	Hart	K6449	7 FTS	RAF Peterborough	A/Ldg. Airm. J.H.Meyer RN.	U
06/06/40	Hart	K4991	7 FTS	RAF Peterborough	A/Ldg. Airm. J.W.Ridley RN.	U
06/06/40	Hart	K6459	7 FTS	RAF Peterborough	A/Ldg. Airm. T.J.Turner RN.	U
06/06/40	Hurricane	P3666	6 OTU	RAF Sutton Bridge	Sgt. R.B.Simm *	I
09/06/40	Hurricane	P3621	6 OTU	RAF Sutton Bridge	Sgt. H.J.Cullen	U
10/06/40	Oxford	L9645	RAFC	S.Rauceby,Sleaford	Plt. Off. C.P.W.Hildyard	I
12/06/40	Hurricane	L1895	6 OTU	RAF Sutton Bridge	Sgt. P.R.C.Macintosh *	U
15/06/40	Hampden	L6008	14 OTU	S of Pickworth	Sgt. D.S.Matthews	U
16/06/40	Hurricane	L1601	3 FPP	Uffington	1st. Off. E.J.Greenside ATA.	U
19/06/40	Blenheim	L1458	23	Terrington St Clements	Sqn. Ldr. J.S O'Brian *	U
19/06/40	Blenheim	L8617	23	The Wash	Sgt. Close	K
24/06/40	Battle	P6684	12 FTS	Gosberton Marsh	Sgt. G.A.F.Edmiston *	U
24/06/40	Hurricane	P2560	6 OTU	1M S RAF Sutton Bridge	Plt. Off. R.W.Foster *	U
25/06/40	Blenheim	N38(6?)21	82	Wrangle, Boston	Plt. Off. E.J.Keeble	K
25/06/40	Hurricane	L1897	6 OTU	Upwell	Sgt. C.F.Cotton	K
27/06/40	Hurricane	L1660	6 OTU	RAF Sutton Bridge	Plt. Off. G.E.Ellis *	U
27/06/40	Hurricane	L2591	6 OTU	RAF Sutton Bridge	Parked, Hit By L1660	
12/07/40	Hurricane	N2468	6 OTU	Moulton Marsh	Flg. Off. J.Gillan *	U
18/07/40	Hurricane	N2616	6 OTU	RAF Sutton Bridge	LAC. Z.Urbanczyk	U
18/07/40	Spitfire	N3244	266	Heckington	Plt. Off. R.J.B.Roach *	U
19/07/40	Hurricane	314	6 OTU	1M N Sutton Bridge	Flg. Off. H.C.Mayers *	U
22/07/40	Hurricane	N2354	6 OTU	RAF Sutton Bridge	Plt. Off. W.Rosycki *	U
29/07/40	Hurricane	L1714	6 OTU	Walsoken, Wisbech	Plt. Off. K.Olewinski	K
31/07/40	Hurricane	N2365	6 OTU	Near RAF Sutton Bridge	Sgt. C.De Scitivaux*	U
05/08/40	Hurricane	L1741	6 OTU	RAF Sutton Bridge	Sgt. J.P.Morrisson *	U
07/08/40	Hurricane	328	6 OTU	RAF Sutton Bridge	Flt. Sgt. R.Grasset	U
08/08/40	Blenheim	L1448	23	Peterborough	Plt. Off. C.F.Cardnell *	K
10/08/40	Blenheim	N/K	23	RAF Sutton Bridge	Plt. Off. A.J.Willans *	U
12/08/40	Master	N7959	6 OTU	Near RAF Sutton Bridge	Sqn. Ldr. G.C.Tomlinson	U
13/08/40	Harvard	P5887	15 FTS	Moulton	Sgt. E.L Hogbin	U
16/08/40	Hurricane	P3528	6 OTU	Wisbech	Sgt. F.A.Sibley *	U
16/08/40	Lysander	L6861	613	Friskney Flats, The Wash	Plt. Off. J.G.Lecky *	U
17/08/40	Hart	K5799	7 FTS	Deeping St Nicholas	A/Ldg. Airm. E.G.Culley RN.	K
18/08/40	Hurricane	L2082	6 OTU	Walpole Cross Keys	Sgt. D.McGee	K

Hurricane N2479, coded US-B at rest between sorties with 56 Sqn. Handed down to 6 OTU it suffered a landing accident at the hands of Sgt. P. Pearson on 3/9/40. Pearson was posted out in October to 238 Sqn. and was k.i.a. in North Africa in 1942. (D.Hannah)

Still bearing the markings of 504 Sqn. Hurricane L1942 is in bits undergoing an overhaul, possibly at 1 CRU, Cowley, before re-issue to 6 OTU. L1942 also served with 79 Sqn., 9FTS, 9 PAFU,and ATA before being s.o.c. on 18/5/44. It reached 6 OTU in mid-1940, suffering damage in a heavy landing by Flg. Off. B.A.Hanbury (Can). Hanbury was posted to 1Sqn. then to 1(RCAF) Sqn. with whom he was killed in 1942. (B.Lowe via Bruce Robertson)

18/08/40	Hurricane	324	6 OTU	Terrington St Clements	Maj. K.Niedswiecki	K
20/08/40	Battle	L5714	6 OTU	RAF Sutton Bridge	Plt. Off. J.Macinski *	U
21/08/40	Dornier Do17Z-3	N/K	KG3	In sea off Skegness	Fw. M.Zimmermann	M
21/08/40	Hurricane	328	6 OTU	RAF Sutton Bridge	Sgt. C.J.Saward *	U
22/08/40	Hurricane	310	6 OTU	RAF Sutton Bridge	Plt. Off. J.Himr *	U
23/08/40	Hurricane	N2354	6 OTU	Walpole St Peter	Plt. Off. J.Macinski *	U
25/08/40	Battle	K9392	12 FTS	Ingthorpe, Stamford	Sgt. H.H.Jennings	U
25/08/40	Blenheim	L1330	29	The Wash	Plt. Off. R.A.Rhodes *	M
26/08/40	Hampden	P1354	83	The Wash	Flg. Off. N.Svendson DFC	U
27/08/40	Hampden	X2909	4 FPP	Potters Eau, Upwell	Flt. Lt. F.C.Gibbs	U
28/08/40	Battle	N2047	12 FTS	5miles NW Bourne	Sgt. A.W.Gear *	U
29/08/40	Hurricane	V7247	303	RAF Sutton Bridge	Flg. Off. W.Lapkowski *	U
30/08/40	Hurricane	L1769	6 OTU	RAF Sutton Bridge	Plt. Off. J.Bryks *	U
30/08/40	Hurricane	L2063	6 OTU	Holbeach	Sgt. N.F.Finch	U
03/09/40	Hurricane	L1654	6 OTU	Wiggenhall St German	Sgt. F. Howarth	K
03/09/40	Hurricane	L1833	6 OTU	Wiggenhall St German	Sgt. K.Stibor	K
03/09/40	Hurricane	L1924	6 OTU	Near RAF Sutton Bridge	Plt. Off. S.Fejfar *	U
03/09/40	Master	N7964	6 OTU	Moulton Seas End	Sgt. G.Hardie *	U
03/09/40	Master	N7805	6 OTU	RAF Sutton Bridge	Sgt. F.J.Twitchett *	U
04/09/40	Battle	L5711	6 OTU	Walton Marsh	Plt. Off. G.Noel-Johnston	U
09/09/40	Hurricane	L1596	6 OTU	RAF Sutton Bridge	Sgt. J.Zaluski *	U
09/09/40	Hurricane	L1727	43	Gedney Dyke	Plt. Off. C.K.Gray *	U
09/09/40	Hurricane	L1986	6 OTU	RAF Sutton Bridge	Sgt. G.Hardie *	U
10/09/40	Hurricane	P3644	6 OTU	RAF Sutton Bridge	Plt. Off. E Jereczek *	U
13/09/40	Magister	N3958	1SIG/SC	Near Spalding	Plt. Off. K.Laverty	U
14/09/40	Hurricane	N2479	6 OTU	RAF Sutton Bridge	Sgt. P.Pearson *	U
14/09/40	Magister	R1817	266	Alwalton, Peterborough	Sgt. R.G.V.Barraclough *	U
16/09/40	Oxford	N4849	RAFC	Gosberton	LAC. D.M.Napier	U
18/09/40	Hurricane	L1942	6 OTU	RAF Sutton Bridge	Flg. Off. B.A.Hanbury *	U
19/09/40	Master	N7803	6 OTU	RAF Sutton Bridge	Plt. Off. R.Barratt	U
24/09/40	Hurricane	L1787	6 OTU	RAF Sutton Bridge	Sgt. E.E.Croker *	U
24/09/40	Master	N7961	6 OTU	2miles SW Sutton Bridge	Flg. Off. K.C.Jackman	U
24/09/40	Oxford	P8829	RAFC	1mile W of S.Rauceby	Sgt. W.R.Clements	K
27/09/40	Hurricane	N2357	6 OTU	Near RAF Sutton Bridge	Sgt. R.L.Baker	I
30/09/40	Hurricane	L1986	6 OTU	Walton, Peterborough	Sgt. J.Kurka	K
01/10/40	Hurricane	L1871	6 OTU	Near RAF Sutton Bridge	Sgt. P.Brazda	U
01/10/40	Master	N7778	6 OTU	RAF Sutton Bridge	Wg. Cdr. A.W.B.Macdonald	U
02/10/40	Dornier Do17	N/K	N/K	Old Leake	N/K	
02/10/40	Hurricane	L1851	6 OTU	RAF Sutton Bridge	Sgt. V.Brejcha *	U
04/10/40	Hurricane	L1927	6 OTU	RAF Sutton Bridge	Sgt. J.F.Plasil *	U
04/10/40	Hurricane	319	6 OTU	RAF Sutton Bridge	Plt. Off. P.S.Merritt	U

Hurricane I, L1732, coded FT-E of 43 Sqn. also laid bare at 1 CRU, Cowley. Plt. Off. W.B.Shimmons collapsed the undercarriage of this aircraft in a heavy landing at 6 OTU, RAF Sutton Bridge on 10/10/40.

(B.Lowe via Bruce Robertson)

04/10/40	Hurricane	L1705	6 OTU	2M from Sutton Bridge	Sgt. R.Stirling	U
04/10/40	Spitfire	P7296	266	Little Bytham	Sgt. S.A.Goodwin *	U
05/10/40	Hurricane	L1766	6 OTU	Walpole ST Andrew	Plt. Off. C.C.H.Davis	I
05/10/40	Hurricane	N2341	6 OTU	RAF Sutton Bridge	Plt. Off. E.Cizek *	U
08/10/40	Hurricane	L2083	6 OTU	RAF Sutton Bridge	Plt. Off. D.C.Browne	K
08/10/40	Hurricane	P3169	1	Spalding	Sgt. N.Cameron *	U
08/10/40	Tutor	K6103	2 FTS	Ancaster, Sleaford	Plt. Off. J.B.Mackill	K
09/10/40	Hurricane	V7376	1	The Wash	Sgt. S.Warren *	M
09/10/40	Hurricane	N2367	6 OTU	RAF Sutton Bridge	Sgt. J.Dygryn *	U
10/10/40	Anson	N4885	12 FTS	Irnham, Bourne	Sgt. J.H.Bevans	U
10/10/40	Hurricane	L1732	6 OTU	RAF Sutton Bridge	Plt. Off. W.B.Shimmons	U
10/10/40	Hurricane	L2045	6 OTU	RAF Sutton Bridge	Sgt. D.S.F.Winsland	U
12/10/40	Lysander	P9104	613	Wainfleet	N/K	N/K
13/10/40	Master	N7962	6 OTU	Near Wisbech	Plt. Off. S.J.Thompson	K
15/10/40	Hurricane	L1713	6 OTU	Near RAF Sutton Bridge	Plt. Off. R.Borovec	I
16/10/40	Hurricane	L2003	6 OTU	RAF Sutton Bridge	Sgt. G.H.Williams	U
16/10/40	Hurricane	N2343	6 OTU	RAF Sutton Bridge	Plt. Off.. S.Bachwek	U
16/10/40	Hurricane	P3318	1	Near Stamford	Sgt. J.Prihoda *	U
17/10/40	Battle	P6632	7 FTS	Langtoft	Sgt. B.J.Balchin	U
17/10/40	Gladiator	N5594	1401 FL	Spalding	Flt. Lt. G.P.Miers	U
17/10/40	Hampden	P2142	44	Ramsey St Mary	Sgt. L.F.Kneil	U
17/10/40	Harvard	N7178	6 OTU	RAF Sutton Bridge	Sgt. A.G.Simmons	U
17/10/40	Hurricane	N2338	6 OTU	RAF Sutton Bridge	Parked, Hit By N7178	
18/10/40	Hurricane	N2365	6 OTU	RAF Sutton Bridge	Sgt. J Wright	U
21/10/40	Hampden	P4418	61	Guyhirne, Wisbech	Plt. Off. H.T.Gilbert	U
21/10/40	Hampden	X2096	61	Tilney St Lawrence	Plt. Off. I.A.Stewart	U
21/10/40	Hampden	X2980	61	North Brink, Wisbech	Sgt. R.G.W.Oakley	U
26/10/40	Hurricane	L1731	6 OTU	1mile N RAF Sutton Bridge	Sgt. S.D.Ormiston	U
26/10/40	Hurricane	L1548	6 OTU	1mile N RAF Sutton Bridge	Plt. Off. J.H.Tavener	U
27/10/40	Hurricane	L1581	6 OTU	RAF Sutton Bridge	Sgt. W.A.Lack	U
27/10/40	Hurricane	L1574	6 OTU	Wingland, Sutton Bridge	Sgt. G.S.Sutcliffe	U
28/10/40	Hampden	X3027	49	S Skegness Pier	Plt. Off. K.Ballas-Anderson	M
29/10/40	Hurricane	P3318	1	Orton, Peterborough	Sgt. W.T.Page	U
30/10/40	Heinkel He111		KG4	Newmarket	N/K	
31/10/40	Anson	N9649	12 FTS	Boothby Pagnell	LAC. T.J.R.Marsham	K
01/11/40	Hurricane	L1851	6 OTU	Tydd St Mary	Sgt. T Patlejik	K
01/11/40	Tiger Moth	N9439	4 FIS	Lords Bridge FLG	Plt. Off. C.Cox	U
06/11/40	Hurricane	L2084	6 OTU	RAF Sutton Bridge	Plt. Off. F.J.Soper *	U
06/11/40	Hurricane	P2822	6 OTU	RAF Sutton Bridge	Sgt. C.R.Glover	U
06/11/40	Hurricane	N2356	6 OTU	RAF Sutton Bridge	Plt. Off. L.E.Price	U
06/11/40	Hurricane	N2591	6 OTU	RAF Sutton Bridge	Parked,Hit By N2356	
06/11/40	Hurricane	L1704	6 OTU	RAF Sutton Bridge	Plt. Off. E.L.Neal	U
07/11/40	Harvard	N7175	6 OTU	RAF Sutton Bridge	Parked, Hit By L1706	
07/11/40	Hurricane	315	6 OTU	RAF Sutton Bridge	Sgt. H.H.Jennings	U
07/11/40	Hurricane	L1706	6 OTU	RAF Sutton Bridge	Sgt. G.B.Hine	U
10/11/40	Tiger Moth	R5212	4 FIS	Lords Bridge FLG	Plt. Off. D.F.Greig	U
11/11/40	Oxford	N6292	14 FTS	1mile N Ryhall, Stamford	LAC. T.C.Hope	K
14/11/40	Battle	L5303	7 FTS	Pinchbeck	A/Ldg. Airm. G.B.O'Flynn RN.	I
15/11/40	Hurricane	310	6 OTU	RAF Sutton Bridge	Sgt. E.G.Mason	U
18/11/40	Hurricane	L1927	6 OTU	RAF Sutton Bridge	Plt. Off. F.D.Snalam	U

The code SD-B identifies Hurricane L2052 as formerly operated by 501 Sqn before being passed to 6 OTU. Czech pilot Sgt. Srom had engine failure on a routine training sortie and crash-landed with wheels and flaps up, at Worths Farm, Wingland near RAF Sutton Bridge.

[B.Lowe, via Bruce Robertson]

19/11/40	Harvard	N7177	6 OTU	Near Sleaford	Plt. Off. J.G.Weir	U
19/11/40	Hurricane	L1659	6 OTU	RAF Sutton Bridge	Sgt. M.Pavlovic	U
21/11/40	Hurricane	L1814	6 OTU	RAF Sutton Bridge	Sgt. A.Y.McCombe	U
22/11/40	Spitfire	X4593	266	Holme, Peterborough	Plt. Off. Penkeith	K
24/11/40	Hurricane	L2052	6 OTU	Wingland	Sgt. Srom	U
25/11/40	Hampden	P1320	106	Tickencote	Sgt. R.S.Bagnall	I
25/11/40	Hurricane	L1552	6 OTU	RAF Sutton Bridge	Plt. Off. E.L.Neal	U
26/11/40	Master	T8397	5 FTS	Uffington, Stamford	LAC. W.Bethell	K
28/11/40	Spitfire	X4589	611	RAF Sutton Bridge	Sgt. D.A.Edwards	U
29/11/40	Hurricane	L2100	6 OTU	RAF Sutton Bridge	Flg. Off. G.M.Robinson	U
29/11/40	Whitley	T4201	51	The Wash	Plt. Off. D.J.Dunn	U
30/11/40	Hurricane	N2468	6 OTU	RAF Sutton Bridge	Plt. Off. K.S.Taylor	U
02/12/40	Blenheim	T1946	235	Holbeach Range Ldg. Grd.	Sgt. Evans	U
04/12/40	Blenheim	T1813	82	E of Denver Sluice	Sqn. Ldr. J.H.McMichael	U
10/12/40	Hurricane	322	6 OTU	Wiggenhall St Mary	Sgt. E.H.Burton	U
11/12/40	Tiger Moth	T5637	22 EFTS	Lords Bridge FLG	Flt. Lt. J.C.Burge	U
12/12/40	Hurricane	L1864	6 OTU	RAF Sutton Bridge	Sgt. A.C.Kelly	U
13/12/40	Hurricane	N2398	6 OTU	2miles SW RAF Sutton Bridge	Sgt. H.B.Almond	U
14/12/40	Master	P8342	6 OTU	RAF Sutton Bridge	Plt. Off. I.R.MacIntyre	U
14/12/40	Whitley	N1485	78	The Wash	Plt. Off. M.L.Stedman	K
17/12/40	Hurricane	L1552	6 OTU	Terrington Marsh	Plt. Off. R.C.Webb	U
17/12/40	Hurricane	L1820	6 OTU	RAF Sutton Bridge	Plt. Off. J.D.Wright	I
17/12/40	Master	N8046	6 OTU	RAF Sutton Bridge	Sgt. A.C.Kelly	U
19/12/40	Hurricane	N2399	6 OTU	RAF Sutton Bridge	Sgt. D.J.Scott	U
19/12/40	Hurricane	L2006	6 OTU	RAF Sutton Bridge	Sgt. G.E.Henderson	U
29/12/40	Battle	P6766	5 FTS	Hubberts Bridge, Boston	LAC. Davies	I
04/01/41	Hurricane	L1741	56 OTU	Hilgay Fen	Sgt. K.A.Worthington	K
14/01/41	Beaufighter	R2129	25	South Brink, Wisbech	Sgt. K.B.Hollowell *	U
14/01/41	Master	T8340	56 OTU	RAF Sutton Bridge	Sgt. K.A.Wigglesworth	U
16/01/41	Hurricane	P5188	56 OTU	RAF Sutton Bridge	Sgt. M.M.Maxwell	U
16/01/41	Hurricane	L2084	56 OTU	RAF Sutton Bridge	Sgt. L Luck	U
16/01/41	Hurricane	L2073	56 OTU	1mile S RAF Sutton Bridge	Sgt. P.J.Taylor	U
17/01/41	Hurricane	L1868	56 OTU	1mile N RAF Sutton Bridge	Sgt. E.M.Williams	K
27/01/41	Junkers Ju88A-5	4D+CT	9/KG30	Fishtoft, Boston	Oblt. F.Rinck	U
02/02/41	Hurricane	L1555	56 OTU	RAF Sutton Bridge	Sgt. F.E.Earnshaw	U
05/02/41	Battle	L5710	56 OTU	RAF Sutton Bridge	Flt. Lt. F.J.L.Duus	U
10/02/41	Hurricane	L1732	56 OTU	RAF Sutton Bridge	Sgt. P.C.Edwards	U
10/02/41	Hurricane	L2052	56 OTU	RAF Sutton Bridge	Sgt. A.S.Arnold	U
10/02/41	Hurricane	N2467	56 OTU	Near Sutton Bridge	Flt. Lt. D.F.Beardon	U
10/02/41	Hurricane	313	56 OTU	RAF Sutton Bridge	Plt. Off. J.L.Briggs	U
10/02/41	Hurricane	N2616	56 OTU	RAF Sutton Bridge	Plt. Off. P.W.Coggins	U
11/02/41	Hurricane	N2196	56 OTU	RAF Sutton Bridge	Flg. Off. H.F.Auger	U
12/02/41	Hampden	X3007	144	Snettisham	Sgt. E.Dainty	U
12/02/41	Henley	L3375	56 OTU	Near RAF Sutton Bridge	Sgt. J.Ketley	U
12/02/41	Hurricane	N2365	56 OTU	RAF Sutton Bridge	Sgt. G.L.Lawson	U
12/02/41	Hurricane	L1601	56 OTU	RAF Sutton Bridge	Sgt. Hard	U
12/02/41	Wellington	T2888	99	Staggs Holt, Wisbech	Sgt. C.T.Robinson	U
14/02/41	Hurricane	L2100	56 OTU	RAF Sutton Bridge	Plt. Off. L.Harper	U
16/02/41	Hurricane	L1666	56 OTU	RAF Sutton Bridge	Plt. Off. J.L.Briggs	U
16/02/41	Master	N8043	56 OTU	Hilgay Station	Sgt. A.J.Burley	K

18/02/41	Hurricane	N2557	56 OTU	Near RAF Sutton Bridge	Sgt. J.C.Moores	K
24/02/41	Hurricane	P3619	56 OTU	Near RAF Sutton Bridge	Plt. Off. V.Sikl	U
24/02/41	Hurricane	L1638	56 OTU	RAF Sutton Bridge	Sgt. A.V.Lewis	U
25/02/41	Hurricane	N2460	56 OTU	1mile S Wiggenhall St Mary	Sgt. J.M.Chambers	K
25/02/41	Hurricane	V7722	56 OTU	Whaplode Marsh	Sgt. A.G.Carless	U
25/02/41	Hurricane	L1769	56 OTU	RAF Sutton Bridge	Sgt. A.S.Arnold	U
25/02/41	Hurricane	L2006	56 OTU	RAF Sutton Bridge	Plt. Off. Jenkins	U
26/02/41	Hurricane	L2006	56 OTU	RAF Sutton Bridge	Plt. Off. F.J.Soper	U
26/02/41	Hurricane	313	56 OTU	RAF Sutton Bridge	Flt. Lt. D.F.Beardon	U
01/03/41	Battle	L5714	56 OTU	Holbeach Range Ldg. Grd.	Plt. Off. P.E.Penfold	U
01/03/41	Hurricane	N2529	56 OTU	RAF Sutton Bridge	Plt. Off. W.W.Swinnerton	U
02/03/41	Hampden	P4394	144	Wainfleet St Mary	Plt. Off. Skinner	I
02/03/41	Spitfire	X4613	266	Gedney Hill	Flt. Lt. S.H.Bazley	K
04/03/41	Anson	N9835	N/K	Wyberton Marsh	N/K	N/K
04/03/41	Defiant	N1794	151	Ketton, Stamford	Flg. Off. P.L.Gordon-Dean	K
04/03/41	Hurricane	L1617	56 OTU	RAF Sutton Bridge	Wg. Cdr. J.B.Lynch	U
04/03/41	Oxford	V1091	15 FTS	Gedney Drove End	LAC. W.F.Read	U
04/03/41	Tiger Moth	N9276	22 EFTS	Stow Bardolph Station	LAC. G.C.John	U
05/03/41	Blenheim	L6602	25	Castle Bytham	N/K	K
05/03/41	Hurricane	L2100	56 OTU	Near RAF Sutton Bridge	Plt. Off. C.K.J.Thompson	U
08/03/41	Hurricane	V7234	151	Burghley Park, Stamford	Sgt. H.E.Bodien	U
08/03/41	Spitfire	X4347	266	Wothorpe, Stamford	Plt. Off. A.H.Humphrey	I
10/03/41	Junkers Ju88C-4	R4+CH	1/NJG2	Terrington St Clements	Oblt. K.Herrmann	U
12/03/41	Hurricane	P3162	56 OTU	RAF Sutton Bridge	Flt. Lt. D.F.Beardon	U
13/03/41	Dornier Do17	N/K	N/K	SE Skegness Pier	N/K	N/K
13/03/41	Hurricane	V7209	56 OTU	Near RAF Sutton Bridge	Flt. Lt. D.F.Beardon	U
14/03/41	Hurricane	N2341	56 OTU	RAF Sutton Bridge	Plt. Off. V.Olson	U
14/03/41	Hurricane	P1935	56 OTU	RAF Sutton Bridge	Plt. Off. O.H.Coen	U
15/03/41	Hurricane	N2591	56 OTU	RAF Sutton Bridge	Sgt. A.H.Sands	U
16/03/41	Master	N8011	56 OTU	RAF Sutton Bridge	Plt. Off. R.W.Waine	U
17/03/41	Hurricane	N1783	56 OTU	RAF Sutton Bridge	Plt. Off. L.F.Read	U
17/03/41	Hurricane	N2457	56 OTU	RAF Sutton Bridge	Sgt. A.M.Morrison	U
17/03/41	Hurricane	P5192	56 OTU	RAF Sutton Bridge	Plt. Off. W.L.Davis	U
17/03/41	Master	N8011	56 OTU	RAF Sutton Bridge	Flg. Off. P.D.M.Down *	U
18/03/41	Hurricane	P5195	56 OTU	New Leake Fen	Plt. Off. W.L.Davis	K
18/03/41	Wellington	R1474	149	Beck Row	N/K	
19/03/41	Hurricane	N2399	56 OTU	RAF Sutton Bridge	Plt. Off. L.L.MacLoughlin	U
21/03/41	Hurricane	L2529	56 OTU	Tilney St Lawrence	Sgt. R.W.Read	U
23/03/41	Hurricane	L1951	56 OTU	RAF Sutton Bridge	Sgt. J.W.Edwards	U
23/03/41	Hurricane	P3884	56 OTU	RAF Sutton Bridge	Sgt. T.S.Scales	U
25/03/41	Hurricane	L1568	56 OTU	RAF Sutton Bridge	Sgt. R.Phillips	U
27/03/41	Hurricane	320	56 OTU	4miles S of Fosdyke	Plt. Off. F.Raw	U
28/03/41	Whitley	Z6477	10	Pickworth, Stamford	Sqn. Ldr. H.A.R.Holford	U
30/03/41	Hurricane	N2502	56 OTU	Near RAF Sutton Bridge	Plt. Off. N.J.Lockyer	U
01/04/41	Blenheim	Z6022	235	Snettisham Beach	Plt. Off. P.A.Annan	U
01/04/41	Blenheim	V5764	235	The Wash	Plt. Off. P.H.Blake	K
02/04/41	Battle	V1204	56 OTU	RAF Sutton Bridge	Sgt. L.J.Barnes	U
02/04/41	Hurricane	L2006	56 OTU	W of RAF Sutton Bridge	Plt. Off. C.W.McColpin	U
03/04/41	Beaufighter	X7541	25	Burghley Park, Stamford	Sgt. H.I.Maxwell	K
03/04/41	Hurricane	L1695	56 OTU	RAF Sutton Bridge	Sgt. B.W.Sanders	U
04/04/41	Hurricane	P5192	56 OTU	RAF Sutton Bridge	Plt. Off. S.Czarnecki	U
04/04/41	Hurricane	P5183	56 OTU	3miles E RAF Sutton Bridge	Sgt. G.K.Tomlinson	U
04/04/41	Master	N8021	56 OTU	RAF Sutton Bridge	Plt. Off. H.S.Fenlaw	U
04/04/41	Wellington	R1470	115	Terrington St Clements	Sgt. Thompson	K
06/04/41	Hurricane	L1831	56 OTU	RAF Sutton Bridge	Sgt. L.J.Barnes	U
08/04/41	Hampden	P1240	14 OTU	Little Bytham	Plt. Off. E.E.G.Crump	U
08/04/41	Hampden	P2092	14 OTU	Little Bytham	Sgt. R.J.Holborrow	K

An early aircraft from the first production batch, Hurricane L1568 is seen here in 1938 outside the splendid WW1 vintage hangars of RAF Digby. Coded 'S' of 73 Sqn., L1568 was transferred to 6 OTU where it survived intact until damaged by Sgt. R.Phillips in a landing accident at RAF Sutton Bridge on 25/3/41. (P.H.T.Green Collection)

09/04/41	Hurricane	L1927	56 OTU	RAF Sutton Bridge	Plt. Off. H.S.Fenlaw	U
09/04/41	Master	N8011	56 OTU	RAF Sutton Bridge	Sgt. A.A.Robinson	U
10/04/41	Harvard	N7175	56 OTU	RAF Sutton Bridge	Plt. Off. A.C.Cochrane	U
12/04/41	Hurricane	L2665	56 OTU	RAF Sutton Bridge	Sgt. Briggs	U
12/04/41	Tiger Moth	BB758	13 EFTS	Lolham, Market Deeping	Lt. Saward	U
13/04/41	Hurricane	N2467	56 OTU	RAF Sutton Bridge	Sgt. G.B.Buist	U
15/04/41	Hurricane	N2665	56 OTU	RAF Sutton Bridge	Plt. Off. P.W.Coggins	U
17/04/41	Hurricane	L2055	56 OTU	RAF Sutton Bridge	Sgt. G.F.Lawrence	U
17/04/41	Hurricane	L1555	56 OTU	Long Sutton	Sgt. J.N.Yates	U
17/04/41	Hurricane	P3785	56 OTU	Gedney Drove End	Sgt. W.R.Rodger	K
17/04/41	Junkers Ju88C-2	R4+BM	1/NJG2	Gedney Hill	Ogefr. W. Beetz	K
18/04/41	Hurricane	L1769	56 OTU	RAF Sutton Bridge	Sgt. R.G.Pascoe	U
20/04/41	Hurricane	N2482	56 OTU	Near Sutton Bridge	Plt. Off. P.W.Coggins	U
23/04/41	Hurricane	W9129	56 OTU	RAF Sutton Bridge	Plt. Off. M.W.Fessler	U
23/04/41	Wellington	R1368	218	Clenchwarton	Sgt. W.S.Adams	U
24/04/41	Whirlwind	P6992	263	Burghley Park, Stamford	Flg. Off. B.Howe	K
25/04/41	Hurricane	L2070	56 OTU	RAF Sutton Bridge	Plt. Off. W.Hopkins	U
29/04/41	Battle	L5769	56 OTU	RAF Sutton Bridge	Flt. Lt. F.J.L.Duus	U
30/04/41	Wellington	T2721	99	The Wash	Sgt. F.Hewitson	K
02/05/41	Hurricane	V6869	56 OTU	RAF Sutton Bridge	Plt. Off. S.R.Edner	U
04/05/41	Hurricane	L2099	56 OTU	RAF Sutton Bridge	Sgt. W.E.Hopkins	U
04/05/41	Hurricane	P3884	56 OTU	RAF Sutton Bridge	Sgt. T.W.Allen	U
04/05/41	Junkers Ju88A-5	V4+BS	8/KG1	Eastgate, Bourne	Uffz. A.Becker	K
04/05/41	Junkers Ju88A-5	3Z+CL	1/KG77	Welney Wash	Lt. J.Wreschnick	U
06/05/41	Hurricane	L1574	56 OTU	Moulton Austendyke	Sgt. J.C.Cox	U
07/05/41	Hurricane	V6860	56 OTU	RAF Sutton Bridge	Sgt. A.Robinson	U
08/05/41	Dornier Do17ZK-10	R4+GK	2/NJG2	Carrington, Boston	Fw. W.Lettenmeier	K
08/05/41	Hurricane	W9114	56 OTU	RAF Sutton Bridge	Sgt. H.L.Stewart	U
11/05/41	Hurricane	N2457	56 OTU	Terrington Marsh	Plt. Off. E.H.Ullah	U
12/05/41	Harvard	N7176	56 OTU	RAF Sutton Bridge	Destroyed In Air Raid	
14/05/41	Defiant	N1610	54 OTU	Thorpe St Peter	Sgt. H.I.Stephen	U
16/05/41	Hurricane	N2717	56 OTU	RAF Sutton Bridge	Plt. Off. M.S.Pujji	U
16/05/41	Oxford	P1814	RAFC	Grimsthorpe Bombing Range	LAC. J.M.Snow	U
17/05/41	Hampden	P2099	106	Uffington, Stamford	Plt. Off. S.J.Harvey	K
17/05/41	Hurricane	V7416	56 OTU	RAF Sutton Bridge	Plt. Off. T.N.Rosser	U
18/05/41	Hurricane	V6999	56 OTU	RAF Sutton Bridge	Plt. Off. D.Bourne	U
18/05/41	Wellington	W5448	218	Hilgay	Plt. Off. B.E.Lymbery	K
22/05/41	Hurricane	W9129	56 OTU	RAF Sutton Bridge	Sgt. D.G.Aurisch	U
22/05/41	Hurricane	P3205	56 OTU	RAF Sutton Bridge	Sgt. J.C.Cox	U
23/05/41	Hurricane	L1989	56 OTU	RAF Sutton Bridge	Plt. Off. D.Bourne	U
26/05/41	Hurricane	V7185	56 OTU	RAF Sutton Bridge	Plt. Off. E.E.Pine	U
26/05/41	Hurricane	V7049	56 OTU	RAF Sutton Bridge	Sgt. A.H.Stuchery	U
28/05/41	Hurricane	P3714	56 OTU	1M N Sutton Bridge	Sgt. C.S.Collins	I
29/05/41	Hurricane	P2919	56 OTU	Holbeach Hurn	Sgt. J.R.Campbell	U
02/06/41	Hurricane	W9114	56 OTU	Walpole St Peter	Flt. Sgt. J.T.Craig DFM. *	K
02/06/41	Hurricane	P3162	56 OTU	Terrington St John	Sgt. Bisgood	K
11/06/41	Hurricane	L2055	56 OTU	West Walton	Sgt. A.M.Duthie	K
11/06/41	Hurricane	N2359	56 OTU	RAF Sutton Bridge	Sgt. Matthews	U
12/06/41	Hurricane	N2665	56 OTU	RAF Sutton Bridge	Sgt. J.Maddox	U
14/06/41	Blenheim	L6726	25	Barnack, Stamford	Sgt. H.F.Gigney	K
15/06/41	Hurricane	V7252	56 OTU	RAF Sutton Bridge	Sgt. A.H.Spier	U
16/06/41	Hurricane	V7287	56 OTU	4miles S Sutton Bridge	Sgt. J.M.Smith	U
16/06/41	Hurricane	V6865	56 OTU	RAF Sutton Bridge	Plt. Off. J.C.Hutton	U
18/06/41	Hurricane	L1740	56 OTU	RAF Sutton Bridge	Sgt. W.M.Kirkup	U

End of another sortie for 504 Sqn. Hurricane P3774 at Filton, Bristol, in 1940. This aircraft can be traced to 56 OTU, RAF Sutton Bridge by its landing accidents on 24/7/41 (Sgt. H.C.Webber) and 17/1/42 (Sgt. J.Omand).

"Upside down and nothing on the clock...!" The unknown pilot of Hurricane V6842 was said to have just 'buzzed' RAF Glatton, near Peterborough, when his engine failed and he had to force land. The aircraft flipped over onto its back with dire consequences as he braked hard to avoid running into the rapidly approaching house.

18/06/41	Hurricane	V6603	56 OTU	RAF Sutton Bridge	Sgt. R.Bastow	U
20/06/41	Hurricane	R2680	56 OTU	RAF Sutton Bridge	Sgt. F.H.Halvorsen	U
21/06/41	Wellington	N/K	N/K	Mouth of River Welland	N/K	
22/06/41	Hurricane	P3380	56 OTU	RAF Sutton Bridge	Plt. Off. N.S.Head	U
22/06/41	Junkers Ju88C-2	R4+JH	NJG2	Deeping St James	Ofw. Otto Weise	K
25/06/41	Hurricane	V7006	56 OTU	Newton Fen,Wisbech	Sgt. J.D.Hayhurst	U
27/06/41	Battle	L5766	56 OTU	Holbeach Range Ldg. Grd.	Sgt. G.B.Reader	U
27/06/41	Hurricane	L1740	56 OTU	RAF Sutton Bridge	Sgt. L.G.Gwill	U
27/06/41	Hurricane	V6993	56 OTU	RAF Sutton Bridge	Sgt. P.Tanner	U
30/06/41	Hurricane	V7111	56 OTU	RAF Sutton Bridge	Sgt. R.Weir	U
02/07/41	Hurricane	P3777	56 OTU	3miles NE Downham Market	Plt. Off. E.B.Gartshaw	U
03/07/41	Manchester	L7427	97	Wykeham, Spalding	Plt. Off. T.W.Dench	U
04/07/41	Wellington	R1589	57	Southery	Sgt. J.C.Irwin	K
05/07/41	Hurricane	L1935	56 OTU	RAF Sutton Bridge	Sgt. A.W Scragg	
05/07/41	Hurricane	P3863	56 OTU	RAF Sutton Bridge	Sgt. C.E.Browne	U
05/07/41	Hurricane	V7170	56 OTU	RAF Sutton Bridge	Sgt. Stewart	U
05/07/41	Master	N7941	56 OTU	Holbeach St Marks	Plt. Off. L.G.Bedford	U
08/07/41	Hurricane	R4217	56 OTU	RAF Sutton Bridge	Sgt. J.G.Nubley	U
08/07/41	Hurricane	V7466	56 OTU	RAF Sutton Bridge	Sgt. H.C.Webber	U
09/07/41	Hurricane	P3225	56 OTU	RAF Sutton Bridge	Sgt. V.Smith	U
09/07/41	Tiger Moth	N6591	25 EFTS	Spalding Common	Sgt. B.Pieslak	U
10/07/41	Hurricane	P2814	56 OTU	RAF Sutton Bridge	Sgt. R.E.Doman	U
11/07/41	Battle	P6571	12	Wainfleet Sands	Flt. Lt. A.D.Gosman	U
11/07/41	Hurricane	P3918	56 OTU	RAF Sutton Bridge	Sgt. J.H.Price	U

Hurricane V6935, DU-W of 312 (Czech) Sqn. being 'buzzed' by squadron contemporaries while undergoing minor checks at Speke in 1940. Re-allocated to 56 OTU, V6935 crashed near Sutton Bridge on 16/8/41, killing the pilot Sgt. M.F.Mills.

Section at readiness. A fine study of pilots and 'planes ready to scramble. Parachute on the wing, placed at just the right height, so that all the pilot needs do is pull on and secure the straps and race to the cockpit. Trolley acc is plugged in and clear of the wheel track with the ground crew huddled round a brazier, muffled against the cold winter air. In the foreground is Hurricane V6609, YO-X of 401 Sqn. in November 1940. Transferred to 56 OTU in 1941, V6609 suffered engine failure and was damaged when Plt. Off. J.W.Hicks force landed at Long Sutton on 14/1/42.

11/07/41	Spitfire	X4504	1 PRU	Nordelph	Flg. Off. S.H.Dowse	U
13/07/41	Hurricane	V7112	56 OTU	Near RAF Sutton Bridge	Sgt. A.J.Mills	U
14/07/41	Argus (Fairchild)	BS817	56 OTU	RAF Sutton Bridge	Plt. Off. G.S.Tobin	U
14/07/41	Hurricane	P5202	56 OTU	RAF Sutton Bridge	Sgt. J.G.Nubley	U
17/07/41	Master	N7560	56 OTU	RAF Sutton Bridge	Plt. Off. J.C.Nelson	U
19/07/41	Hurricane	V6869	56 OTU	RAF Sutton Bridge	Plt. Off. J.O.Daniels	U
19/07/41	Hurricane	V7000	56 OTU	RAF Sutton Bridge	Plt. Off. M.S.Vosburg	U
19/07/41	Hurricane	W9233	56 OTU	RAF Sutton Bridge	Plt. Off. A.C.Marchbanks	U
19/07/41	Hurricane	Z4036	56 OTU	RAF Sutton Bridge	Sgt. R.F.Southern	U
19/07/41	Hurricane	V6603	56 OTU	RAF Sutton Bridge	Sgt. J.Fullalove	U
21/07/41	Hurricane	P3713	56 OTU	N/K	Sgt. A.J.Mills	U
22/07/41	Tiger Moth	T5810	17 EFTS	4miles from Peterborough	Sgt. A.E.Hartley	I
24/07/41	Hurricane	V7446	56 OTU	Walpole St Peter	Plt. Off. J.C.Nelson	I
24/07/41	Hurricane	P3774	56 OTU	RAF Sutton Bridge	Sgt. H.C.Webber	U
25/07/41	Master	N7510	56 OTU	The Wash	Plt. Off. F.A.Grove	K
26/07/41	Wellington	R1617	300	Leverton,Boston	Sgt. M.Kostecki	U
26/07/41	Wellington	W5627	214	Jordens Lane, Spalding	Sgt. G.J.Joseph	U
26/07/41	Wellington	R1148	11 OTU	Wygate, Spalding	Plt. Off. R.M.Hill	K
27/07/41	Hurricane	V6940	56 OTU	2miles NE RAF Sutton Bridge	Plt. Off. H.Quilliam	U
28/07/41	Master	N7884	56 OTU	RAF Sutton Bridge	Plt. Off. S.F.Whedon	U
29/07/41	Hampden	AD795	83	Drayton, Swineshead	Sgt. Linacre	U
30/07/41	Hampden	AD970	106	The Wash	Sgt. Lockyer	I
30/07/41	Hurricane	T9535	56 OTU	Holbeach St Marks	Plt. Off. G.Garlet	U
31/07/41	Hurricane	V6882	56 OTU	RAF Sutton Bridge	Sgt. E.P.Greenhough	U
02/08/41	Hurricane	V7064	56 OTU	Lutton, Long Sutton	Plt. Off. W.T.O'Regan	I
04/08/41	Hurricane	V7126	56 OTU	2miles N Whittlesey	Plt. Off. M.C.Blanchard	U
06/08/41	Hurricane	V7019	56 OTU	RAF Sutton Bridge	Sgt. Gates	U
06/08/41	Hurricane	V6822	56 OTU	RAF Sutton Bridge	N/K	U
07/08/41	Hurricane	V6842	56 OTU	RAF Sutton Bridge	Plt. Off. R.L Wolfe	U
08/08/41	Blenheim	V6522	114	North Wooton Station	Plt. Off. S.R.Orichmond	I
08/08/41	Blenheim	R3743	114	Near Kings Lynn	Flt. Lt. Patterson	U
08/08/41	Hurricane	V6735	56 OTU	RAF Sutton Bridge	Plt. Off. A.Poznanski	U
09/08/41	Hampden	AE259	61	Algarkirk, Boston	Plt. Off. L.W.Methcalfe	U
09/08/41	Hurricane	R4081	56 OTU	RAF Sutton Bridge	Plt. Off. L.S.Loomis	U
11/08/41	Hurricane	V7465	56 OTU	RAF Sutton Bridge	Plt. Off. J.M.Bryan	U
13/08/41	Blenheim	N/K	17 OTU	Wilburton, Ely	N/K	K
13/08/41	Blenheim	V5758	17 OTU	New Fen, NNE Upwood	Sgt. G.P.Kerr	U
14/08/41	Hurricane	P3307	56 OTU	Lutton Marsh	Plt. Off. D.H.Hone	U
14/08/41	Stirling	N6043	15	Ramsey St Mary	Sqn. Ldr. J.Foulsham	U
16/08/41	Hurricane	P3028	56 OTU	RAF Sutton Bridge	Sgt. J.M.Dixon	U
16/08/41	Hurricane	V6935	56 OTU	2miles SE Sutton Bridge	Flt. Sgt. M.F.Mills	K
17/08/41	Hurricane	N2665	56 OTU	1mile NE Sutton Bridge	Sgt. G.H.N.Davey	U

18/08/41	Defiant	N3328	151	RAF Sutton Bridge	Sgt. J.A.Denys	U
19/08/41	Hurricane	P3888	56 OTU	RAF Sutton Bridge	Plt. Off. A.C.Marchbanks	U
20/08/41	Hurricane	V7648	56 OTU	RAF Sutton Bridge	Sgt. F.C.Coneybeare	U
20/08/41	Hurricane	V7591	56 OTU	RAF Sutton Bridge	Sgt. R.R.Chesterfield	U
20/08/41	Hurricane	V7076	56 OTU	RAF Sutton Bridge	Sgt. K.Bunting	U
20/08/41	Hurricane	V6538	56 OTU	RAF Sutton Bridge	Sgt. Miller	U
21/08/41	Hurricane	P3605	56 OTU	RAF Sutton Bridge	Plt. Off. R.L.Pewitt	U
21/08/41	Hurricane	P6938	56 OTU	RAF Sutton Bridge	Plt. Off. Dooley	U
22/08/41	Battle TT	L5708	5GP TTF	7miles NNE Boston	Flt. Sgt. J.K.Shreeve	I
27/08/41	Hurricane	P3225	56 OTU	RAF Sutton Bridge	Plt. Off. A.C.Marchbanks	U
28/08/41	Hurricane	W9130	56 OTU	Goosetree, Peterborough	Sgt. A.J.J.Hawley	U
29/08/41	Blenheim	L3734	17 OTU	3miles W Whittlesey Range	Plt. Off. J.G.C.Grieve	U
31/08/41	Hurricane	V7507	56 OTU	RAF Sutton Bridge	Sgt. W.Brown	U
01/09/41	Hurricane	R4091	56 OTU	RAF Sutton Bridge	Sgt. P.Keeping	U
03/09/41	Hampden	AE314	83	Wildmore, Coningsby	Sgt. Dennis	U
03/09/41	Hampden	AE194	49	10miles S Coningsby	Sgt. Gillies	U
06/09/41	Hurricane	W9225	56 OTU	Baston Fen	Sgt. A.C.McGuire	U
09/09/41	Tiger Moth	T5464	241	Needham Hall, Wisbech	Flg. Off. R.F.H.Pughe	U
10/09/41	Wellington	R1767	25 OTU	1mile N of Chatteris	Flg. Off. J.S.Willis	K
12/09/41	Hurricane	V6822	56 OTU	3miles W Kings Lynn	Sgt. H.R.Grinrod	U
17/09/41	Blenheim	V5651	56 OTU	RAF Sutton Bridge	Wg Cdr. H.J.Maguire	U
17/09/41	Hurricane	P3093	56 OTU	RAF Sutton Bridge	Sgt. Hall	U
17/09/41	Hurricane	W9178	56 OTU	RAF Sutton Bridge	Sgt. A.H.Kerr	U
17/09/41	Tiger Moth	N6595	17 EFTS	Willesden Av, Peterborough	Plt. Off. H.H.Chandler	I
20/09/41	Hurricane		56 OTU	Near RAF Sutton Bridge	Plt. Off. J.R.Owen	I
21/09/41	Wellington	R1539	103	Holbeach	Sgt. A.H.Rex	K
22/09/41	Hurricane	W9159	56 OTU	Wiggenhall ST Peter	Sgt. J.Swartz	K
25/09/41	Hurricane	P2919	56 OTU	Holbeach Hurn	Sgt. J.R.Campbell	U
27/09/41	Tiger Moth	T7040	17 EFTS	Holbeach	N/K	N/K
28/09/41	Manchester	L7375	97	Frithville	A/Flg. Off. H.S.Blakeman DFM.	U
28/09/41	Tiger Moth	T5638	22 EFTS	Near Hilgay	LAC. H.Bacon	U
30/09/41	Hurricane	W9180	56 OTU	Friskney, Boston	Sgt. R.D.Shuman	U
01/10/41	Tiger Moth	N9460	17 EFTS	Flag Fen, Peterborough	A/Capt. T.A.Bourn(Army)	K
03/10/41	Anson	R3310	14 OTU	Sutton St James	Plt. Off. B.J.A.Rennie	U
07/10/41	Blenheim	V5762	42 OTU	Flag Fen, Peterborough	Plt. Off. D.B.Allen-Williams	K
11/10/41	Defiant	AA281	409	Wolferton, Kings Lynn	A/Flt. Lt. F.S.Watson	K
11/10/41	Whitley	Z9204	58	The Wash	Sgt. E.E.Jones	I
12/10/41	Beaufighter	X7630	25	Barnack, Stamford	Flg. Off. R.C.Setchell	K
13/10/41	Whitley	Z6761	102	Deeping St James	Sgt. J.W.Steel	U
14/10/41	Blenheim	Z7278	114	Clenchwarton	Sgt. W.J.Anstey	U
16/10/41	Hurricane	V7465	56 OTU	RAF Sutton Bridge	Sgt. W.N.Fraser	U
20/10/41	Hurricane	V6690	56 OTU	Kings Lynn	Plt. Off. N.J.Choppen	K
21/10/41	Manchester	R5783	97	Friskney	Flt. Sgt. G.H.Hartley	U
25/10/41	Hampden	P1254	14 OTU	4miles N of Benwick	Plt. Off. J.Lowrie	I
27/10/41	Hurricane	R2688	56 OTU	RAF Sutton Bridge	Sgt. S.H.Spallin	U
29/10/41	Oxford	L4626	RAFC	Near Rauceby, Sleaford	LAC. J.H.Birtwell	K
30/10/41	Hurricane	P2992	56 OTU	RAF Sutton Bridge	Sgt. G.A.Johnstone	U
30/10/41	Hurricane	P3888	56 OTU	RAF Sutton Bridge	Plt. Off. Mckillop	U
30/10/41	Hurricane	P3039	56 OTU	RAF Sutton Bridge	Sgt. Zadworthy	U
03/11/41	Hurricane	R4076	56 OTU	RAF Sutton Bridge	Plt. Off. R.Hosking	U
03/11/41	Master	T8286	56 OTU	RAF Sutton Bridge	Plt. Off. J.A.Gray	U
03/11/41	Tiger Moth	T7175	22 EFTS	Near Southery Church	LAC. W.S.Grayston	U
06/11/41	Hurricane	P2814	56 OTU	Burtoft, Boston	Sgt. D.C.Goudie	U
06/11/41	Hurricane	V7004	56 OTU	Low Fen, Upwell	Sgt. J.Ipsen	I
07/11/41	Hurricane	P5202	56 OTU	RAF Sutton Bridge	Sgt. T.J.Francis	U
08/11/41	Blenheim	N3626	17 OTU	Holme Fen, Peterborough	Plt. Off. J.Lang	U
09/11/41	Hurricane	V6865	56 OTU	RAF Sutton Bridge	Sgt. C.H.Baker	U
11/11/41	Anson	N5371	3 OTU	1mile S Sleaford	Plt. Off. F.R.J.D.T.Minster	U
17/11/41	Hurricane	P3209	56 OTU	Wingland, Sutton Bridge	Plt. Off. G.Murray	U
22/11/41	Tiger Moth	T5697	17 EFTS	Lutton Marsh	Cpl. F.G.Humphrey	U
24/11/41	Hurricane	V6864	56 OTU	Walpole St Andrew	Sgt. G.A.Johnstone	K
24/11/41	Hurricane	V7060	56 OTU	RAF Sutton Bridge	Sgt. M.Munro	U
24/11/41	Manchester	R5792	97	Walpole St Andrew	Flg. Off. H.T.Hill	K
24/11/41	Tiger Moth	N6482	17 EFTS	Spalding Common	Sgt. A.E.Hartley	U
24/11/41	Wellington	Z8863	115	2miles NW March	Sgt. G.R.Bruce	K
25/11/41	Hurricane	P2822	56 OTU	Lakesend, Wisbech	Plt. Off. P.Brouwer	U
25/11/41	Hurricane	V7177	56 OTU	RAF Sutton Bridge	Plt. Off. E.H.Bicksler	U
26/11/41	Wellington	Z1144	75	Midville, N Boston	Sgt. J.R.Giddens	U
27/11/41	Tiger Moth	T6703	17 EFTS	Wragg Marsh, Spalding	N/K	U
30/11/41	Hurricane	P5198	56 OTU	RAF Sutton Bridge	Sgt. J.L.Rayner	U
30/11/41	Hurricane	W6702	56 OTU	RAF Sutton Bridge	Plt. Off. P.Brouwer	U
04/12/41	Battle	L5781	56 OTU	Holbeach Range Ldg.Grd.	Sgt. G.L.Bradley	I

06/12/41	Blenheim	L4894	17 OTU	Gas Works, Ramsey	Plt. Off. C.H.Woodworth	K
08/12/41	Battle	L5770	56 OTU	Holbeach	Sgt. G.L.Bradley	U
08/12/41	Blenheim	L4922	9 MD	Lutton, Spalding	Flg. Off. B.G.Collyns	U
11/12/41	Hurricane	P5209	56 OTU	RAF Sutton Bridge	Sgt. Clark	U
11/12/41	Spitfire	AD291	412	Ruskington	Plt. Off. J.G.Magee	K
12/12/41	Hudson	AM619	407	Potterhanworth 'Q' Site	Sgt. W.Shankland	U
13/12/41	Hurricane	P3809	56 OTU	Friday Bridge, Wisbech	Sgt. N.C.Pow	K
15/12/41	Wellington	X3170	11 OTU	NW of Upwood	Sgt. A.K.Sanderson	K
17/12/41	Havoc Turbinlite	BD120	1453FLT	Deeping St Nicholas	Sgt. J.L.Sudders	K
18/12/41	Hurricane	W9153	56 OTU	RAF Sutton Bridge	Plt. Off. A.M.Maclaren	U
18/12/41	Whitley	Z6841	58	Tydd St Mary	Plt. Off. Maudene	U
27/12/41	Hurricane	V7626	56 OTU	RAF Sutton Bridge	Sgt. P.C.Miller	U
27/12/41	Hurricane	P3812	56 OTU	RAF Sutton Bridge	Parked, Hit By V7626	
28/12/41	Blenheim	Z5984	17 OTU	North Wooton Range	Sgt. H.S.Thomas	K
05/01/42	Hurricane	V6734	56 OTU	Cranmer Lane, Holbeach	Sgt. R.Lalonde	K
07/01/42	Hurricane	V7469	56 OTU	Walpole St Peter	Plt. Off. J.F.Zerovnicky	K
07/01/42	Hurricane	W9180	56 OTU	Walpole St Peter	Sgt. F.Pokorny	I
11/01/42	Hurricane	V6752	56 OTU	RAF Sutton Bridge	N/K	U
14/01/42	Hampden	AE292	106	Butterwick	Sgt. D.Lawson	U
14/01/42	Hurricane	V6609	56 OTU	Long Sutton	Plt. Off. J.W.Hicks	U
17/01/42	Hurricane	V6865	56 OTU	N of Earith Bridge	Plt. Off. D.M.Browne	K
17/01/42	Hurricane	P3774	56 OTU	Gedney Drove End	Sgt. J.Omand	U
17/01/42	Stirling	W7467	7	Earith Bridge	Flt. Sgt. R.W.Taylor	K
20/01/42	Hurricane	V6869	56 OTU	Walpole St Peter	Sgt. R.Thomas	I
21/01/42	Hurricane	W9206	56 OTU	Clenchwarton	Sgt. E.Eves	K
26/01/42	Hampden	P1186	14 OTU	Pinchbeck Station	Plt. Off. J.M.Marok	K
10/02/42	Spitfire	AR283	611	RAF Sutton Bridge	Sgt. F.R.Johnson	U
15/02/42	Hampden	L6020	14 OTU	Gosberton Clough	Plt. Off. P.Chinn	U
02/03/42	Hurricane	P3397	56 OTU	RAF Sutton Bridge	Sgt. L.Walker	U
04/03/42	Wellington	X9920	419	Shippea Hill	Flt. Sgt. T.H.Thompson	U
06/03/42	Spitfire	AA912	412	Ruskington Fen	Plt. Off. E.R.Taylor	U
09/03/42	Hurricane	P3739	56 OTU	Walpole St Andrew	Sgt. G.Brereton	K
09/03/42	Master	DK890	17 PAFU	Willoughby, Sleaford	Sgt. R.H.Cope	I
12/03/42	Hurricane	L2026	56 OTU	RAF Sutton Bridge	Plt. Off. A.H.Smith	U
13/03/42	Manchester	L7495	61	2miles S Wittering	Plt. Off. J.R.Hubbard	U
15/03/42	Hurricane	V7645	56 OTU	RAF Sutton Bridge	Sgt. B.Strachan	U
15/03/42	Hurricane	P3515	56 OTU	RAF Sutton Bridge	Sgt. W.E.Hughes	U
18/03/42	Hurricane	P2915	56 OTU	RAF Sutton Bridge	Sgt. L.G.Fisher	U
20/03/42	Lancaster	L7570	97	Butterwick Marsh	Flg. Off. E.E.Rodley	U
23/03/42	Hurricane	V7164	56 OTU	RAF Sutton Bridge	Sgt. L.A.C.John	U
23/03/42	Hurricane	V7222	56 OTU	RAF Sutton Bridge	Sgt. W.W.Fell	U
23/03/42	Master	DK827	RAFCFTS	1mile S Wainfleet	Flt. Sgt. V.J.Dubourgel	U

Chapter Four

SAILOR'S TOP GUNS

Sqn. Ldr. Allan Wright DFC and Bar lay prone in the cramped bombaimer's compartment of a Hampden bomber. It was March 10, 1942 and far removed from the aeroplane to which he was accustomed. Spitfires were more in his line being a veteran, at the age of 22 years, of air battles over Dunkirk and the south of England flying with 92 Sqn.

It was, however, Allan Wright's first trip in a Hampden and he was enjoying the ride. His brother, Flt. Lt. C.M.Wright was at the controls and knowing he was in capable hands Allan relaxed in the warmth of the sun through the perspex nose. A panoramic view of the geometric patchwork of Fenland fields, criss-crossed by rivers and dykes, unfolded below him.

Sqn. Ldr. Wright had been picked up from RAF Wittering for the short, 25 minute, trip to RAF Sutton Bridge to begin his new job as Chief Instructor of the newly-formed Pilot Gunnery Instructor Training Wing of the Central Gunnery School (CGS).

The River Nene drifted into view and in the distance, sunlight reflected on the vast expanse of The Wash. In a few minutes they would be touching down.

Suddenly, the nose dropped. Where there had been blue sky and brown fields now an almost vertical view of the river was rushing towards him.

With no time to reflect on what was happening, the Hampden flattened out, roaring between those high river banks, skimming just above the surface of the water. Now, a surge of power and noise! He registered a fleeting glimpse of two lattice structures. The nose pointed skyward once more, until the pilot levelled out at a more respectable height for the approach to Sutton Bridge, just coming into view to starboard.

Mandeville Wright had decided to show his brother Allan just how competant a pilot he was by flying under the electricity power lines spanning the Nene four miles upstream from the airfield. With the lines sagging in the middle, he estimated that clearance for the Hampden was not much more than 10 feet above and below but with a 'generous' 20 feet to spare between the banks on either side.

That was Alan Wright's unusual introduction to RAF Sutton Bridge where he was to spend the next six months as deputy to Wg. Cdr. A.G.'Sailor' Malan DSO DFC, engaged in the joint, demanding task of getting the Pilot Gunnery Instructors Wing off the ground - in more ways than one!

The philosophy behind the CGS can be summed up simply. To be successful at anything requires the process of learning to be continous. If learning ceases, failure sets in. In safe occupations failure may be a slow process but for the air-gunner, especially in war, failure can be sudden and irreversable not only for himself but possibly for his crew too.

If this holds true for the air-gunner in a bomber it is equally relevant for the pilot of a fighter. All the pilot's skill is of little use if shots go wide of the target.

A gunner can only retain his expertise by constant practice; by continually getting to grips with new problems resulting from new air tactics, improved aircraft performance or increased armour protection on his opponents. Much of the knowledge necessary to keep standards high comes from the experiences of others who have already proved their ability in these fields. Furthermore if the first hand experience passed on is gleaned from a succession of such 'teachers', then that knowledge keeps pace with current developments in the field of combat and at both tactical and command levels.

Recognising this need for continued and advanced instruction the RAF, in addition to its ordinary gunnery schools, established a Central Gunnery School at which those trained would return to their units to impart new techniques and tactics to other aircrew colleagues.

Formed on November 6 1939, under the command of Gp. Capt. W.H.Poole AFC MM, RAF Warmwell was the first home for CGS.

Originally CGS efforts were directed towards air-gunners. Staff pilots, loaned to the school by Bomber Command, had to develope training methods on their own initiative and aeroplanes were only reluctantly released for this purpose. From among those first instructors, Sqn. Ldr. John Grandy was to rise to the pinnacle of Command in the post-war RAF. Just four officers and twelve airmen comprised the first CGS course in April 1940 and training concentrated on turret-gunnery techniques.

Early in 1942 CGS moved to RAF Chelveston near Northampton then, on April 1 it upped sticks to relocate to RAF Sutton Bridge, where it remained for the next two years. CGS's short stay at Chelveston may well be due to a decision in March 1942 selecting that station as home for the 50th Bombardment Group of the US Army Air Force (USAAF), one of the Groups forming in the USA for service in the European Theatre of Operations (ETO). In the event, 50 BG did not actually use Chelveston but the station was occupied by other 8th Air Force units.

The CGS 'Bomber Wing' therefore came in from Chelveston to Sutton Bridge with Wellingtons and Hampdens and it was in one of these latter that Allan Wright had that most exhilarating flight with his brother. In the meantime, 'Sailor' Malan after many months of lobbying senior officers, finally received the go-ahead to set up a 'Fighter Wing' at CGS.

It was the opinion of one of the leading fighter pilots of the day, Alan Deere (later Air Commodore DSO,DFC), destined himself to become CO of CGS in 1944, that the foresight of Malan in pressing for a Fighter Gunnery School to be established was one of the most productive steps in fighter pilot training in WW2. He also considered it was to the credit of AVM Trafford Leigh-Mallory, the then AOC 12 Group, that he backed Malan's idea even though Malan had

Handley Page Hampdens, AE257 and AE252 of 44 Sqn. over the flat lands of Lincolnshire. War-weary Hampdens were in regular use by the Bomber Gunnery Wing of CGS at Sutton Bridge and it was through the glazed nose of this aircraft that Sqn. Ldr. Allan Wright had his first view of the airfield to which he was appointed CFI in March 1943. The camouflage pattern on these two aircraft is different and KM-X has a row of eight mission symbols painted on the nose below the cockpit. In addition to incidents at CGS a number of Hampdens were lost by operational Squadrons in air accidents in the Fenland region.
(Don Hannah)

disagreed strongly with the former's favourite 'Big-Wing' concept. South African Adolph Malan had proved himself an excellent shot as his tally of 29 enemy aircraft testifies, so he knew what he was talking about. His Ten Golden Rules of Air Fighting were pinned to many a squadron notice board.

It was a logical step thereafter to press for both Wings to be co-located to facilitate co-operation in their practical gunnery exercises. This was how both components of CGS: the Gunnery Leaders Course and the Pilot Gunnery Instructors Course, came to be at RAF Sutton Bridge in April 1942.

When 56 OTU departed for northern climes there was a further change at the top with the arrival on May 7 of Gp. Capt. Claud Hilton Keith as Station Commander. This post at Sutton Bridge had recently been upgraded to a Gp. Capt. appointment and Keith brought with him a fearsome reputation as an experienced bomber operation and gunnery training specialist.

It was as a result of the latter that he had been posted to Picton Air Base as OC the only RAF Air Gunnery and Bombing School in Canada. Recalled to England in April 1942 he was, according to his autobiography (*I Hold My Aim,* Allen & Unwin, 1946; the title of which was taken from the motto of CGS), unable to ascertain why. As a result he was *"...going begging with no immediate job",* when the AOC 25 (Armament) Group sent him to command CGS. The AOC told him his new command was *"...dirty, unhappy and inefficient."* Gp. Capt. Keith recalled: *"I flew to Sutton Bridge and confirmed the truth of this".*

It is essential to remember that training at CGS was run on different lines to that encountered at the basic Air Gunnery schools. Gp. Capt. Keith clarifies this difference by explaining that Central Gunnery School *"....provided post-operational training for air gunners and fighter pilots. Its pupils were those who had already gained experience on active operations and shown themselves sufficiently successful to justify their being given an advanced course in air gunnery, lasting a period of one month."* Quite what were the criteria for being rated as 'sufficiently successful' is not explained.

He continued: *"Each course catered for 10 fighter pilots and 32 air gunners and with a 50% overlap there were always twice those numbers of airmen on the station."*

CGS activity at Sutton Bridge began with Numbers 35 and 36 Gunnery Leaders courses and Number 5 Pilot Gunnery Instructors course, courses 1 to 4 having been held at RAF Wittering.

Fighter boys went to the Fighter Wing, under the command of the famous 'Sailor' Malan. According to

Gp. Capt. Keith: *"...he was a first-class exponent of air gunnery and lived up to it but he was not ever very interested in what the air gunners of bombers did. These latter were trained by the Bomber Wing, commanded by Wg. Cdr. J.M.Warfield, (ironically, an ex-Malta campaign fighter pilot) but he was succeeded on June 25 by an old hand on bombers, Wg. Cdr. J.J.Sutton."*

It was, in Gp. Capt. Keith's view, *"...intended that the School was the last word in everything to do with air gunnery. Although instruction was never as complete as I would have liked it to have been, undoubtedly pupils did benefit considerably and could go back to operational stations to preach their added knowledge to others with good effect and to go into the air to tackle the enemy with added confidence."*

People like 'Sailor' Malan knew exactly what to do in an air scrap and at CGS they passed on this knowledge first hand. It was intensive training with air-gunners manning the turrets of a bomber while being attacked by fighter pupils. Instructors in the bomber watched what was being done and taught such things as the concept of 'fire-control' for example, where one gunner - positioned either in one of the turrets or in the astro-dome - would act to co-ordinate and direct via the inter-comm all gunfire in the bomber against a potential attacker. Miles of cine film were exposed, by air gunners using camera guns fitted to their turrets and by fighter pilots alike, with exhaustive viewing and evaluation sessions after each sortie. Ground training also included the theory of ballistics, discussion of tactics, aircraft recognition and later on, clay pigeon shooting, - this latter was ideal for deflection training.

All of this was supported by the use of towed targets, courtesy of the Henley and Lysander aeroplanes of 1489 Target Towing Flight, formerly known as Station Flight, who were kept very busy. Station Flight had been re-designated 1489 Flight in September 1941 but the cadre of this unit subsequently moved out to RAF Matlaske in April 1942 when CGS arrived and the latter began to operate its own integral Target Towing Flight.

Among the workhorses of the School have been identified: Henleys L3267, L3273, L3310, L3320, L3335 and L3375; Lysanders: T1429, T1459, T1618, V9496, V9813 and W6955. Holbeach Marsh Range continued to provide the airspace and ground targets for air-to-air, air-to-ground and low-level strafing practice.

A 'clipped-prop' mark of Spitfire! An unidentified Spitfire after its return to RAF Sutton Bridge displaying graphic evidence of flying just a bit too low during a ground-strafe exercise over Holbeach Marsh - and getting away with it. There could have been only inches between the underwing radiator, Mother Earth and oblivion. (Gp. Capt. A.R.Wright)

On the subject of ground attack exercises, Allan Wright remembered they included a 'minimum exposure' run-in and get-away. The run-in was usually at a very low level across the marshes, before a quick climb and dive on the target. One day after making such an attack one of the trainees, an American, called up on his R/T to say his engine was running roughly and losing power and he was returning to the airfield. He made a good landing and taxied to the parking area. On switching off the engine, to everyones surprise, most of all the pilot, his propeller was only two thirds of its proper size. The end of each blade was splintered and its length reduced. No damage was found to the engine nor elsewhere on the Spitfire. The pilot had simply flown that bit too low on his run-in, scrubbed off the ends of the prop on the ground but got clean away with it!

Elsewhere, in May 1942, momentous events in the operational arena were to filter down even to training unit level and CGS was proud to take its slice of the action.

Much has been written and argued about the 'Thousand Bomber' raids. It is not proposed, however,

Summary of air target flying activity Oct 1941 to March 1942.

Date	Hours Flown	Targets Streamed	Qty of Aircraft firing Air-to-Ground
Oct 1941	43	161	51
Nov 1941	33	134	37
Dec 1941	31	84	28
Jan 1942	45	49	11
Feb 1942	36	20	6
Mar 1942	125	291(see note)	12

Note: Of the 291 targets streamed that month it was recorded that 276 aircraft fired, 9 targets were lost or shot away and 6 targets were not fired upon.

In a special photo sortie near Sutton Bridge in June 1943, Central Gunnery School Spitfire IIA, K-L, breaks away from a simulated fighter attack on CGS Wellington IA N2887. Streaked with stains from machine gun exhaust gases, the underside of the Spitfire's wings confirm regular weapons firing by these CGS aircraft. With turrets unmanned and its pilot keeping a wary eye on the photo aircraft, on this occasion the weather-worn N2887 looks easy meat but on a real 'shoot' Wellington pilots would delight in making their bombers a far more unco-operative target.

to repeat or debate those discussions at length here, only to set the background to CGS involvement.

'Area Bombing' was a new RAF strategic policy adopted early in 1942 after acceptance of the limited ability of RAF bombers to find and destroy individual targets at night. This new policy marked a major turning point in Bomber Command operations when much larger geographic areas of German industrial towns would become a target instead of pinpoint installations such as specific factories or railway yards. No longer would there be any concession for residential or cultural areas under the Area Bombing concept; all would be legitimate targets now and most of a raiding force, sent out as a cohesive stream of aeroplanes, could be expected to hit some part of such a large target.

Initially the new policy was put into practice with a large raid on Lubeck in March and repeated attacks on Rostock in April 1942. Although post-war analysis of raids on these two targets suggests they were not as successful as the public was lead to believe at the time, they did test Sir Arthur Harris's Area Bombing concept successfully and allowed him to push forward with his revolutionary idea for a massive 1000-strong bomber attack on either Cologne or Hamburg. In the event it was weather conditions which finally persuaded Harris to chose Cologne for this first 'Thousand Raid' on the night of May 30/31 1942.

How, then, did Central Gunnery School come to be involved in this attack?

In order to achieve the magic 1000 aeroplane figure, Harris had to pull in men and machines from every unit in Bomber Command, right down to the Command's own OTU's. When Coastal Command, who originally agreed to contribute 250 bombers, were ordered out of the raid by the Admiralty - the result of a long-running political argument between the two Services - Flying Training Command, of which CGS was a part, was also scoured for suitable aircraft.

It is recorded in the book *Bomber Command War Diaries* (Middlebrook & Everitt, Viking 1985) that just four Wellingtons were contributed by Training Command, largely because most of that Command's bombers were inadequately equipped for night bombing operations or so 'tired' they were incapable of making a sustained journey.

This is where RAF Sutton Bridge, in the form of CGS, made its small contribution to the momentous Operation Millenium. Three CGS Wellingtons were detached on May 26 to RAF Feltwell "...for special operational co-operation with Bomber Command". Pilots, wireless operators, air-gunners and complete ground crews were supplied by CGS on detachment for the few days around the raid date. When the attack began, these three CGS Wellingtons took off from Feltwell in company with 44 other Wellingtons; 20 from 57 Sqn., 23 from 75 Sqn..and one other from an unidentified Training Command unit.

According to the books *Operation Millenium* (Eric Taylor, Robt Hale 1987) and *The Thousand Plan* (Ralph Barker, Chatto & Windus, 1965) it certainly was a motley collection of tired old aircraft and green crews drawn from the second line units.

For example, at RAF Cottesmore instructors with 14 (Bomber) OTU who no doubt thought they had escaped the near-certainty of death on ops were now pressed once more into service but this time faced crewing up with 'green' students for this op. This OTU lost five crew members on the raid. Meanwhile, over at RAF Moreton-in-the-Marsh, 21 OTU also sent its battered, war-weary Wellingtons. Patched up and with dodgy engines they were flown by students - pilots and crews who had just two or more solo cross-country flights to their name. RAF Lichfield could even claim to have contributed the oldest aeroplane in the raid, in the shape of a Wellington from among the first half-

Over the range. With the distinctive black diagonal bars painted on the yellow undersurface of the mainplane, this Target Tug Westland Lysander, T1444 G-5, is believed to be operating with CGS. Just discernable stretched taut beneath the tailwheel is the target cable and the hatch through which the targets were streamed can be seen open beneath the rear cockpit. It was on just such a towing sortie as this that a Lysander was lost over The Wash in a mid-air collision with a 411 Sqn. Spitfire on 21/1/43.

dozen built and it was said to have taken off with no guns installed!

Forty-one aircraft were lost that night from a total of 1047 despatched and RAF Sutton Bridge took its share of those casualties too.

Wellington 1A, N2894, of CGS was reported missing. It was the last bomber to be despatched from Feltwell, at 23.47 on May 30 and was not heard from again. Four of the crew of six were members of CGS staff and there was a mood of sadness on the Station for the loss of Plt. Off. David Johnson who went along as aircraft captain; Flt. Sgt. J.R.Connor, WOp/AG; Flt. Sgt. J.M.McLean, AG and Flt. Sgt. S P.W.Waddington-Allbright, rear gunner. Providing operational experience and acting as second pilot for the trip was WO. A.Jambar (Czech) with a spare navigator, Acting Flt. Lt. H.A.C.Batten, both from Feltwell. Later, it was discovered that, having successfully bombed Cologne, the aeroplane strayed from the prescribed return route and was shot down near Arnhem by a night fighter. All the crew, except Waddington-Allbright who was made POW, died and were buried at Uhelan, near Apeldoorn in Holland.

With training activity now beginning to settle down it was not long before the inevitable procession of accidents began, too.

RAF Sutton Bridge made its small but important contribution to the historic 1000-Raid with N2894, a companion of CGS Wellington IA, N 2887 seen here over the feature-less Fens a year later.

The dubious distinction of having the first mishap with a CGS aeroplane from Sutton Bridge fell to Canadian Flt. Sgt. D.R.Morrisson on April 13. Trying to find his way back to Sutton Bridge in Spitfire II, P8279, he encountered hazy weather. While attempting to climb above it he became lost and only regained his bearings when he reached the Humber Estuary - roughly 100 miles north of the station! Setting course south once more, unfortunately he ran out of fuel before reaching the airfield and crash landed at Wyberton near Boston. Morrisson was unhurt. There were the usual reasons for these crashes; engine failure, burst tyres and undercarriage collapses were among the most common, although one Wellington managed to hit a tree and stagger back to base without crashing. This was P9209, flown by WO. D.J.North-Bomford, a staff pilot and one of the many colourful characters to serve at CGS. Son of an earl, according to former member of the Sergeant's Mess staff, Vic Goodman, 'Bomber' was *"...noted for his 'natty' line in richly-lined uniforms, sporting a large ginger handlebar moustache and with a penchant for wearing exotic headgear such as a wide-brimmed Stetson or a jockey hat!"*

First CGS Hampden to record a mishap was P2084 which suffered hydraulic failure, leaving the undercarriage and flaps useless. Flt. Sgt. E.H.Noxon managed to pump down the flaps with the emergency system and bring the aeroplane down on the airfield for a 'repairable' belly-landing.

Further confirmation of the gestation and subsequent activities of CGS comes from the pen of ground crew mechanic, Aircraftman Douglas Broom. During his wartime RAF service Douglas, a native of Crowland, Lincs, kept a meticulous diary which became the basis of a series of articles by this writer published in Flypast magazine in 1990.

As a keen 20 year-old airman in 1941 Douglas began his service as an engine fitter with 651 Army Observation Post Sqn. at Old Sarum, working on Taylorcraft-Austers. He returned to home territory on March 6, 1942 when the diary records his posting to RAF Wittering. Extracts from Mr.Broom's diary for the period are reproduced here, edited to clarify or expand specific events and providing an excellent view of life in general at CGS Sutton Bridge during 1942 and 1943.

"On 6 March I was posted. I'm off to Central Gunnery School (CGS) at RAF Wittering together with AC's Hayter, Colby, McIntyre, Abraham, Easthope and Reynolds. On the way I stop off at nearby Peterborough to see my wife, then arrive at Wittering only to find my billet is in Burghley Park, about a mile from the camp.

The next couple of days were quiet so at night I thumbed a lift home and borrowed a bike to get back

Above: Flying searchlights. One of the more bizarre devices to combat Luftwaffe forays into Fenland airspace during 1941/1942. Seen here at Collyweston, the RAF Wittering satellite, is Douglas Boston III, Z2184, converted to Turbinlite Havoc NFII, personal mount of Spalding-born pilot Flg. Off. Jack Cheney. The distinctive arrow-head and other antennae of the airborne radar equipment, AI Mk.IV, can be seen mounted on the nose and forward fuselage. Aircraft of 1453 Flight, later re-designated 532 Sqn., were frequent users of Fenland skies both on night operational patrols and on Night Flying Tests(NFT) during daylight hours. (J. Cheney collection)

Right: The business end of the Helmore Turbinlite - an airborne searchlight mounted in the nose of a converted Boston light bomber. Powered by a bomb-bay stuffed full of batteries the light could be switched on for a total of about two minutes. Having no room for offensive armament the Havocs had to work in conjunction with co-located squadrons of Hurricanes but were singularly ineffective and withdrawn from service by end-1942. (Simon Parry)

to camp. I did the same the next night but the bike went for a Burton on the way back. These were the first of several unofficial jaunts home - well it was too good an opportunity to miss!

On 12 March some of our Spitfires began to arrive and I was put on P7818, a Mark IIA, with AC. Hebson and Cpl. Durkin. I was quite proud when 'my' kite flew off to Blackpool, piloted by none other than the OC CGS Fighter Wing, Wg. Cdr. 'Sailor' Malan.

I was put on coal fatigues later in the month and this gave me an opportunity to watch some of the other aircraft operating from Wittering at that time. These included lots of Bostons from 1453(Turbinlite)Flight, the Defiants of 151 Sqn. and Hurricanes from both these units.

Off we went again on 27 March when CGS moved to RAF Sutton Bridge, near the Wash, in South Lincolnshire. It was a deadly place with terrible food - an important yardstick in those days.

The first day there I did a Daily Inspection (DI) on a Lysander Target tug and watched all our Spitfires and Masters arrive. A couple of day's later a Blenheim IV, Z5494, from 17 OTU at Upwood, crashed in a field close to the camp. It had engine trouble and although the pilot, Sgt. Heagety, tried to get into Sutton Bridge, he undershot and flew into the raised bank at the perimeter. It was a 'Cat E' job but the pilot got away with it.

At the end of the month I was put onto the Servicing Flight with Abe, Tich and Sgt. Milton. It was a good scrounge but I sailed a bit close to the wind on 4 April when I left work at 13.00 to cycle home. The Sarge asked for me a few times but each time the lads covered for me by saying I was in the lavatory. Had a great time at home and stayed overnight.

In April I was moved yet again, this time onto 'D' Flight. This was the Fighter Combat Flight and I began to come into contact with heaps of highly decorated pilots passing through the courses. I was also getting settled into the daily servicing routine and now felt no qualms in carrying out '40 hour' inspections on our Spitfires.

A reminder of the hazards to the flying boys came when first one Spitfire IIA, (P8250,with Sgt. M.C. Falcard on board), crash-landed on 29 May, followed by another Spit. down on 2 June."

A Famous Spitfire.

In comparison to famous pilots arriving at Sutton Bridge the arrival of yet one more anonymous Spitfire IIA among so many would hardly turn anyone's head at CGS. Spitfire P7350, however, was destined to lead a life far more exotic than any of her stable-mates and of a length undreamed-of in those hectic days of war.

Built at Vickers Castle Bromwich factory she is believed to have been only the fourteenth Spitfire off its production line. Issued first to 266 Sqn. on September 6, 1940, P7350 saw Battle of Britain service with 266 and 603 Sqn before being damaged in combat during October and forced to crash land. Repaired over the winter of 1940 this Spitfire was then re-issued to 616 Sqn in March 1941 then 64 Sqn. in April 1941 before being sent to various third-line units until April 1942. On April 27, 1942 P7350 was flown to RAF Sutton Bridge where she spent the next ten months in the service of CGS, chasing Wellingtons and her contemporaries rather than Bf109's and He111's.

What is it that makes this particular Spitfire so worthy of comment? Well, P7350 managed to survive to this day as the oldest airworthy Spitfire in the world and is currently operated by the RAF Battle of Britain Memorial Flight. Furthermore, not only does she thrill modern-day airshow crowds more than fifty years after she first took to the air but being based at RAF Coningsby in Lincolnshire, P7350 is still a frequent sight and sound in that very Fenland sky in which she spent the longest period of service with any wartime unit.

In common with Hurricane L1555 mentioned in the previous chapter, P7350 illustrates that this story is not just about people but about the interaction of men, machines and historic events.

Douglas Broom continues: *"There was a big 'flap' on which resulted in a lot of work for the Wellington ground crews in the Gunnery Leaders Wing. This was the first 1000 bomber raid on Cologne on 30 May and*

A famous Spitfire survivor. Spitfire IIA, R7350, which served with Central Gunnery School at RAF Sutton Bridge in 1942/1943 seen here in immaculate condition more than fifty years on, flying with the Battle of Britain Memorial Flight, based at RAF Coningsby. (by kind permission of Steve Barker and BBMF)

kites were being pulled in from all over the place. CGS provided three Wimpies for this raid but we lost one to flak; bad show.

I had another treat about a week after the big raid, when Jock Richardson and I each had a flip in one of the CGS Master's. We had a great time doing rolls and loops above the wide open Fens around Wisbech and March. After half an hour of stunting though, I started to get a bit queasy and was pleased to get down again.

June was a pretty good month, with lots of DI's and a 40 hour inspection to keep me busy. This reflected the constant flying programme run by CGS to keep up the flow of aircrew cramming our little station. I drew two 48-hour passes and the month drew to a close with a 'Purple' air-raid warning, as Jerry started to nose around again.

Occasionally we had unusual visitors at Sutton Bridge, often to undertake trials work down at the firing range on nearby Holbeach Marsh, at the edge of the Wash. One such visitor was a Hurricane which flew in on 1 July, carrying what looked like four bombs under each wing. A terrible disaster struck this aeroplane, flown by a Wing Commander, on the way to the range. Just as it passed over the town, the port mainplane ripped off and it crashed behind the cookhouse of the camp extension on the edge of town. The pilot was killed instantly. I learned later that those 'bombs' were actually rocket projectiles and this was the first installation trials aircraft up from Farnborough for live firing tests."

Douglas Broom's version of this story naturally only deals with the accident itself. It can be seen, however, as an illustration of the wider role which RAF Sutton Bridge and Holbeach Range played, as a venue for experimental aero-armament tests, in addition to its more conventional gunnery training role. As mentioned in the previous chapter, in the latter stages of the Battle of Britain for example, 20mm cannon armament for fighter aircraft was being tested over the Holbeach Range.

Back in mid-1941 British military mission representatives in Moscow witnessed a demonstration by the Soviet Air Force of a rocket projectile (RP) which was fired directly forwards from beneath the wings of an aircraft. It was said to be able to be used against air, ground and sea targets. The British were agreeably surprised by the consistancy of this weapon's trajectory and arranged for a Russian aircraft, equipped with this device, to be sent to England in October that year. In the event the Russians backed out and nothing materialised. There had already been a little work on this subject undertaken in this country by the Directorate of Armament Development, specifically for the evaluation of its anti-tank potential. When the Russian report materialised, this project was

Below A Hurri with 'attitude'. The menacing Hurricane II A, Z2415 sporting its six experimental rocket projectile rails, designed to carry 3inch RPs. Just discernable above the port wing rails and beneath the taped over gun ports, is a metal panel fitted to protect the wing undersurface against the effects of flame from the rocket propellant. Z2415 was destroyed by a mid-air explosion near Sutton Bridge on 1/7/42. (BAe)

Right:From little acorns..... Airborne rocket projectiles developed into a potent weapon against land and sea targets. Here is a Mark III installation loaded with four 3inch/60lb solid head RPs and mounted beneath the wing of a Hawker Tempest. (RAE Farnborough)

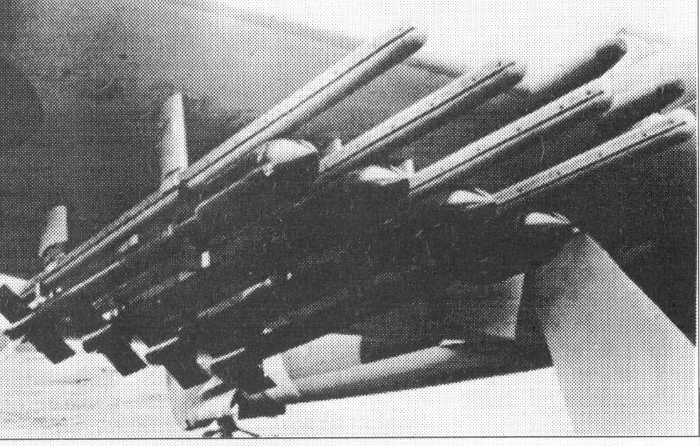

immediately given high priority.

While the Aircraft & Armament Experimental Establishment (A&AEE) Boscombe Down undertook development of a 3-inch solid-head projectile, RAE Farnborough set about testing first the vulnerability of the underside of a Hurricane wing to flames from the RP propellant when it was fired, then to design and construct suitable carrier rails for a Hurricane. The specification was for three rails underneath each wing. Trials installations were to be complete by October 24, 1941 when A&AEE would begin air-sighting tests to settle the harmonisation of the RP and gunsight and to give the test pilots experience of the weapon.

By December flight trials over ranges near Exeter and Bridgewater had proved the viability of the weapon and the lack of flame effect on the carrier's wings. However, these ranges were not so well-equipped or convenient as the Holbeach Marsh / Sutton Bridge combination.

Testing progressed slowly until mid-1942. Wg. Cdr. A.F.R.Bennett was on the Special Duty List attached to Farnborough specifically for the RP trials. Two Hurricanes were allotted for these trials, Z2415 and Z4993 and Bennett's team comprised two other pilots: Flt. Lt.'s Letts and Martin, operating under the banner of Instrument, Armament and Defence Flight, RAE Farnborough.

Previously Hurricane Z2415 had been used for terminal velocity trials and high altitude research and its main wing spar was specially strengthened for those projects. Because of this, it was deemed a suitable test bed for the wing mounted RP trials.

Bennett flew Z2415 to RAF Sutton Bridge in the late afternoon of June 30 where, making the most of the light evenings, he immediately put in more than two hours of trial firings at Holbeach Range.

July 1 dawned fine again and Z2415 was loaded with six RP for more trials. Wg. Cdr. Bennett took off and headed towards the range. As Douglas Broom then described, the aeroplane had just cleared the village when the air was rent by an explosion and bright flash. When the smoke cleared the Hurricane was found to have crashed on Bridge Farm, littering wreckage over a wide area. Bennett died in the crash and two civilian women were seriously injured by flying debris.

In such circumstances life must go on and next day Flt. Lt. Martin flew Z4993 to Sutton Bridge, did a 30-minute sortie to the range then returned to Farnborough.

After the accident, trials of airborne RP increased considerably until by August 1942 in addition to Z4993 other Hurricanes were allocated to the task: Z2457, Z2320, Z2895, Z3564 and Z2961 but for reasons probably due to the contention with CGS for range air-space which the increased testing would bring, the venue for firing tests was moved to RAF Warmwell.

This sad incident closed with the removal of Wg. Cdr. Bennett's body by train en route for burial in Brookwood cemetary. But it was to be a grim week as Douglas Broom now takes up the narrative again...

"It was a bad time for 'prangs', for the very next day another of our Spitfires, P8583, was lost. Sgt. C.I.Scott, a pupil from RAF Matlaske, was killed when his aircraft collided with a Hampden from 14 OTU, a few miles South of Spalding. Around this time several of our Wellingtons and Hampdens also suffered mishaps in the air and on the ground and I suppose this was inevitable with the amount of flying these kites had to do at the School."

It was not over yet for on the 4th, Flg. Off. N.S.Dunkerton was chauffeuring trainees to Holbeach Range in Wellington IA, N2893 when hydraulic failure cut short the sortie. He had to use the emergency system to lower the undercarriage but landing without flaps and with the undercart unlocked, he pulled off a creditable landing in which only the tailwheel suffered total collapse.

There was a narrow squeak for youngsters of the Dawsmere School the very next day. Returning from a target-towing sortie in Lysander T1618, staff pilot Sgt. W.M.L.Penny narrowly missed hitting the school when he had to force land due to running out of fuel.

On the 6th, WO. North-Bomford, with a crew of air-gunner trainees on board, got into difficulty in Wellington L7774 while on their way to the Range. Failure of a piston caused oil pressure to drop in the port engine and it caught fire. Unable to maintain height, North-Bomford could not make it back to the airfield so he force landed at Basses Farm, Wingland. He and the crew, some of whom were slightly injured, scrambled clear before the Wellington went up in flames and was completely burned out.

Douglas Broom noted at this point that Jerry had started to stooge around the area in daylight.

"Some of our fighter chaps jumped at the chance to go up and see if they could catch one but they had no luck. However, there came a rude awakening when, on July 24, a Dornier dropped four bombs on the camp during the night. One of these hit the armoury and sent loads of bullets and cannon shells whizzing all over the place.

Part of a bullet even landed on my bed and there was bags of panic, with people crashing round in pyjamas and steel helmets. The small fire was put out within minutes but there was not much sleep afterwards, though. In our billet we had to sleep three chaps in two beds because McIntyre's bed was saturated by the fire extinguishers. The war came jolly close that night...!"

Next morning Douglas was up early to view the damage. One Hampden and several Spitfires and Masters, eight aircraft in all, had been damaged by four 500lb HE bombs. In addition to completely demolishing the armoury, many hundreds of thousands of ammo rounds went sky high in a huge pyrotechnic display.

Sqn. Ldr. Alan Wright and his boss Wg. Cdr. Malan, were both living off the station with their families at this time; Alan being only recently married and in temporary accomodation in the nearby village of Terrington St. Clements. It was a grim sight which greeted them when they arrived for work to find the Fighter Wing office and lecture rooms totally demolished and much of their equipment destroyed.

A contemporary of Douglas Broom, 18 years old Aircraftman Norman 'Taff' Warren recalled there was some concern for the safety of the duty armourer who should have been in the armoury at the time of the

The sleek but menacing shape of a Dornier 217. The Luftwaffe made a dozen attempts to knock out RAF Sutton Bridge but only two raids were on target. A Do217 like this one is most likely to have been responsible for the attack on 24 July 1942. Apart from generally missing the airfield itself, some of these raiders were also caught and destroyed by local RAF nightfighters. One notable combat involved this particular Do217E-4, F8+CN of 5/KG40 on 23/7/42. Werk Nr 4279 was caught over Spalding and shot down near Fleet Fen by a 486(NZ)Sqn. Hurricane from RAF Wittering flown by Flt. Lt. Harvey Sweetman. (Bundesarchiv)

attack. Fortunately for him he was not at his post but it is not known if he was put on a charge or whether a blind eye was turned on the matter in the circumstances.

Two hangars, a decomtamination centre and the orderly room were also damaged but despite all this, only one airman was critically injured and three others slightly hurt.

Two nights later another Red Warning was sounded and AC1. Broom went off to the shelter *"... feeling really scared, but nothing happened."*

Midst all this gloom it could not have passed unnoticed to the airmen of the Station that the population rose substantially with the arrival in May of no less than 2 officers and 181 other ranks of the Womens Auxiliary Air Force (WAAF). It was recorded in the Station 'Form 540' that on July 3 Section Officer S.Ottaway was posted in to command the WAAF detachment.

Among the first WAAF contingent was Corporal(W) Olive Moule (now Mrs Olive Denis) who has memories, both fond and sad, of RAF Sutton Bridge during her service there in 1942/3.

At first she worked in the photographic section, helping to process those *"...miles of cine-gun film"* before transferring to the Bomber Wing with its Wellingtons and air-gunners. Here Olive was corporal in charge of a gun turret - one which remained firmly fixed to the ground - an early example of a simulator.

Air-gunners sat in this turret while Cpl. Moule moved it with random operation of a set of levers and cams. While counter-acting the motion of the turret, gunners 'fired' at a screen displaying cine-film images of attacking fighters. Of this turret, Olive said: "I recall it was necessary for quite a bit of climbing on and off this apparatus and a monkey couldn't have done it better than me after a while."

Located in the village across the river, close to the small dock, was the 'WAAF-ery', a group of Nissen huts which were so close to the river that, when the

The victor, Flt. Lt. Harvey Sweetman, left, with Wittering Station C.O. Gp. Capt. Basil Embry, centre and another 486 Sqn. pilot, Bob Roberts. Behind the group is a Hurricane IIA of 486 Sqn. in sooty-black nightfighter camouflage. 486 Sqn's claim for the Fleet Fen Dornier was hotly contested by a 409 Sqn. Beaufighter crew but evidence clearly supports Sweetman as the victor. [P.Sortehaug]

Nene carried a really high tide, they were prone to flooding. Other WAAF accomodation was situated on open ground near New Road.

"Amenities for us WAAF's were so basic", said Olive, *"that we had to have a rosta for baths. They were the old-fashioned 'hip'-type, where either your feet stuck out over one end or you just stood upright in them. We were allowed one a week and it was all very communal. I was a bit shy of bathing with so many other girls so I used to slide my bath to the back part of the bath house. One day, when my turn came round, the other girls waited for me to sit down in the regulation 3-inches of water then a group of them rushed up, picked up the bath with me in it and dumped me in the yard outside. That certainly knocked the shyness out of me!! Thereafter I made certain I bathed in the middle with the rest."*

Olive Moule also knew sadness at Sutton Bridge. She met and married a young air-gunner while at CGS. Their wedding was on April 10, 1943 but one week later her husband was killed over Germany on what would have been his last op before being posted as an instructor. Olive left CGS after a while, having made up her mind as she put it *"... to get my own back"* and in July 1943 she re-mustered as a Radar operator.

It was Olive who brought to light another *"who flew under the Bridge?"* story. While seeking corroberation of the 1930 incident, mentioned at the beginning of this book, Olive responded with her eye-witness account not of the 1930 incident but of another in 1943.

She wrote: *"I think it was a Canadian pilot. Several of us watched him do it, with sheer horror, as we stood somewhere near the old railway station or at* the WVS, both of which were by the side of the river Nene and close to the bridge. The reason for us being there was probably because we went to the WVS around mid-day to avoid the awful cookhouse food!" On the latter emotive subject the CGS '540' had recorded that on October 10 1942 "...a new Cookhouse was opened on No.2 Site and the old one at the Camp closed down. It is a great success, being much brighter and more efficient." That seems to have been a matter of opinion!

Olive was quite adament she saw an aeroplane fly beneath the bridge but sadly there is no firm indication as to who the dare-devil might have been. Is it just possible that it may have been that most rebellious of Canadian pilots George 'Buzz' (or 'Screwball') Buerling, who was actually serving as an instructor at CGS Sutton Bridge between May and July 1943?

'Taff' Warren was among many airmen who were moved out of the Station and billeted in the village. He was not sure whether this was a safety measure as a direct result of the bombing raids or the result of the influx of the WAAF - but more likely the latter.

He had the pleasure of staying with Mrs Sage in Custom House Street, about half a mile from the Camp. Widow of the former railway Station Master, Mrs Sage had Taff and one other airman under her roof, receiving the sum of six shillings (30p) a week from the RAF for doing so.

Inevitably the airmen and WAAFs quickly got on good terms and Taff Warren was no exception. He worked as a fitter on 'C' Flight with Lysander target tugs and he met his future wife at the Station where she

Turret gunnery was equally important at CGS and here an air-gunner gets the feel of his turret in a working model firmly fixed on the ground. This photo, taken in 1943, gives a good impression of the levers and hydraulics needed for turret mobility and how little room there was when an airman was encumbered by flying clothing.

Top Gun pioneers. Wg. Cdr. A.G. Sailor Malan DSO DFC, OC (right) and Sqn. Ldr. Allan Wright DFC, (left) seen in relaxed mood outside the office and training room of the Pilot Gunnery Instructor Training Wing (PGITW), Central Gunnery School, RAF Sutton Bridge, May 1942. This building was destroyed by a bomb during the air raid in July. (Gp. Capt. A.R.Wright)

worked as an armourer, the Station armoury being located adjacent to 'C' Flight dispersal.

Returning again to Douglas Broom's story of events, he wrote:

"On 27 July there were more attack warnings all day long, a pattern continuing over the next two months. Our kites were always eagerly scrambled but could find nothing to have a go at. The alarms went on into that night and we were all restless for over two hours. More Red Warnings next day and our Spitfire boys went off after Jerry but still without success.

Another Spitfire, P8090, crash-landed on the 'drome although the pilot, Plt. Off. D.H.Forrest, was unhurt. A defective tyre had gone flat after he took off on a tactical exercise. This was spotted when he returned to base and lowered his undercart, but he could not be warned because his R/T was 'duff'. When he landed, the wheel spat clogged up and the starboard oleo leg was torn off. I think someone got a rocket for not finding both faults during a Daily Inspection.

On 2 August Jerry was still active and yet more Red warnings were issued during the day and night. That same night Spalding was bombed pretty badly. I went on leave on the 3rd. after three warnings had gone off that morning. Just as I reached Peterborough, blow me, if there was yet another to greet me. This time, though, I saw a Spitfire chasing a Jerry plane and the local AA guns also let loose. Back from leave and I was on duty crew in the early hours of 11 August. A Lancaster landed at 02.00 after a minelaying raid on Kiel. One engine was dead, the bomb doors had been shot away and there was much other flak damage. The pilot and crew were all safe but he had only enough fuel for another five minutes flying and was dead lucky to drop into Sutton Bridge - just in time for the inevitable air-raid warning!

We lost another Hampden, P1163, together with the pilot, Flt. Sgt. S.L.Vinton, a New Zealander. He was on his first solo on the type, in the local area when he hit some trees and a house before finishing up in flames at Wingland, a few miles from the camp. The occupants of the house, a woman and her child, were slightly hurt.

That was on 17 August and on the 18th. a Spitfire, P7670 suffered a collapsed undercart on landing. Plt.

A cornucopia of experience. Gp. Capt Charles Beamish, second from left, photographed in June 1943 with senior members of his CGS staff. Fighter Wing CO, Wg Cdr. P.G.R.Walker is second from right, Sqn. Ldr. R. C. Dafforn is on the left of the group and the celebrated Flg. Off. George 'Screwball' Beurling is on the right.

My, how the grass has grown! In April 1992, fifty years on, former LAC Norman Taff Warren, on the left, is re-kindling old memories with his wartime CGS mates Jack Berrington and Frank Pringle outside what is left of their old 'C' Flight dispersal office.

Off. Bevan walked away unhurt from that one.

As far as my work was concerned, I was becoming quite confidant and had recently even done a '40-hour' on a Spitfire with no problems. In spite of being busy and having all these air-raid alerts, I was pretty fortunate, with overnight passes and 48's, especially useful as I was so close to home and my new wife, but such journeys were often quite eventful in wartime.

The 'liberty' bus to Peterborough was cancelled on 28th. so I caught another bus to Spalding, 14 miles, then walked another 8 miles to Crowland where I phoned for my father to come and pick me up for the last 8 miles. Good old dad came in his car (running on paraffin!) and I was able to stay the night. I missed the train back to camp and had to walk to Thorney, 8 miles, then hitched a lift to Wisbech and thence to Sutton Bridge. I arrived back way overdue and the work parade had long since passed, so I went sick and luckily got away with it.

To mark the passing of the third year of the war, on September 3rd a special open air service of prayer was held at the camp, with Gp. Capt. Keith in charge for his last official duty. On September 5, 1942, Gp. Capt. Charles Beamish DFC, took over command of CGS while, shortly after, the Fighter Wing was commanded by Wg. Cdr. P.G.R.Walker DSO,DFC., who would have memories of Sutton Bridge before the war when he visited for summer camps.

The original CGS team was moving on, having seen their new 'baby' begin to grow. Wg. Cdr. 'Sailor' Malan was now posted to command Biggin Hill Wing and subsequently the Station itself while Sqn. Ldr. Alan Wright joined three other highly experienced RAF fighter pilots on a tour of the USA to instruct American fighter pilots in combat tactics suitable for European skies.

'Sailor's' final duty at Sutton Bridge was to lead the local parade marking the anniversary of the Battle of Britain on September 20.

As was mentioned earlier, when Sqn. Ldr. Alan Wright relinquished his post as CGS Fighter Wing CFI, he was posted along with three others to tour the USA. This mission returned to England on November 23, 1942 and shortly afterwards one of its members, also a former CGS Instructor, Wg. Cdr. James Rankin DSO DFC, was posted to command the Fighter Wing at Sutton Bridge. Alan Wright received a Commendation for his work at CGS and was awarded an AFC in 1944.

Life on the base was still hectic for ground crew like Douglas Broom and Taff Warren and 16 September was probably one of their busiest day's so far.

"In all," said Douglas, *"we had 37 aircraft to service, including Blenheims, Whitleys, Wellingtons, Troop carriers and some Yankee P38 Lightnings. Three Lightning pilots joined the course on 18th and their machines were much admired and said to be very fast. The pilots showed them off to us after dinner.*

When pilots were posted to Sutton Bridge for the Gunnery Courses, they often brought their own aircraft with them as the demand often exceeded the quantity of aeroplanes available at the School. This is why we occasionally had Yank types and others such as Mustang Mk1's from some of the Army Co-Op units.

There were still regular 'prangs' to lighten the daily routine.

Spitfire P7851, Plt. Off. Chandler, landed with the wheels up on 20th and on 25th. Hampden P5341, Sgt. Vern, swung so violently during take off that the undercarriage collapsed. Both pilots were unhurt. Also on 25th in Spitfire P8087, Flg. Off. Thwaites got a bit too low over the perimeter ridge and the undercarriage was neatly torn off. He pulled off a

Lockheed P38 Lightning twin-engined USAAF fighters were regular visitors to Sutton Bridge. Pilots of the 20th Fighter Group, whose P38J, 43-2843 Jeanne was based at Kings Cliffe near Stamford, sometimes dropped in to this welcome refuge after long operational sorties. Also a number of American pilots attached to CGS courses often brought their P38's with them thus adding to the immense variety of aircraft types seen in the district. (Merle Olmsted)

belly-landing and was unscathed. Next day a Master, DL684,spun in near Wisbech. The control column had seized up but the pilot, Flg. Off. Lardner-Burke DFC and his pupil, Flt. Lt. St.C.Reid managed to bale out safely.

The Americans were by now, beginning to mount their first bombing raids and had been putting in much practice flying at both low- and high-level in our vicinity. Sadly on 2 October, one of their Fortresses crashed near Spalding, killing many of the crew, their bodies being taken to the RAF mortuary at Peterspoint, Sutton Bridge and thence to Brookwood for burial."

This incident refers to B-17F, 41-24492, 367BS, 306BG, from Thurleigh, with 1/Lt.W.W.Ely in command. A gunner suffered oxygen failure on a practice high level formation flight at 24,000 feet over The Wash and the aircraft disintegrated when the pilot pulled out of a power dive to reach lower altitude.

Douglas Broom continues: *"These Yank formations were pretty impressive to watch as they wheeled over The Wash area during assembly before setting off on their raids. Another B-17 made quite an arrival when it landed on our small 'drome. It was one of 20 aircraft which set off to bomb shipyards at Lorient. The mission was aborted due to bad weather and they headed back for The Wash to get rid of their bombs on Holbeach Range. This aeroplane had to get down quickly when a survival dinghy blew out of its housing during flight, fouling the elevator. It landed safely and we chatted to the crew while they waited for a transport to collect them. They were a friendly bunch and shared some of the emergency rations from the wayward dinghy with us. On the morning the pilots were due to take off from our little field, word had spread and hundreds of villagers lined the perimeter road to watch the spectacle. With its roaring engines run up to full throttle and the noise shaking camp buildings and nearby houses, it sprang forward off the brakes, thundered down the longest run and leaped into the air amid cheers from the watching crowd." (This aeroplane was B-17F, 41-24460; 423BS, 306BG also from Thurleigh).*

Sutton Bridge represented a welcome haven for returning 'lame ducks' of both Air Forces for on October 14 Halifax W1102 of 35 Sqn. made a forced landing on the way home from a night op to Kiel.

As the CGS was the temporary home of several American pilots drawing on the experience of the RAF, it was also a target for VIP visits. An example of this aspect occurred on 22 October, when a Douglas C47 Skytrain landed, bringing with it Brigadier-General James Doolittle (he of Tokyo Raid fame) and an entourage of American 'brass-hats, including Colonels

Boeing B17F Flying Fortress in the markings of 306 Bomb Group, WW-A, based at Thurleigh. The 306th. was the second US bomber group to reach England in Sept. 1942 and its crews trained hard in the Fenland sky to become combat ready. They suffered several losses through accidents and the first of these occured above Weston Hills, near Spalding on 2/10/42, when 41-24492 crashed with the loss of eight of its crew. (Harry Holmes)

Turner and Vandenberg.

There was no formal parade as they were there to look at training methods at CGS and fit in some air firing experience for themselves in Spitfires. Anyway I wasn't bothered by all this as I had been sent off on a 'Backers-up' course. This consisted of bayonet drill, grenade throwing and an assault course - complete with six-foot high walls, jumps and loads of barbed wire! Am I still in the RAF? It was a very tough ten days but I felt much fitter as a result and got a seven-day leave chit at the end of it, so it wasn't all in vain."

"November saw the arrival of the first of those thick Fenland fogs and all our kites were grounded on the 12th. The level of flying activity slackened off in general but one compensation was that it enabled me to get home quite frequently.

On 25 November a Wimpey, L7785, Flt. Sgt. V.P.Friese-Green, crashed on landing at Sutton Bridge. These Wimpeys were hammered pretty hard and this one's undercart had suffered in earlier heavy landings. This time the starboard leg just got tired and folded on touch-down but the crew were unhurt.

Two days later the undercarriage of a Spitfire, P7440, could not be locked down and the pilot, Sqn. Ldr. P.J.E.Ritchie, had to belly-land. It was messed up quite a bit.

After those fogs came the hard frosts of December but even so the air bombing war became much more evident judging by all the activity in the sky around the camp. On 6 December I watched bags of British and American fighters and bombers, pass overhead on a big daylight raid, said to be on Lille.(AJG: A diversion to cover a 2 Group raid on the Philips factory in Eindhoven).

"There were still monotonously regular crashes at Sutton Bridge, as evidenced by the demise of Hudson, N7404, on 9 December. The pilot was under instruction on the type and the 'plane swung on take off. It got dicey when the starboard leg collapsed and punctured the petrol tank. The aircraft caught fire and in a short time it was a burned out wreck but fortunately the crew escaped in time." Apparently this was a common result in such circumstances due to the design of the Hudson having a 'wet' wing fuel tank immediately above the oleo leg and near the engine.

"This was followed on 17th. by Lysander, V9496, making a rough landing causing the undercarriage to collapse and the undercart of Master, W9056, with a Belgian and a Yank on board, refused to lower. The 'Lizzie' just collapsed in a heap and the Master bellied in, with both crews getting away with cuts and bruises. I was attending church parade on the 20th., when another Spitfire crash-landed. They seemed to make a habit of doing that during church parades!

I drew guard duty regularly throughout December and latched onto the wheeze of sleeping in a Spitfire. Very Cosy! Christmas rolled round again and on the 24th. I caught an evening train home to Peterborough and stayed (unofficially) overnight. Christmas dinner was grand and we even had chicken. Good old Dad drove me back to camp in good time for work parade. The festivities were rounded off that night with a trip into Wisbech with the boys. We all got pretty merry."

While Douglas enjoyed home-cooked fare those back at Camp celebrated Christmas Dinner in the traditional Service manner with meals being served by the Station Commander, Gp. Capt. Beamish, his officers and senior NCO's.

"I was on duty ground crew for the next two days but it started to snow and apart from one P38 Lightning, which called at the watch office, there were no visitors at all.

By 31 December about four inches of snow had fallen and the year closed with yet another tragedy when two Spitfires collided in mid-air near Kings Lynn, killing both pilots."

"The weather improved a little on January 3. I was on duty crew again with plenty of visiting aircraft to attend to. It snowed hard again, however, on the 6th, and my mates and I were called out from 20.30 to midnight to picket down the kites out on the airfield. The howling wind and driving snow mixed with rain was horrendous and I was dog tired and soaked to the skin when I finally turned in. Next morning, being slightly late on duty at the Flight the lovely Sgt. Stafford put me on a charge. I was up before Wg. Cdr. Fletcher and got four days Confined to Camp. My pals 'Titch' Hebson, Taylor and 'Jelly', were all on charges and received Jankers too. We had the bind of reporting in full kit to the guard room at 06.30, 13.00, 18.30 and 22.00 each day for our sins. What a bind!

The weather turned foul again in mid-January. After hail, snow and rain, for good measure, there was thick fog too. Out on the airfield it became waterlogged and we had to push all the kites into hangers for protection.

By comparison with the aircraft operated by CGS predecessor 56 OTU, W9056 was a Miles Master II powered by a 870hp Bristol Mercury radial engine. This aeroplane suffered a landing accident at RAF Sutton Bridge on 17/12/42. It did, however, live to fight another day and is seen here in post-war markings.
(Mike Hooks)

"A large force of our aircraft....." A formation of 29 American B17 Flying Fortress bombers of the 379th Bomb Group, outward bound from its Kimbolton base. Such sights as these became commonplace after 1943 as day bombers formed up over the Fens and The Wash before setting course for enemy targets. (Harry Holmes)

There was a one-day 'Backers-up' exercise on 13 January and I had to cook food under 'field' conditions. It reminded me of my far-off days down at Sherbourne with the Army flyers but it was a jolly sight colder and more miserable up here. It was good to see Gp. Capt. Malan pay a flying visit to the station that same day.

The weather improved and on 18 January there was the first flying for a fortnight. The 'drome, however, was still badly waterlogged and on 23rd all our Spitfires went u/s on their first trips. This was due to water damaging their flaps as they landed back and hit the great puddles out on the field.

One of the teaching techniques used at CGS was to show students actual combat film, taken by cameras mounted in fighters and synchronised to work when the guns were fired. I had an opportunity to see some of this when I attended a talk about fighter sweeps, given one evening by Wg. Cdr. Rankin.

Flying activity gathered pace once more after the spell of bad weather. On 27 January I counted 57 high-flying Fortresses going over the camp, heading out towards The Wash. (AJG: This was probably a view of the Eighth Air Force's first raid on Germany, which took place on that date, the targets being Emden and Wilhelmshaven. Aircraft of the 1st.Bombardment Wing were based mainly on airfields in Hunts and Northants and assembled in formation over the Fens adjacent to The Wash). *Shortly afterwards, over 70 Bostons, Mitchells and Venturas shot over at roof-top height. What a wonderful sight that was.*

It started to rain heavily on 29 January and the wind was very rough, so that by the beginning of February the 'drome was waterlogged and rendered u/s again.

Many more Fortresses flew over on 4th. February (AJG: to Emden) *and three Typhoons beat up the airfield before landing. These are potent looking machines.*

Our kites were heavily used but with the relatively small size of the maintenance facilities available for such a large number of aeroplanes, aircraft servicability was always a problem on the station. On the 9th, for example, even working flat out all day, we could still only get 20 aircraft servicable out of 60 on the 'drome.

A new and exciting sight, in the shape of two sleek Mosquitoes, dropped in one day, in amongst heaps of other visiting aircraft such as Typhoons, Venturas, Battles and Stirlings. The Yanks were now much in evidence and some US P47 Thunderbolts, back from a bomber escort mission, showed off their paces with stunts over the airfield.

I was on duty crew on 13 February when the telephone rang with a frantic report of an aeroplane crash at Cowbit, a few miles South of Spalding. Upon our arrival at the site, all that remained visible was the fin and tailplane. It was a real mess. Only after bags of digging was it identified as an Oxford. The poor pilot and his Aircraftman crew had no chance and there was not much we could do." (AJG: This was V3948 from 14 PAFU at Ossington.It was on a cross-country and is believed to have stalled in a turn and spun in. The pilot was a Canadian, Plt. Off. Reid and

The Jug. Republic P47C Thunderbolt, 42-8369, HE-V of 61 Fighter Sqn. 56 F.G. based at Halesworth, Suffolk. This USAAF fighter operated mainly from bases well south of The Wash but strayed into Fenland skies when their weary pilots, lost or struggling to bring home damaged aeroplanes, perhaps in bad weather, tried to find a friendly airfield. They also knew there would always be plenty of flat fields to drop into in a real emergency. 42-8369 was one of the unlucky ones and it crash-landed at Salters Lode, near Wisbech on 28/1/44.
[Jerry Scutts]

his WOp was AC2 Jones). *We returned to Sutton Bridge just in time for another 'buzzing' session by US Thunderbolts. It seems to have become a regular habit of theirs!*

There was more panic that night when a Wimpey, evidently in trouble, droned round and round the airfield for almost an hour. As our field was still u/s, he was directed to Marham where, it transpired, he landed safely. While on duty crew again the following day, RAF Mustang, AP230, flown by one of our New Zealand pupils, Flg. Off. Dooley, developed a coolant temperature rise during take off. The coolant return pipe hose blew off at the cylinder block and glycol fumes filled the cockpit. Almost blinded, the pilot did a quick circuit and dropped the machine on the deck causing the undercart to fold beneath him. He walked away unscathed.

A Stirling passed overhead also in trouble and eventually it force landed near Kings Lynn. One of the CGS Wellingtons dropped a first aid kit for the crew but I believe they were all unhurt. (AJG: Stirling W7451 from 1657 HCF at Stradishall, pilot Sgt. R.Watson. He was on a full load climb test and could not retract the undercarriage. Unable to gain height and with one engine on fire he headed for the Wash to jettison the bomb load. His troubles increased when he found the bomb doors would not open and finally managed to pull off a wheels down forced landing at Saddlebow).

There were heaps of Thunderbolts over again on 16 February (AJG: Escorts for a US raid on St. Nazaire). *Two of this type landed on the 'drome on 18th. They are 'tubby' but very powerful-looking aircraft compared to our dainty Spitfires. More of them came over on 26th., this time together with some Mitchell bombers, off on a daylight raid* (AJG: Wilhelmshaven?). *As duty crew that night I had to wait up late for one of our pupil's, a Yankee pilot, who lost his bearings and ended up way down on the South Coast. I took a dim view of this!*

The next day another CGS Yank pilot took off and nearly went straight through a parked Lysander. It was a close shave but he managed to get airborne in time, only slightly damaging his Spitfire and the 'Lizzie's' tailplane in the process.

On 1 March 1943, Flt. Lt. 'Wimpey' Wade DFC, our Flight Commander, was promoted to Sqn. Leader.

The catalogue of crashes continued unabated when, on 7 March a Master smashed its mainplane during a particularly heavy landing. There were a couple of visiting Mosquitoes in during that day too.

It was quite eerie, during night guard duty, to listen to the sound of hundreds of our bombers droning overhead - this time on their way to Munich (AJG: 9/10 March). *I was quite pleased to get away on seven days leave but when I returned to Sutton Bridge, it was business as usual. A white 'Wimpey', LB230, of No.3 Coastal Command OTU, based at Cranwell, lay out on the field badly smashed up. The accident happened on 14th, as the aeroplane dropped in over the threshold. It had hit a pillbox and having lost the port wheel, Flg. Off. Hollinson belly-flopped the Wellington onto the airfield, where it ground-looped ripping off the starboard leg before finally careering to a halt.*

Two days later, on 22nd., one of our CGS Wellingtons, N2876, crashed at Terrington Marsh, near Kings Lynn, when first the starboard then the port engine cut out. In the ensuing crash one of the air gunners, Flt. Sgt. Davies, was killed and the rest of the crew badly injured. This was followed on 24th., by Master, W8969, which had it's undercarriage collapse on landing causing the prop to go for a Burton'. A Spitfire, with 2/Lt. Cole, USAAF, on board caused a lot of panic just after take off. The pilot thought one of his tyres had a possible puncture and perhaps a damaged u/c leg. He was ordered to do a circuit, which confimed his suspicions and pulled off a great landing in spite of one flat tyre. All this excitement certainly kept us groundcrew on top line trying to put the pieces together again.

I heard the bombers off on another big raid on the night of 26 March and again on 27th. I think it was the biggest raid, so far, on Berlin. (AJG: Duisberg,26th; Berlin,27th.).

Our Wellington crews did their bit for the Wings For Victory Week effort by laying on a low-level formation flypast over the town of Wisbech.

Just to show that even senior officers are not immune from bending aeroplanes, a Yank Lt/Col made a rough landing in a Spitfire. The undercarriage prettily folded up and the machine slid along, nose down, for many yards, in danger of flipping over onto it's back, before the tail thumped down again. The

Its June 1943 and above long straight roads and patchwork fields of south Lincolnshire are the workhorses of the CGS in formation for the press. In the foreground Wellington N2887 looks like a grand old lady, with patches and scratches, chaperoning two flighty youngsters in the elegant shape of a Spitfire IIA and a North American Mustang I. Machine guns have been removed from the bomber's turrets to be replaced by less potent camera guns.

prop and the Colonel's pride were badly damaged."

It was bad enough that pilots should have to live with the possibilty of an aero-accident but on one occasion an American trainee had a very narrow escape from death in the icy waters of The Wash.

A contemporary of Douglas Broom at CGS in 1943 was LAC (Armourer) Eric Joyce who recalled the day he and this American met on the bleak Wash marshes.

" One sunny February afternoon in 1943, I biked round the perimeter road heading for 'B' Flight dispersal. I was going to work on the front turret of a Wellington; the rotating service joint of which was leaking. As I propped up my bike the Tannoy blared out my name - and others - to report immediately to the Orderly Room. Fearing the worst I did as ordered and was relieved to find I was detailed to go to an aircraft which had force-landed on the sand off the out-marsh at a place called Fosdyke about ten miles from Sutton Bridge. The panic was due to the fact that the tide would cover the aircraft at 5 o'clock. This would not do the aeroplane any good!

One man from each trade, including me as armourer, was instructed to get as much off the aircraft as possible in the time available. Grabbing some tools at random, off we raced in a lorry, being met by some civvies near the village church, two of whom were to act as guides for the dangerous trek out onto the marsh. That was a god-forsaken place. Miles from anywhere, shifting sands, mud, deep sometimes hidden creeks, leading out to flat sands as far as the eye could see, with the sea way out beyond that. The danger was from the tide which raced in and crept up the creeks behind you but this all passed over my head at the time.

Two miles out onto the marsh and there was our aeroplane, perched on a narrow strip of shining sand. It was a Spitfire and bearing a single white American star on the fuselage. The pilot, Lt. Wallace a pupil at CGS on attachment from the USAAF, stood alongside dressed only in a thin shirt and slacks. Airborne over the Range for gunnery practice in Spitfire Vb W3133, his engine packed up and he force-landed on the sand at low tide. The aeroplane seemed quite undamaged but we all set about our tasks at once. Even if the other fellows helped, with the few tools at my disposal there was no possibility of removing the two 20mm cannon - I was a Wellington fitter, I had no Spitfire spanners! After an hours concentrated effort I had coaxed the machine guns to drop from their mountings onto the sand.... that is, all except the fourth gun. I noticed it dropped with a splash. When I looked up, to my horror the sand had gone - nothing but water as far as the eye could see! On the skyline in the direction of Fosdyke was the sea bank and the small figures in the distance legging it for all they were worth were my so-called comrades! Oblivious to my surroundings, I had not heard my mates shout that they were off and neither had the Yank. The tide was racing in by the minute; too deep even now to risk falling in a creek if we set off for the bank.

Only three hours ago I had a cushy little job to do on a Wimpy and could 'pan it out' until the NAAFI wagon came but now there was just me and a Yank, marooned in The Wash with this damned Spitfire. As the water rose, we sat side-by-side astride the cockpit canopy and waited. Nonchalantly, Lt. Wallace produced a couple of "ceegars" and offered me one

56 Sqn. was based at RAF Matlaske in north Norfolk from August 1942 to July 1943 and its aircraft could be seen roaming Fenland skies on training sorties or occasionally dropping in at Sutton Bridge after anti-shipping patrols. These two flights of Hawker Typhoon IA's are typical of those noted by Douglas Broom in his diary. The squadron lost Typhoon R7644 during a training sortie over south Lincs on 18/8/42. This crash was believed to have been caused by structural failure of the rear fuselage and the pilot, New Zealander Sgt. J.S.Jones died in the accident. (Don Hannah)

but I didn't smoke and didn't feel like starting either. As the light faded, the wind picked up and grey water crept upwards, first covering the star then lapping at the tops of my gumboots. Wallace must have been half-frozen because, even with my oilskin on, I was miserable and getting numb with cold and fear.

Suddenly a voice came out of the gloom, "Hold yew on hard, bor, we'll soon git yew out of it!" There was a boat, not more than twenty feet away, with two men in it. Rowing right up to the cockpit, all we had to do was slide off and into the sancturary of the dinghy. Talk about relief!

I had had the foresight to stow the four machine guns inside the cockpit and I wasn't about to let them go now, so these were retrieved, together with the small red canister with a pull-tape, known as 'Bomb, aircraft destroying', which I stuffed in my mac pocket. We reached a type of tug vessel which turned out to be the river Nene Catchment Board boat, used to inspect banks and navigation channels. Its snug wardroom and mugs of hot cocoa made it seem like heaven. The skipper, however, was not amused when the bomb fell from my coat pocket and rolled about the deck. In no uncertain terms he told me, Air Force property or not, to "get rid of that.... infernal thing in the sea!"

Tying up at Fosdyke Bridge quay, the American and I were taken to a nearby pub for a wash and a meal. We were being regally entertained by the locals and well 'oiled' when the door burst open and in walked my mates - with a load of excuses for their unseemly departure. They had had to hoof it back over the mud and looked a sorry mob. Well, mates can't fall out so we had a few more beers all round before the lorry from Sutton bridge arrived to take us back to 'reality'."

Spitfire W3133 had lead a chequered life. First flown in April 1941, it was operated by 91 Sqn, repaired at 1 CRU Morris Motors then re-issued to 65

English aircraft - American markings!

A Spitfire MK.V of the 308th Fighter Squadron with pilot and ground crew. It was an aircraft similar to this that ended up on the sands... *[USAF]*

Sqn in June 1942. In August of that year it was handed over to the USAAF but in November it is recorded as being operated by 332 (Norwegian) Sqn at RAF North Weald. As mentioned above it was clearly marked with US insignia and attached to CGS at the time of this accident in February 1942, so the Norwegian interlude is intriguing. As a result of the 19/2/43 incident, W3133 was originally classified as Cat.B - repairable at MU but, after The Wash had finished with it, it was subsequently re-classified as Cat.E - a write off- "salvage impossible."

Back on the station Douglas Broom takes up the story again.

"On 1 April, a most appropriate date, two Thunderbolts puzzled us by making about six circuits of the airfield. They evidently decided they could actually land on our little pocket handerchief and the first one touched down without difficulty. The second, however, also touched down but believing he would overshoot, the pilot slammed on his brakes. That great windmill of a prop dug into the turf as the tail shot upwards. This pilot was also lucky as it too did not turn over. (AJG: He was 1/Lt. Calvin Webb from 82 FS,78 FG at Goxhill in P 47C 16389)

That might have been considered an amusing enough April Fool day event but imagine my panic when later that day I received a telegram asking me to go home urgently. It was from my family and rushing round like a madman I managed to get ten days compassionate leave. I arrived home to find I was the father of a bonny baby boy! Then, as if to top even this, I received yet another telegram on 3 April, ordering me to return to Sutton Bridge at once. I rang the station to establish just what the flap was all about only to find that I was posted. The good news was that I was allowed to finish out my leave.

Back at the Station, my time there drew to a sad close, with two very bad, fatal crashes. In the first, on 8 April, one of our Spitfires was making a dummy attack on a 'Wimpey'. The pilot failed to pull out of his dive in time and ran into the Wellington, which crashed killing all on board. The Spitfire pilot also crashed and was seriously injured. This tragedy was followed on the 10th, when Spitfire, P7678, dived straight into the ground at Tholomas Drove, near Wisbech. The pilot was a New Zealander, Flg. Off. Thomas, from 486 Sqadron who was briefed to practice stern attacks and evasions on a 'Wimpey'. I was one of the recovery detail sent to the site. We dug down in the running silt soil to a depth of about 18 feet but the machine was smashed beyond recognition and very little of the pilot was found. It was thought he may have blacked out, poor fellow.

This dismal period closed with us parading for the burial of one of the Wellington crew in Sutton Bridge Churchyard. It was on this sad day, after just over a year at the CGS, that I received my clearence chit, signed ready for my posting the next day. I stayed the following night at my home in Peterborough and listened to that now familiar sound of hundreds of aeroplanes passing overhead, bound this time for a target in Italy.(AJG: La Spezia)."

LAC Douglas Broom was posted to RAF Moreton Valence (Glos), then Hartfordbridge (Blackbushe). He went to France after D-Day and on into Belgium, finally being de-mobbed in January 1946.

From among the many famous names to pass through the gates of RAF Sutton Bridge, one in particular stands out in 1943. Flg. Off. George Beurling's name became synonymous with the air battles over Malta - indeed his autobiography is entitled *Malta Spitfire.* Although many other pilots achieved prominence in the defence of the island, Beurling became by far the leading scorer with 24 enemy aircraft claimed as destroyed. This, together with his two earlier claims over France, earned him a commission a DSO,DFC and two DFM's.

According to his contemporaries, among them top 'ace' J.E.'Johnnie' Johnson, key to Beurling's success was the combination of personal attributes such as excellent eyesight, phenomenal shooting skill, particularly in the art of deflection and an aggressivness which drove him to engage the enemy whatever the odds. Over Malta in 1942 the RAF was almost always at a disadvantage from numerical and tactical viewpoints and this imbalance could only be made up by men displaying just such attributes as Buerling's, often forced to fight alone, on their own initiative. Those conditions suited a loner like Beurling but returning to the European theatre in October 1942 he found the teamwork and discipline necessary under the different tactical conditions hard to settle down to. After a spell of leave in his native Canada and having raised his score to 31 e/a destroyed he now enters the narrative of CGS.

Arriving at RAF Sutton Bridge for instructor duties on May 27 1943, George Beurling, known to some as 'Buzz' and others as 'Screwball', in his brief six-week stay made his mark in the minds of young and old on the Station and in the locality. He is generally portrayed as a tough, hard-living, unruly and undisciplined, individual. In the circumstances in which he carved out his reputation perhaps such an attitude was appropriate, although it was often distained, it is said, by other flyers. In any event he was a very effective fighter pilot at a time when results counted. There is no evidence from his time at CGS to suggest he thought himself special; on the contrary, for a supposed loner he seems to have been approachable and appears to have joined in local activities as the 'quiet' celebrity. More than five years later upon his untimely death in an air crash in Italy in 1948, the *Lincolnshire Free Press* was moved to say of him:

" ... he was a familiar and popular figure in the Sutton Bridge district. Flg. Off. Beurling is particularly remembered for his attendance at the Spalding Wings for Victory Week events and only a day after baling out of a blazing Spitfire he still found time to judge an aeromodelling competition in the Corn Exchange and visit cadets of 1406(Spalding)Air Training Corps Sqn."

There are even some airmen and airwomen who served at CGS who claimed Beurling was *"the crazy Canadian pilot who flew under the Bridge"*, a story which is still repeated among the locals. With his combat background and the view of life generally credited to him, a routine training job might very easily become boring to him. Undoubtedly he had the nerve

Flg Off. G. F. Beurling DSO, DFC, DFM

to try such an escapade and eyewitness accounts, such as that of WAAF Olive Moule mentioned earlier in the chapter, match the time Beurling was at CGS. In a Spitfire is stretching imagination but a Master or Magister, both of which were available, is feasible.

Could an attempt on the Bridge, coupled with him removing three Spitfires from the RAF inventory in the space of six weeks, have been too much for the 'Brass' to tolerate even from a national hero?

Those six weeks also brought 'Buzz' three more brushes with the 'grim reaper'. Taking off after lunch on June 8, Flg. Off. Beurling intended to carry out what was described officially as "a tactical evasion exercise." Less than an hour later Beurling was floating to earth beneath his parachute and Spitfire II, P7913 had buried itself deep into Fenland subsoil on a farm at Middle Drove near Wisbech.

This was not the first escape by parachute Beurling had made but he was unscathed in this latest descent. Invited by a local man into his house nearby, George was given a cup of tea while the incident was reported to CGS and transport arranged to collect him.

It is said locally, that during the walk to the cottage, Flg. Off. Beurling said something to the effect that *"...the aeroplane was going to claim someone's life as it was all but worn out and to prevent this happening (he) buried it!"* His official report claims he abandoned the aircraft when the engine caught fire due to a glycol leak.

Whether this is an accurate story or just another 'Beurling myth' is hard to say but in 1985 some evidence came to light which seemed to lend weight to the story. After a long search, members of the Fenland Aircraft Preservation Society (FAPS) found the site of the crashed Spitfire and mounted a recovery dig. It was to prove one of the most productive and most difficult they had yet undertaken.

In the course of the dig, in addition to copious amounts of twisted fuselage and wing material, items such as rudder pedals, compass, pilot seat, control column, gunsight and even the 'Form 700' with other documentation - still readable - emerged as the excavator went ever deeper. At 18 feet depth a larger digger was obtained which was able to take the hole down to 26 feet.

It was at this depth that the most significant find emerged from the all-embracing blue clay - the virtually intact Merlin 12 engine. Close inspection showed there was no sign of any fire damage to either the engine or the cockpit area. In fact so complete and in good condition was the engine that the Society decided to restore it.

After more than 700 man-hours of painstaking work FAPS produced a beautifully restored engine, capable of being turned over manually. It is now displayed in their own museum near Wisbech where it is much admired by the public and a credit to the ingenuity of this reputable group of aviation archeologists.

George Beurling was back in the air very quickly but two weeks later, on June 24 up-ended Spitfire II, P7496 when the undercarriage locking pin seized and cracked its housing, so that the wheels would not lock down. On touch down at Sutton Bridge the undercarriage collapsed and pitched the aeroplane onto its nose. Beurling was unhurt.

His final mishap was to write off Spitfire, P8010, when the engine seized up after loss of oil pressure. This time he was out over The Wash but, fortunate that the tide was out, managed to glide it to a crash landing on Pandora Sand.

On that day Flg. Off. George Beurling was posted out from CGS, to 61 OTU, but he certainly made an impact while he was there and will never be forgotten.

Officers Commanding Central Gunnery School 1942 to 1944.

Station Commanders RAF Sutton Bridge.

7 May 42 to 5 Sep 42	Gp. Capt. C.H. Keith.
5 Sep 42 to 26 Nov 43	Gp. Capt. C St. J. Beamish.
26 Nov 43 to 22 Feb 44	Gp. Capt. Dwyer.

Officers Commanding Pilot Gunnery Instructor Training Wing, CGS.

Mar 1942 to Sep 1942	Wg. Cdr. A.G. Malan
Sep 1942 to Dec 1942	Wg. Cdr. P.R. Walker
Dec 1942 to Jun 1943	Wg. Cdr. J. Rankin
Jun 1943 to Oct 1943	Wg. Cdr. P.R. Walker
Oct 1943 to (Feb 1944)	Wg. Cdr. A.C. Deere

Officers Commanding Gunnery Leader (Bomber) Wing, CGS.

Mar 1942 to Jun 1942	Wg. Cdr. J.M. Warfield
Jun 1942 to Jun 1943	Wg. Cdr. J.J. Sutton
Jun 1943 to Dec 1943	Wg. Cdr. Claydon
Dec 1943 to (Feb 1944)	Wg. Cdr. A.E. Lowe

Chief Instructors Fighter Wing, CGS.

Mar 1942 to Sep 1942	Sqn. Ldr. A.R. Wright
Oct 1942 to Feb 1943	Sqn. Ldr. P.W. LeFevre
Feb 1943 to Jun 1943	Sqn. Ldr. T. Balmforth
Jun 1943 to Sep 1943	Sqn. Ldr. R.C. Dafforn (K)
Sep 1943 to (Feb 1944)	Sqn. Ldr. A. Winskill

Another Malta 'old-boy' and both a former instructor at 56 OTU and a pupil at CGS, Sqn. Ldr. Bob Dafforn arrived once more at Sutton Bridge at about the same time as George Beurling. Awarded the DFC in the Battle of Britain, he was shot down and wounded over Malta from where he was invalided home in August 1942, returning to flying duties in November that year.

Bob, a six-foot six-inch Old Harrovian was a highly experienced fighter pilot with over 1000 flying hours to his credit when he was posted, in June 1943, to replace Sqn. Ldr. T.Balmforth as CI of CGS.

Educating fighter gunnery pupils was a task involving both ground and air duties and it was essential for the CI to keep his hand in. It was one such training sortie that was to cost Sqn. Ldr. Dafforn his life. Sadly there would be occasions when vast experience and having survived all the enemy could throw at him, was to no avail. Tiredness, a momentary lapse of concentration or both was all it needed.

On September 9, 1943 Bob Dafforn had just completed an air-to-air firing sortie over Holbeach Range in Spitfire, P7289. He was seen at very low level between the range and the village of Long Sutton, in a steeply banked turn in which the port wing hit the ground. P7289 cartwheeled into the ground in a welter of earth and debris at Redhouse Farm, killing its pilot.

Replacing Bob Dafforn would not be easy but Sqn. Ldr. Archie Winskill was an excellent choice. Destined, post-war, to rise to command the Queen's Flight, he reached Air Commodore rank and became a Knight into the bargain. One month later the command of CGS Fighter wing changed again and Sqn. Ldr. Winskill found himself deputy to one of the foremost fighter pilots in the RAF at that time: Wg. Cdr. A.C. Deere.

Of his term of office as last CO of CGS Fighter Wing in its days at RAF Sutton Bridge, Air Commodore Alan Deere DSO DFC OBE, wrote in 1993:

"I first heard of my appointment to CGS from Gp. Capt. 'Sailor' Malan who was, at that time, commanding RAF Biggin Hill. It was great news as, having been the 'Biggin Wing' Leader for the previous nine months, I expected a posting to a desk job, a prospect which held no appeal for me whatsoever.

RAF Sutton Bridge was a station known to me already, having landed there for air-firing practice on a number of occasions pre-war, while flying Gloster Gladiators with 54 Sqn. How it had grown in the intervening years.

Holding a training post was a new experience for me but I knew my recent operational record would carry some weight with the student intake. It was comforting, though, to have the support of two excellent deputies:- Sqn. Ldr. Roy Morant, in charge of ground training and Sqn. Ldr. (later Air Commodore Sir) Archie Winskill as CI.

Gp. Capt. Charles Beamish, the Station Commander, was an old friend from pre-war RAF rugby football circles. In modern parlance, Charles was very 'laid-back' but very much 'on the ball' too; he never interfered but was always there to encourage and advise when needed."

In fact, as a trained fighter pilot, one of Gp. Capt.

CGS Fighter Wing's last CO before it left RAF Sutton Bridge in April 1944 was another pre-war pilot and Battle of Britain ace, New Zealander, Wg. Cdr. Alan Deere.

Beamish's first acts on taking command had been to join Gunnery Leaders Course No.45 to see for himself just how the Bomber Wing operated.

Alan Deere continued: *"We had a pretty intensive training schedule, tied in of course with the Bomber Wing, whose pupils would benefit enormously from having to handle fighter 'attacks' from staff pilots with formidable records and pupils with great potential. At this time the Bomber wing was commanded by Wg. Cdr. 'Lofty' Lowe, a pre-war NCO with a distinguished operational record. Lofty in size and nick-name, he was a real 'go-er'.*

Competition for places on the Fighter Course was intense and such was the calibre of pilot that there were few, if any, failures. In my opinion, there is no doubt that our training scheme gave those pilots a greater awareness of the art of air gunnery and an edge when it came to applying that training in subsequent combats.

Quite a lot of these fellows succeeded and one example in particular springs to mind from my period in command. He was a young American, from the 8th Air Force (we took pilots from all the Allies) who expressed an outspoken determination to become the best shot in his squadron. He achieved that ambition

Instructors of the CGS Fighter Wing at RAF Sutton Bridge June 1943. From the left: Flg. Off. Conway; An unknown Polish Officer; Flg. Off H.G.R. Thomas; Flt. Lt. J.M.B. Beard DFM; Sqn. Ldr. R.C. Dafforn DFC. Fighter Wing CI.; Wg. Cdr. P.G.R. Walker DSO,DFC,CdeG. Fighter Wing CO.; Gp. Capt. C.E.St J. Beamish DFC. CGS CO & Station Commander.; Sqn. Ldr. E. Mayne AFC.; Flt. Lt. R. Morant; Flg. Off. W.E.Gaunt; Flg. Off. W.L.Johnston; Flg. Off. A.S. Harker DFM; Flg. Off. G. Buerling DSO,DFC,DFM&Bar.

with something like twenty confirmed victories. His name escapes me now but I remember he was known as 'Willie' and he spoke in one of those 'Deep-Southern' American drawls. I met him a few times after the war, although I lost track of him in the 1960's. In our conversations he always gave the credit for his success to the training he received at CGS.

Alan Deere recalled: *"They were happy months for me at Sutton Bridge, staying in post long enough to move the School to RAF Catfoss, 12 miles NE of Hull, in Yorkshire. I am unsure why we had to move but I suspect it was because, with the gradual build-up of the US 8th and 9th Air Forces, the sky over East Anglia became a bit too congested and the relatively clearer sky over Yorkshire offered safer areas for daytime training. After the move was completed I was posted to a staff job at HQ No11 Group."*

After several visits by Gp. Capt. Dwyer to finalise details, the move to RAF Catfoss took effect from February 23, 1944 and was completed by the end of that month. Suddenly once more, RAF Sutton Bridge reverted to a Care & Maintenance basis for a period until a new role could be found. This was not long in coming and training would still be the order of the day. While the sound of foreign tongues, however, was destined to be heard again in the village, this time the aircrew would not be the cream of the fighter profession but instead included the fledglings of what was to become the nucleus of the post-war French Air Force.

Air Incidents in the Fenland region 1942 to 1944

Date	Aircraft Type	Serial	Sqn/Unit	Incident Location	Pilot	Fate
23/03/42	Hurricane	V7164	56 OTU	RAF Sutton Bridge	Sgt. L.A.C.John	U
23/03/42	Hurricane	V7222	56 OTU	RAF Sutton Bridge	Sgt. W.W.Fell	U
23/03/42	Master	DK827	RAFCFTS	1m S. Wainfleet	Flt. Sgt. V.J.Dubourgel	U
23/03/42	Spitfire	P8131	CGS	Marholm,Peterborough	Plt. Off. F.Wiza	I
27/03/42	Beaufighter	T3142	409	Leverton, Boston	Sqn. Ldr. B.A.Hanbury	K
29/03/42	Blenheim	Z5494	17 OTU	Nr RAF Sutton Bridge	Sgt. J.L.M.Heagety	I
29/03/42	Defiant	AA384	151	1m N. Stamford	Plt. Off. H.W.Hart	K
11/04/42	Hampden	AT187	144	Gedney Marsh	Sgt. D.H.Smith	I
13/04/42	Spitfire	P8279	CGS	Wyberton, Boston	Flt. Sgt. D.R.Morrisson	U
13/04/42	Spitfire	K9947	CGS	West Winch	Sgt. W.S.Johnson	I
13/04/42	Wellington	DV437	304	March	Sgt. A.Lozowici	I
20/04/42	Wellington	T2834	3(C)OTU	N. Rauceby,Sleaford	Plt. Off. H.E.Rath	K
23/04/42	Stirling	W7473	218	Clenchwarton	Sgt. S.V.Davidge	K
24/04/42	Typhoon	R7654	266	Gt. Casterton,Stamford	Plt. Off. N.N.Allen	K
13/05/42	Blenheim	V5384	17 OTU	Butchers Fm,Thorney	Plt. Off. H.G.Zavadowski	K
20/05/42	Tiger Moth	T7867	17EFTS	Deeping St. Nicholas	Plt. Off. R.R.Reed	U
23/05/42	Tiger Moth	R4858	268	West Fen, Nr. Ely	Plt. Off. N.C.Pye	U
26/05/42	Master	W8531	16 FTS	King St, Bourne	LAC. B Tomaszewski	U
30/05/42	Spitfire	P8250	CGS	RAF Sutton Bridge	Sgt. M.C.Falcard	U
31/05/42	Halifax	W1013	78	Whitemoor, March	Plt. Off. G.Foers	I
31/05/42	Hampden	P5321	14 OTU	Whitemoor, March	Sqn. Ldr. D.Falconer	K
31/05/42	Wellington	N2894	CGS	Holland (On Ops)	WO. A.Jambar	K
03/06/42	Beaufighter	R2479	409	Holdingham	Plt. Off. R.H.Hedger	I
03/06/42	Spitfire	P8583	CGS	RAF Sutton Bridge	Flt. Lt. D.H.Foxmale	U
21/06/42	Hampden	P2084	CGS	RAF Sutton Bridge	Flt. Sgt. E.H.Noxon	U
26/06/42	Dornier Do217E-4	U5+ML	1/KG2	The Wash	4 X N/K	K
01/07/42	Hurricane	Z2415	RAE	Sutton Bridge	Wg. Cdr A.F.R.Bennett	K

02/07/42	Hampden	P2067	14 OTU	Deeping St. Nicholas	Flt. Sgt. F.Hill	U
02/07/42	Spitfire	P8583	CGS	Cloot Drove, Postland	Sgt. C.I.Scott	K
04/07/42	Wellington	N2893	CGS	RAF Sutton Bridge	Flg. Off. N.S.Dunkerton	U
05/07/42	Lysander	T1618	CGS	Gedney Drove End	Sgt. W.M.L.Penny	U
06/07/42	Wellington	L7774	CGS	Wingland	WO. D.J.North-Bomford	I
15/07/42	Spitfire	P7603	CGS	Old Somerby	Plt. Off. A.H.Sagar	U
21/07/42	Lancaster	R5576	106	Benington Seas End		
25/07/42	Spitfire	P8048	CGS	RAF Sutton Bridge	Plt. Off. G.D.C.Bell	U
30/07/42	Junkers Ju88 A-4	1T+CR	7/KG26	Green Drove, Thorney	Ofw. V.Bechthold	K
31/07/42	DornierDo217E-4	U5+ET	9/KG2	Conington, Peterborough	Fw. K.Lauss	K
31/07/42	Hampden	AE192	14 OTU	1 m NW Mkt. Deeping	Plt. Off. C.E.MacIntosh	U
31/07/42	Hampden	P5397	14 OTU	1 m NW Mkt. Deeping	Sgt. A.R.Grubert	U
01/08/42	Spitfire	P8090	CGS	RAF Sutton Bridge	Plt. Off. D.H.Forrest	U
08/08/42	DornierDo217 E-4	U5+DR	7/KG2	Revesby, E.Kirkby	Oblt. R.Thun-Hohenstein	I
11/08/42	Hampden	AE155	14 OTU	Edenham, Bourne	Sgt. R.P.Davies	K
11/08/42	Lancaster	N/K	N/K	RAF Sutton Bridge	N/K	
12/08/42	Wellington	N2959	CGS	Sutton Bridge	Sgt. R.V.Parker	U
17/08/42	Hampden	P1163	CGS	Terrington St Clements	Flt. Sgt. S.L.Vinton	K
17/08/42	Oxford	AB648	12 PAFU	West Pinchbeck	Sgt. G.D.Perks	U
18/08/42	Spitfire	P7670	CGS	RAF Sutton Bridge	Plt. Off. D.Bevan	U
18/08/42	Stirling	W7589	419	1m S. Southery	N/K	
18/08/42	Typhoon	R7644	56	Moulton, Spalding	Sgt. J.S.Jones	K
21/08/42	Blenheim	N/K	17 OTU	Ramsey St. Mary	Sgt. T Mair	U
24/08/42	DornierDo217 E-4	U5+CK	2/KG2	East Walton Wood	Obfw. R.Bodenhagen	K
31/08/42	Hampden	P1205	14 OTU	Grimsthorpe Range	Sgt. K.R.Fisher	I
07/09/42	Master	DL849	7(P)AFU	West Walton	Sgt. D.D.Knott	K
07/09/42	Master	DL838	7(P)AFU	West Walton	Sgt. K.Letch	K
17/09/42	Dornier Do217		N/K	Shernborne, K Lynn	N/K	
20/09/42	Spitfire	P7851	CGS	RAF Sutton Bridge	Plt. Off. E.B.Chandler	U
23/09/42	Halifax	W7814	N/K	Holland Fen, Boston	N/K	U
25/09/42	Hampden	P5341	CGS	RAF Sutton Bridge	Sgt. D.G.Vern	U
25/09/42	Spitfire	P8087	CGS	RAF Sutton Bridge	Flg. Off. B.J.Thwaites	U
26/09/42	Master	DL684	CGS	Gorefield, Wisbech	Flg. Off. H.P.Lardner-Burke	U
26/09/42	Whitley	Z6757	3(C)OTU	Wainfleet Beach	Plt. Off. F.W.Smith	U
30/09/42	Wellington	DV672	1483GTF	RAF Sutton Bridge	Plt. Off. Burgess	U
02/10/42	B17F	41-24492	306BG	Weston Hills	1/Lt. W.W.Ely	K
13/10/42	Master	N7962	CGS	Near Wisbech	Plt. Off. S.J.Thompson	K
21/10/42	B17F	41-24460	306BG	RAF Sutton Bridge	N/K	
27/10/42	B17F	41-24508	306BG	Near The Wash	1/Lt. R.J.Check	U
29/10/42	Stirling	BF386	15	Salters Lode	Flt. Lt. H.B.Salter	K
08/11/42	Hampden	P5343	CGS	RAF Sutton Bridge	Flt. Sgt. A.Digby	U
19/11/42	Halifax	BB209	158	Castle Bytham	Sgt. S.Benford	U
25/11/42	Wellington	L7785	CGS	RAF Sutton Bridge	Flt. Sgt. V.P.Friese-Green	U

Short Stirling W7451, MG-D, is photographed while on the strength of 7 Sqn. based at RAF Oakington. The immense size of this aeroplane can be judged by comparison with its crew standing nonchalantly by the bomb trolleys beneath the towering nose of the bomber. W7451 was transferred to 1657 Heavy Conversion Unit (HCU) at RAF Stradishall but witnessed by Douglas Broom as it struggled over Sutton Bridge on 14/2/43, its career was interrupted by a forced landing with engines on fire near Kings Lynn. The pilot on that occasion was Sgt. R. Watson who fortunately, together with his crew, escaped unharmed. (Canadian Armed Forces Archive)

27/11/42	Spitfire	P7440	CGS	RAF Sutton Bridge	Sqn. Ldr. P.J.E.Ritchie	U
01/12/42	Hudson	N7404	CGS	RAF Sutton Bridge	Flt. Lt. C.T.Boxall	U
04/12/42	Defiant	N1786	29 OTU	Near Sleaford	Flt. Sgt. R.McGladdery	U
11/12/42	Tiger Moth	DE765	316	RAF Sutton Bridge	Sgt. A.Murkowski	U
14/12/42	Master	DL879	7 PAFU	1m S. Swineshead	Sgt. F.Barwise	U
17/12/42	Lysander	V9496	CGS	RAF Sutton Bridge	Sgt. Giles	U
17/12/42	Master	W9056	CGS	RAF Sutton Bridge	Flt. Lt. G.E.F.Dieu	U
20/12/42	Spitfire	P8663	CGS	RAF Sutton Bridge	Flg. Off. C.A.King	U
24/12/42	Spitfire	N/K	CGS	RAF Sutton Bridge	Flt. Lt. McMillan	U
01/01/43	Spitfire	EP289	167	The Wash	Flg. Off. J.K.A.Pickering	K
01/01/43	Spitfire	EP235	167	The Wash	Plt. Off. P.F.Franklin	K
01/01/43	Spitfire	EP289	167	The Wash	Flg. Off. J.K.A.Pickering	K
01/01/43	Spitfire	EP235	167	The Wash	Plt. Off. P.F.Franklin	K
15/01/43	Master	DL196	RAFCFTS	Willow Fm, Spalding	Flt. Lt. A.B.Watkinson	U
21/01/43	Lysander	V9797	3(C)OTU	The Wash	Flt. Sgt. W.E.Atkins	K
21/01/43	Spitfire	AA754	411	The Wash	Sgt. J.A.McMillan	K
26/01/43	Wellington	DV927	3(C)OTU	North End, Swineshead	Sgt. P.V.Jerome	K
28/01/43	Master	T8668	7 PAFU	Wisbech St Mary	Flt. Lt. R.A.Couchman	U
29/01/43	Lancaster	ED503	9	Sibsey	Flt. Lt. R.F.Lind	K
01/02/43	Whitley	Z9135	3(C)OTU	Hubberts Br, Boston	Sgt. G.C.Wright	I
02/02/43	Master	DL288	7 PAFU	2m NE Chatteris	Sgt. D.Ditcher	K
11/02/43	Manchester	L7391	1485GTF	Fishtoft Drove, Boston	Flt. Sgt. R.Eyres	U
13/02/43	Oxford	V3948	14 PAFU	Queens Bank, Cowbit	Plt. Off. D.R.Reid	K
14/02/43	Mustang	AP230	613	RAF Sutton Bridge	Flg. Off. Dooley	U
14/02/43	Stirling	W7451	1657HCU	Saddlebow, K.Lynn	Sgt. R.Watson	U
17/02/43	Master	DL846	7 PAFU	3m NE Bourne	Sgt. G.G.Jones	U
19/02/43	Spitfire	W3133	CGS	The Wash	Lt. Wallace	U
22/02/43	Mosquito	DZ434	109	Tongue End, Bourne	Flg. Off. F.R.Jackson	K
04/03/43	Lancaster	W4333	103	Yaxley, Peterborough	Flg. Off. N.Kujundzic	K
04/03/43	Master	W9059	7 PAFU	Chestnut Fm,Wisbech	Flg. Off. G.L.Lloyd	U
05/03/43	Mustang	AP170	41 OTU	Holbeach Range	Flt. Lt. Burra-Robinson	U
05/03/43	Wellington	BK390	29 OTU	Coates, Whittlesey	Sgt. K.H.Long	K
08/03/43	Spitfire	P7886	AFDU	Friday Bridge, Wisbech	Flt. Lt. B.G.Collyns	U
11/03/43	Halifax	DK117	1660HCU	Leasingham, Sleaford	Sgt. W.J.King	I
12/03/43	Master	DM220	RAFCFTS	Baston Fen, Bourne	LAC. J.F.Wooley	U
14/03/43	Wellington	LB230	3(C)OTU	RAF Sutton Bridge	Flg. Off. Hollinson	U
19/03/43	Dornier Do217E-4	U5+AH	I/KG2	Ongar Hill, K.Lynn	Uffz. H.Toifel	K
19/03/43	Mosquito	DZ427	109	Tongue End, Bourne	Flt. Lt. C.R.Henry	K
22/03/43	Wellington	N2876	CGS	Terrington Marsh	Plt. Off. H.J.Soares	I
24/03/43	Master	W8969	CGS	RAF Sutton Bridge	Flt. Lt. W.L.Johnston	U
24/03/43	Spitfire	N/K	CGS	RAF Sutton Bridge	2/Lt. Cole	U
29/03/43	Liberator	FL950	224	Whittlesey	Flg. Off. C.Moore	U
01/04/43	P47C	41-6379	78 FG	RAF Sutton Bridge	Lt. C. Webb	U
06/04/43	Wellington	BJ979	16 OTU	The Wash	Flt. Sgt. J.J.Britton	M
09/04/43	Spitfire	P7678	CGS	Tholomas Dr, Wisbech	Flg. Off. G.G.Thomas	M
10/04/43	Lancaster	ED478	50	The Wash	Sgt. P.G.McGrath	M
11/04/43	Master	DL956	7 PAFU	Marholm, Peterboro	Sgt. P.A.Walton	U
15/04/43	Lysander	T1429	CGS	Holbeach Rge Ldg Grd	Sgt. A.George	U
19/04/43	Wellington	W5352	14 OTU	Langtoft	Sgt. B.Jones	U
20/04/43	Spitfire	P8279	CGS	RAF Sutton Bridge	Flg. Off. J.A.Hall	U
24/04/43	Spitfire	P7754	CGS	RAF Sutton Bridge	Flg. Off. Z Buchowiekiz	U
01/05/43	Spitfire	P8048	CGS	RAF Sutton Bridge	Flg. Off. J.A.Hall	I
03/05/43	Mustang	AM231	169	RAF Sutton Bridge	Flg. Off. J.G.Thompson	U
05/05/43	Blenheim	L1224	12 PAFU	Near Sleaford	Flg. Off. Abbott	K
05/05/43	Lancaster	ED715	156	Near Chatteris	A/Sqn. Ldr. B.L.Duigan	U
11/05/43	Beaufighter	V8370	141	Burghley Pk,Stamford	Flt. Sgt. R.Judge	K
11/05/43	Lysander	W6955	CGS	Holbeach Rge Ldg Grd	Flt. Sgt. W.S.Johnson	U
12/05/43	Spitfire	P7840	CGS	RAF Sutton Bridge	Flg. Off. W.J.Hibbert	U
12/05/43	Wellington	BK123	29 OTU	Scottlethorpe	Sgt. F.T.Allen	K
13/05/43	B17F	42-29752	96 BG	The Wash	Capt. D.Rogers	K
16/05/43	Spitfire	P8279	CGS	RAF Sutton Bridge	Sqn. Ldr. R.W.Barton	U
20/05/43	B17F	42-29786	306 BG	Dunsby Fen	1/Lt. M.V.Judas	U
21/05/43	Stirling	EF365	218	Nr Downham	Plt. Off. D.R.Rich	U
26/05/43	Wellington	L7796	CGS	RAF Sutton Bridge	Flg. Off. A.J.Muir	U
04/06/43	Master	AZ811	CGS	Three Holes Bridge	N/K	
04/06/43	Whitley	207	51	The Wash	Plt. Off. D.B.Dunn	U
08/06/43	Spitfire	P7913	CGS	Middle Drove	Flg. Off. G.F.Beurling	U
09/06/43	Lysander	V9011	29 OTU	Holbeach Rge Ldg Grd	Flt. Lt. A.R.Dunn	U
09/06/43	Master	DK801	7 PAFU	Needham Lge, Wisbech	Sgt. I.W.McKnight	U
09/06/43	Spitfire	P7524	CGS	Near Holbeach Range	Flt. Sgt. T.R.G.Bryant	I
16/06/43	Halifax	HR832	405	Clenchwarton	Flt. Lt. C.D.Lawson	K
18/06/43	Lancaster	ED439	83	S Of Sleaford	Sgt. M.F..Cummins	K

18/06/43	Master	AZ361	7 PAFU	Hardy Farm, Crowland	Flt. Lt. N.R.Norfolk	U
18/06/43	Master	DL858	7 PAFU	Wiggenhall St Mary	Plt. Off. H.J.Andrews	K
19/06/43	Spitfire	P8037	CGS	Middle Drove	Sqn. Ldr. R.R.Ferguson	I
24/06/43	Spitfire	P7496	CGS	RAF Sutton Bridge	Flg. Off. G.F.Beurling	U
25/06/43	Spitfire	P8591	CGS	RAF Sutton Bridge	Flt. Lt. R.H.Golightly	U
26/06/43	Lancaster	W4830	61	Baston	Sgt. D.H.Pearce	I
28/06/43	Wellington	HE922	166	Wigtoft	Plt. Off. W.B.McGinn	U
01/07/43	Spitfire	BL655	416	Dorrington Fen	Flg. Off. N.A.Watt	K
05/07/43	Wellington	N2996	N/K	N/K	N/K	
06/07/43	Spitfire	P8010	CGS	The Wash	Flg. Off. G.F.Beurling	U
07/07/43	Master	T8776	7PAFU	Glinton, Peterborough	Sgt. A.T.Lord	U
09/07/43	Lancaster	ED360	106	Parson Drove	Flt. Sgt. A.G.Bristow	M
26/07/43	Lysander	T1459	CGS	Holbeach Rge Ldg Grd	Flt. Sgt. R.P.Wilson	U
28/07/43	Mustang	AM113	2	Terrington St Clements	Plt. Off. P.A.Hay-Neeve	U
07/08/43	Master	T8565	7 PAFU	Near RAF Peterborough	Sgt. C.H.Atkin	I
14/08/43	Boston	BZ367	13 OTU	RAF Peterborough	Sgt. W.C.Duff	I
19/08/43	B17F	42-30172	96 BG	The Wash	2/Lt. J.A.Attaway	U
19/08/43	Master	T8659	7 PAFU	Priory Rd, Westwood	Sgt. A Duquette	U
29/08/43	Whitley	T4215	N/K	N/K	N/K	
31/08/43	Halifax	JD201	78	Nr. Murrow Station	Flt. Lt. A.F.Short	K
02/09/43	Master	AZ792	7PAFU	3m N Crowland	Sgt. D.R.Davies	I
09/09/43	Spitfire	P7289	CGS	Long Sutton	Sqn. Ldr. R.C.Dafforn	K
14/09/43	Lancaster	DS780	115	Wiggenhall St Mary	Flt. Sgt. E.A.Bradford	K
23/09/43	B17F	42-3183	92 BG	Deeping St Nicholas	2/Lt. H.M.Ogburn	U
28/09/43	Lysander	V9813	CGS	Near Holbeach Range	Sgt. H.Mantell	I
07/10/43	Master	DK975	CGS	RAF Sutton Bridge	Flt. Lt. G.J.Grey	U
11/10/43	Spitfire	EN944	3501 SU	Heacham	Plt. Off. J.Whelan	U
17/10/43	Stirling	EH960	196	Gat Sand,The Wash	Flg. Off. J.L.Deans	M
21/10/43	Whitley	EB348	24 OTU	Cottenham	Sgt. W.J.Christie	K
03/11/43	Halifax	LK954	428	South Kyme	Plt. Off. R.G.Eaton	K
08/11/43	Gladiator	N2309	521	Wiggenhall St German	Flt. Lt. G.Watson	U
09/11/43	Hurricane IV	KW800	AFDU	Sedge Fen	Flt. Sgt. R.H.Brown	I
09/11/43	Stirling	LK380	90	Sedge Fen	Flt. Lt. R.Y.Rodger	K
24/11/43	Mosquito	HX978	21	1m S Newborough	Flt. Sgt. N.R.Deakin	K
09/12/43	Lancaster	ED811	1660 HCU	Blankeney Fen	Flt. Sgt. E.E.Franks	I
11/12/43	Gladiator	N2310	521	1m E Old Leake	Sgt. W.McKay	U
15/12/43	Lysander	W6955	CGS	Holbeach Rge Ldg Grd	Sgt. T.J.Fogg	U
16/12/43	Lancaster	JB369	405	Near Ely	Flg. Off. B.A.McLennan	K
16/12/43	Lancaster	JB482	97	Near Ely	Plt. Off. R.L.Mooney	U
16/12/43	Lancaster	JB531	97	North Of Wyton	Plt. Off. F.Smith	U
17/12/43	Halifax	LL120	161	The Wash	WO. W.A.Caldwell	U
17/12/43	Lancaster	JB282	156	Earith-Sutton Road	Flt. Sgt. W.H.Watkings	K
20/12/43	Spitfire	P8660	CGS	RAF Sutton Bridge	Plt. Off. R.C.Bridger	U
31/12/43	B17F	42-31073	384 BG	Whittlesey	1/Lt. G. Stier	K
02/01/44	Lancaster	DV345	550	Whaplode Drove	Flg. Off. R.H.Mawle	K
07/01/44	B17F	42-29821	351 BG	Whaplode Drove	1/Lt. H.J.Anderson	K
09/01/44	Tiger Moth	N/K	25 EFTS	Near Sutton Bridge	N/K	N/K
13/01/44	Lancaster	ED826	15	The Wash	Flt. Sgt. W.Houston	K
20/01/44	Lancaster	ED918	617	Snettisham Beach	A/Flt. Lt. T.V.O'Shaugnessy	K
21/01/44	Wellington	HE286	27 OTU	Morborne, Peterborough	Sqn. Ldr. E.A.Hudson	U
28/01/44	P47C	42-8369	56 FG	Salters Lode	N/K	U
06/02/44	Spitfire	N/K	CGS	RAF Sutton Bridge	N/K	N/K
10/02/44	B24H Liberator	41-29254	453 BG	Hilgay	1/Lt. R.B.Bickerstaff	U
10/02/44	P38J Lightning	42-67729	20 FG	Friday Bridge	Lt. J.Taylor	K
27/02/44	Spitfire	N/K	CGS	RAF Sutton Bridge	N/K	

Spitfire VB, AA754, photographed as DV-L of 129 Sqn.. This is the aircraft which collided with Lysander V9797 over The Wash range on 21/1/43, with fatal consequences for all concerned. At the time of the collision AA754 was operated by 411(Canadian) Sqn. from RAF Digby, near Sleaford.

Chapter Five

THE SKY IS NEVER STILL

Making his first public appearance since being appointed AOC RAF Flying Training Command, Air Marshal Sir Arthur Coningham KCB, DSO, MC, DFC, AFC, reviewed the passing out parade of No.6 (French)Course at RAF Peterborough. Accompanying AM Coningham on that chilly morning of November 6 1945 was his contemporary from the French Air Force, General-de-Brigade De Vitrolles, who flew in from Le Bourget with his entourage.

This parade was the culmination of three months RAF-style flying training for 27 French Naval and Air Force pilots. Now they were ready to join others of their similarly trained countrymen in laying the foundations of the post-war French Air Force.

By mid-1944 RAF Sutton Bridge had become a satellite to RAF Peterborough (Westwood) but it by no means took a back seat when it came to flying training. Courses handling specifically the training of French pilots began at Peterborough in September 1944 and between that date and November 1945, including No.6 Course, 198 French airmen had passed through both stations to reach RAF Wings standard.

But what had been happening at Sutton Bridge and around the shores of The Wash in the intervening period?

From the end of 1943 it is reasonable to consider Fenland sky as the domain of the bomber. However, with Wash Range and local air activity conducted at the intensity required by Central Gunnery School it became obvious that this could not continue without serious interference to the 8AF bomber training programme and a hazard risk to both parties. With such numbers of aircraft milling around in that piece of sky it was just asking for trouble.

Central Gunnery School, therefore, was moved

Above: The VIPs. Air Marshal Sir Arthur Coningham, AOC RAF Training Command (4th from right) with his French opposite number General de Brigade De Vitrolles (5th from right) and their respective entourages at RAF Peterborough. The group was photographed at the passing out parade of No.6 French course at 7 SFTS on 6/11/45. Accompanying AM Coningham is Air Cdre. Duncan West VC (at right); Gp. Capt. J. R. Addams, OC 7 SFTS, 2nd from right and Air Cdre. J.G. Hawtry, 3rd from right. Col. Coustie, 6th from right, was OC French Air Force in England. [via Joy Baxter]

Left: Paraaaade.....'SHUN! Accompanied by Gp. Capt. Addams, General De Vitrolles inspects RAF airmen in a guard of honour drawn up in bright winter sunshine on the apron at RAF Peterborough. (via Joy Baxter)

RAF Sutton Bridge was ideally placed to receive 'lame-ducks', particularly those of the USAAF which was a prolific user of The Wash airspace during the latter stages of the war. The grass surface was a benefit in this respect although the small dimensions of the airfield could be a drawback as these photographs illustrate.

On 8 July 1944 this B17G Flying Fortress, 43-37799 of the 447 Bomb Group, had to put down at Sutton Bridge for unknown reasons and was halted abruptly as it ground-looped at the edge of the airfield. (Stuart Evans)

north to Catfoss and for a short time RAF Sutton Bridge came under the temporary control of RAF Peterborough before being revived as a satellite first for RAF Newton then, in August 1944, RAF Peterborough once more. Flying activity in this role, however, was far less intensive than during the old CGS days being composed mainly of night flying training. Later on in 1944 the role of Sutton Bridge was further extended to become the base for 7SFTS's 'French Air Force SFTS' and it also continued as a base for the Holbeach Range air weapons facility.

At this point it is relevant to note that USAAF operational bombing and air gunnery standards upto the end of 1943 were judged by Command to be in need of much improvement. As Roger Freeman put it (*Mighty Eighth War Manual,* Janes, pp 125/6): *"...several (RAF) ranges were offered for American use. An immediate problem (though) was safety. The high altitude at which (their) bombing and gunnery would be carried out increased the possibility of error and danger to civilians and property in the vicinity of these ranges. As 8AF grew in strength so did the problem of acquiring suitable ranges. Only Brest Sand, in The Wash off Kings Lynn, was acceptable to become the first range used by B17's in 1942/43. Later in 1943, as more ranges were created elsewhere, it was alloted specifically to First Air Division Bomb Groups. For air-to-air gunnery practice, the Americans set up their first range at Snettisham, on the eastern shore of The Wash. Other ranges, established elsewhere in the UK, were a long way from USAAF East Anglian bases; involving long transit times and complicating practice mission logistics. Bombing and Gunnery Ranges in The Wash area, on the other hand, proved ideal both in terms of environment and convenience; thus accounting for the high level of US activity in this area."*

Congestion, though, was always a problem, even in an area with 500 square miles of 'free' air space. Before very long Snettisham range became over-stretched and in 1943 another range - which had to operate simultaneously with Snettisham, Brest Sand and Holbeach Marsh - was established for the USAAF over on the west shore at Wainfleet Sands (between Boston and Skegness). Wainfleet had been in use as an RAF bombing range since 1938; in WW2 by 5 Group and notably, had been used by the Dambusters at various times. It seems likely that by late-1943, Wainfleet fulfilled an air-to-air and other US-fighter general gunnery training role, while Snettisham, designated No.1 Combat Crew Gunnery School (1CCGS), specialised in ground-to-air firing practice for US bomber gunners (Freeman states specifically: "... B17 gunners..."). With 'traffic' in The Wash at its current level and rising, it was now impractical to carry out this latter activity as an entirely airborne operation. Brest Sand continued to soak up both inert US practice bombs and 'discarded' live loads, while Holbeach Marsh as described in the previous chapter, served CGS - which itself included USAAF fighter pilots among its pupils - and other RAF needs.

Having decided to do something to improve its air gunnery the 8AF found it had neither targets nor target-towing aircraft with which to achieve it. Turning to the

A rare photo of a Boulton Paul Defiant TT4 in USAAF service. Serial number DR945 was one of a pair of this type to see service with the USAAF in a Target Towing capacity and was operated over the Snettisham range. It is seen here whilst operating with the 94th Bomb Group at Bury St Edmunds. [via Dr. Harry Freidman]

RAF for assistance, a US target-towing organisation soon became operational from mid-1943, using mainly Lysanders and a few Miles Masters transferred from RAF towing units. They even acquired at least a couple of venerable Defiant TT4's which are known to have seen service over Snettisham range during late 1943.

The USAAF also enlisted the talent of movie star Clark Gable, whose brief period of combat flying service in England in late 1943 was designed to promote the need to improve gunnery back in the USA primarily through the medium of film (viz *Combat America*). While it was necessary to take steps to improve gunnery in the combat zone, it was also seen as vital to save time by working on that aspect before crews actually left America.

Of the three US target-towing units originally established, 2nd and 3rd Gunnery & Tow Target Flights (2/3 G&TTF) were activated at RAF Goxhill on the Lincolnshire coast north of Grimsby and regularly flew target sorties over The Wash. The third unit, No.1 G&TTF, began life in Wales in August 1943 but from May to November 1944, took up residence at RAF Sutton Bridge, when CGS had moved out and from where it co-operated with 1CCGS at Snettisham.

It was during this period that Vultee A-35B Vengeance aeroplanes were assigned to Tow Flights as the standard replacement for their ageing Lysander and Master tugs. Originally designed as a two-seat dive-bomber, the Vengeance was supplied by US to the RAF early in the war, serving principally in the Far East. It was mainly the later Mark IV (RAF) version which, being surplus to requirements, was converted for target-towing duties.

Some were transferred to the USAAF, still retaining their RAF roundels, including those which served with No.1 G&TTF at Sutton Bridge. Evidence of the latter is provided by a photograph of Vengeance 41-31384 taken on June 12, 1944 near Castle Rising. Engine failure en route Sutton Bridge to Snettisham forced 2/Lt. Maurice Harper to crash land 41-31384 at Knights Hill, fortunately with only minor injuries to himself and his winch operator, Cpl. Theo Brand.

When, in late April 1944, Central Gunnery School moved north it left Sutton Bridge facing an uncertain future for the first time in a number of years. Such was the scale of air war operations in the area around The Wash that, coupled with other factors such as the physical constraints of the airfield and the long term demand for aircrew slowing down, a major review of

"This Vengeance is mine..." saith the USAAF - even though the roundel betrays its former RAF ownership. Vultee A-35 Vengeance 41-31384, based at RAF Sutton Bridge with 1st. Gunnery & Target Towing Flight USAAF, suffered an engine failure en route to Snettisham range for a towing sortie on 12/6/44. It force landed near Kings Lynn without mishap to the crew. (Stuart Evans)

A representative formation of the types of training aircraft operated by 7SFTS at Sutton Bridge and Peterborough in the final stages of the War. From left to right are Miles Master III W8667, Airspeed Oxford I, DF233 and Miles Magister N3838.

its role became inevitable. However, RAF Sutton Bridge had, as has been shown, performed its wartime duty with an enviable vitality and was, despite its limited size, functioning as a well-oiled establishment. This latter situation was due in no small part to the succession of exceedingly able and energetic Station and Unit Commanders.

In fact, the future of RAF Sutton Bridge was assured for a few years yet but would now become largely dependant upon its neighbour, RAF Peterborough.

Home to No.7 (Pilot) Advanced Flying Unit (7(P)AFU), with upwards of 130 Miles Masters, 15 Hurricanes and over 200 pilots to cope with, resources at Peterborough, too, were being stretched to the limit at this time. (P)AFU flying training programmes were designed to bring the basic flying skills of pilots trained under the Empire Air Training Scheme, upto European theatre standards. In effect overseas-trained pilots were shown in about four weeks how to (try to) cope with operating in poor weather, at night in the blackout and to navigate under wartime conditions.

In January 1944 discussions had already taken place between RAF Peterborough and RAF College SFTS, one of Cranwell's units, with a view to doing a 'swop' of location to try to relieve the pressure. It was decided, however, that this move was not a practical proposition. Furthermore, on February 4, 1944, word came down from on high that 7(P)AFU would have to undertake the duties of parent unit for a Care and Maintenance party which was to take over RAF Sutton Bridge when CGS moved out. In true military style, before C&M was implemented the 'brass' changed its mind! Sutton Bridge was now allotted as satellite station to 16(P)SFTS based at RAF Newton (Nottingham) but only for the duration of repair work to the latter's airfield surface.

Despite this somewhat confused situation, at least flying training would continue at Sutton Bridge but the harsh realities of the profession were never far away. 'Rookie' pilots hadn't changed much over the years and within a month all three of the above-mentioned units (7PAFU; RAFC SFTS & 16SFTS) had sustained casualties, some fatal, within the region.

On February 23 for example, RAF College SFTS lost Flt. Cdt. C.A.Vose, killed when the Master he was flying (DL893) flicked out of a tight turn at 1500 feet over Swineshead and dived into the ground. Two weeks later a 7(P)AFU pupil, South African 2/Lt. J.A.Cronje, lost his life when Master EM376 dived into the ground between the villages of Werrington and Glinton, near Peterborough.

Sqn. Ldr. Douglas Allison AFC, a former CFI at Peterborough and who played a considerable part in laying the foundation of an Accident Investigation system for the RAF, conducted a detailed examination of this and many other Fenland crashes. On this occasion, however, he was unable to find a tangible reason for the accident.

Since those far-off nights, back in 1941 and 1942, when German intruders roamed the skies of East Anglia, there had been a considerable period of time when such activity by the Luftwaffe was minimal. At the beginning of 1944, however, in concert with its Operation Steinbock bomber offensive, Me410's of Luftwaffe intruder unit KG51 also took to English skies once again. Between March and May 1944 their disruptive effect far outweighed the actual losses involved to both sides.

While primarily targeting RAF and US bombers, these heavily-armed Me410's took whatever opportunity presented itself and one such example caused consternation at 7PAFU Peterborough in the early hours of April 21st.

Dawn was just about breaking and it should have been a routine local-area training flight, one of the first of the day, for Flg. Off. J. Bannister. Having made a killing a couple of nights earlier and being about to surpass even that against the Americans 24 hours later, a '410 of KG51 caught Bannister in his Master shortly

For students at an advanced stage of training, 7(P)AFU at Peterborough still had some of the oldest Hurricanes on charge. Evidence of this is L2087, seen here at Peterborough in late-1944. Flt. Sgt. M.E. Quayle was flying L2087 on a local exercise on 9/11/44 when it ran out of fuel and he was obliged to force land, with the wheels up, near Crowland. L1721, also an elderly Hurricane Mark I serving with 7(P)AFU, met with a similar mishap during October near the village of Eye, Peterborough. (Bernard Baines)

after take-off. One concentrated burst of fire was all it took. Plunging into marshy ground about a mile from the airfield it proved difficult for rescuers to do any more than remove the body of the pilot from the aeroplane before it sank into the morass. Bullet holes in the fuselage, however, left them in no doubt as to the cause of the crash. Flg. Off. Bannister was taken to the mortuary of nearby Westwood crematorium where, on closer examination of the body, a bullet wound was found.

Lost once more on the tide of war, this incident became just a vague memory. Until, that is, February 1974 when workmen, building on the now extensive Bretton housing estate, unearthed the remains of of an aeroplane. Examination of components revealed it to be a Miles Master and together with its location it was identified as that aeroplane in which Flg. Off. Bannister was shot down.

While associated with 16 SFTS several Masters and a Polish pilot course were transferred from Newton to Sutton Bridge. It was not long before it was quite like the old days of 6 OTU with the Poles 'dropping in' again on local farmland. Eight crashes, including one fatal, were recorded by this Polish unit while based at Sutton Bridge between March 13 and May 16. Even averaging one mishap per week was, sadly, not excessive by current flying training standards. About one month after the fatal accident - when on May 16, LAC. Z. Czaplicki in Master DK857 spun in at Long Sutton - the detachments from RAF Newton ended.

Yet another change of system on June 21 saw night flying training for 7(P)AFU - previously conducted from Peterborough airfield, with occasional use of Sibson and Wittering - also being transferred to RAF Sutton Bridge. This was only a temporary relief arrangement for Peterborough as shortly afterwards Sutton Bridge actually went onto a Care & Maintenance basis under the command of Flt. Lt. W.F.Carson, pending yet another re-assessment of its future. It was the demise of Peterborough's current satellite, RAF Sibson, which finally brought this C & M period to a close in August 1944 and with it brought a modicum of stability for a couple of years. Two main factors were responsible for this change.

First, on July 4, in order to speed up throughput of aircrew, the basis of flying training at 7(P)AFU Peterborough changed to a 'course-based' system. This meant that each 'Flight' at Peterborough was made responsible for both day and night training of a complete 'course' of (at that time) about 37 pilots for a four-week period. Various administrative changes were also proposed, all with the aim of using main and satellite airfields more effectively, particularly in respect of accomodation issues.

Second, at the end of July, Sibson airfield's grass surface, having taken a lot of wear and tear, was declared unfit for use and in need of re-seeding. This was a lengthy, time-consuming process so Flying Training Command took the easier option by giving up Sibson and declaring that Sutton Bridge, being immediately available, would take on the role of satellite for Peterborough. This decision was implemented on August 8, 1944, although Sibson actually still remained designated as a Relief Landing Ground (RLG).

It was on that day (Aug 8) that Gp. Capt. Addams, OC RAF Peterborough, had the misfortune to become one of his own accident statistics. Taking off in Hurricane AG284, after visiting his new satellite, the engine cut out at 50 feet and he had to force land just outside the airfield perimeter with the wheels up.

As the incident table shows, between July and September, mishaps involving Masters from 7(P)AFU flying from both Peterborough and Sutton Bridge continued to occur at regular intervals. Of the seven recorded, three had fatal consequences.

Activity at the (P)AFU peaked by mid-1944 after which output from the Overseas Schools began to reduce. Such was the optimism about the outcome of the war that by the end of 1944 the Empire Air Training scheme was virtually at an end.

With fewer conversion students to cater for, the specific task of 7(P)AFU itself also drew to a close. Pilot training continued of course but at Peterborough it now took on a more general and extended nature than before.

With the arrival of September 1944 came yet another change for Sutton Bridge. Ever destined to be associated with foreign pilot training, RAF Sutton Bridge's final lease of life was now as home to part of the intake for No.1 Course of what became known as the 'French SFTS'.

Fifteen new instructors were posted in from RAF Newton on September 13, for the specific purpose of

From mid-1945 Masters were replaced at 7 SFTS by the North American Harvard. These Harvard IIB display post-WW2 three-letter aircraft codes - in this instance as operated by 3 FTS at RAF Feltwell, a Flying Training station at the eastern edge of the Fens.

training French pilots at Sutton Bridge. Airspeed Oxford twin-engine trainer aeroplanes would be transferred to the airfield although, at least initially, servicing work on them would be carried out at Peterborough.

By mid-November there were located at Sutton Bridge sufficient aeroplanes to equip three Oxford Flights, plus a few specialist Oxfords for bombing and beam-approach duties and some Masters for gunnery training. Over at Peterborough another three Flights had also been established, equipped with Masters.

At this point there was effected a final major organisational change when 7(P)AFU was re-titled 7 SFTS and the term 'French SFTS' disappeared.

By the time No.1 Course of 32 pilots passed out in February 1945, the pattern of training French pilots had evolved into single-engine students (one-third of the Course complement) based at Peterborough and twin-engine students (two-thirds) at Sutton Bridge. Miles Masters were phased out upto June 1945, being replaced by the North American Harvard.

Ken Taylor, a former ATC cadet with 1406 (Holbeach) Detached Flight, remembered this period as a very happy time. *"RAF Sutton Bridge was an 'open house' to us cadets,"* he said. *"We used to bike to the airfield most Sundays and went up in anything that was going. I had been in the ATC since the days of 56 OTU and CGS and had loads of trips in Maggies, Tiger Moths, Battle and Lysander target tugs, Hampdens, and Wellingtons. On one or two sorties in the latter I had a chance to sit in the rear turret and watch the Spits beat us up. Great times!"*

Ken also recalled a trip in a 7 SFTS Oxford with a French pupil and an English instructor. The instructors

Airspeed Oxford I, HN324 is typical of the type flown by French pupils from RAF Sutton Bridge in 1945 and 1946. This particular Oxford survived a potential accident at Sutton Bridge on 30/10/45 in the hands of one of the future graduates of No.6 (French) course. Matelot Henri Bartholomei forgot to lower the undercarriage as he approached RAF Sutton Bridge for a landing. It was only when the propeller blades shuddered with their impact with the ground that he realised his mistake. Slamming open the throttles he recovered and went round again, this time landing without mishap. (Michael Gibson)

spoke little or no French and vice versa and with his schoolboy French Ken found himself acting as interpreter on more than one occasion. One quite unnerving experience occured while Ken sat on the main spar watching the pupil bringing the Oxford in for a landing. *"If the undercart was not down as the aircraft dropped below 100feet, then a klaxon would sound off as a warning. This student was concentrating so intensely that he simply didn't hear the klaxon wailing. In the end the instructor knocked the pupil's hands away from the controls and aborted the landing and I had to explain to the distraught Frenchman what was going on!"*

While epitomising this period of Sutton Bridge history, one fatal air accident in particular also played its part in forging a permanent bond between the community and the French nation.

Among sixty military headstones arranged in their neat rows in the village churchyard, stands a cross bearing the inscription:

MOITESSIER G G
MATELOT FRENCH AIR FORCE
MORT POUR LA FRANCE
LE 13.8.1945

The war was over but No.6 (French) Course of 7 SFTS was well into its stride.

From Sutton Bridge on August 13, 1945 Oxford PH414 took off, with Cpl. V. Maestracci and Matelot Moitessier aboard. Briefed for a routine dual sortie of 45 minutes duration in the local area, they were to land at the end of that time and change places, prior to making another sortie. It was quite usual for competant pupils to be briefed to fly as a crew without the presence of an instructor.

This exercise was destined never to be completed. Nearing the village of Clenchwarton, PH414 was last seen emerging from low cloud in a spin from which it did not recover. Hitting the ground at speed it was completely destroyed and both Frenchmen died instantly. Despite speculation, as on so many occasions, no real cause for the accident could be established. Maestracci's body was returned to France for burial while Moitessier, whose family home was in Morocco, was buried with full military honours in Sutton Bridge churchyard.

In the immediate post-war years, in common with towns and villages across the nation, monuments to the fallen were being erected. Particularly with its connections to the RAF airfield, Sutton Bridge was no exception and the churchyard, last resting place of so many brave young men from all parts of the world, was honoured with a Commonwealth War Grave Memorial Cross.

At a ceremony in 1947 this Memorial was unveiled and consecrated. Making the long journey from his home in Casablanca to be present on that emotional occasion was Monsieur Henri Moitessier, father of that young pilot killed two years earlier.

Returning now to that chilly morning at RAF Peterborough in November 1945, it was to a stirring rendition of La Marseillaise, played by 21 Group HQ Band, that the review programme began in the more comfortable climate of one of the hangars.

Gp. Capt. J.R.Addams AFC, OC 7 Service Flying Training School (7SFTS), opened proceedings with his

At peace. In a tranquil corner of a typically English village churchyard are the graves of some sixty airmen, friend and foe, drawn together by fate from all corners of the warring world.

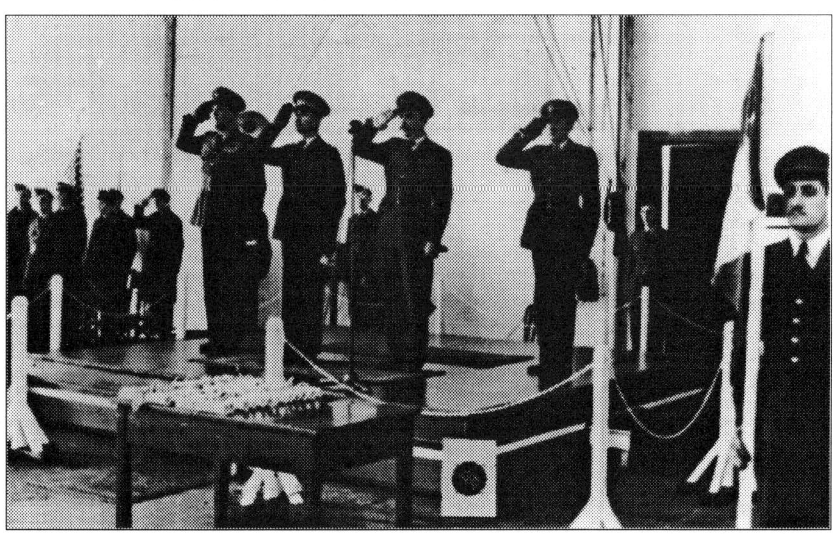

General Salute. The Reviewing Officers for the graduation ceremony, assembled on the saluting dais prior to the presentation of Wings certificates to pilots of No.6 (French) course at RAF Peterborough, 6/11/45. From left: AM Coningham, General De Vitrolles, Gp. Capt. Addams and Air Cdre. Hawtry. The certificates can be seen laid out on the table in front of the dais. (via Joy Baxter)

Course Report. Providing a useful insight to the organisation of the SFTS at that time, he referred to Courses being divided into two Squadrons; No.1 Squadron stationed at Peterborough, training with single-engined Harvards while No.2 Squadron, based at Sutton Bridge used twin-engined Oxford aeroplanes. Nine pupils, he said, had passed on Harvards and eighteen on Oxfords. Names of these graduates and the senior officers present at the ceremony, are listed in the accompanying table.

General De Vitrolles then presented Wings and certificates and addressed his fellow countrymen. AM Coningham in his own speech, said it gave him particular pleasure, on this his first engagement in his new post, to be among Frenchmen once again. He reminded his audience that he had had French squadrons under his command in North Africa and after the invasion, with 2TAF in Europe. General De Vitrolles took the salute at the marchpast of all units present and the afternoon closed with VIP's being entertained to tea in the Sergeants Mess.

The value of flying training undertaken by both RAF Sutton Bridge and Peterborough at this period cannot be overstated, since from aircrew trained at these two airfields was born the nucleus of post-War French military aviation.

In April 1946, in a shrinking military situation, RAF Sutton Bridge and RAF Peterborough were required to perform their sterling service no longer. Both stations were stood down from active flying duties when 7 SFTS moved north to Kirton Lindsey.

In the case of RAF Sutton Bridge, the airfield at the heart of this story, twenty years of flying history had come to a close. The station still continued to provide storage facilities for 58 Maintenance Unit for a number of years to the mid-1950's. In addition

No.6 (French) Course, RAF Peterborough, 6 November 1945.
Passing Out Parade.

Reviewing Officers:
Air Marshal Sir Arthur Coningham,
AOC Flying Training Command, RAF.
General-de-Brigade De Vitrolles,
AOC Training, French AF.
Air Commodore J.G.Hawtry,
AOC 21 Group RAF.
Air Commodore J.West VC,
Director Allied & Foreign Liason RAF.
Colonel Coustie,
CinC French AF in England.

Senior Staff of 7 SFTS
RAF Peterborough
and RAF Sutton Bridge:
Group Captain A.R.Addams,
Station Commander and OC 7SFTS.
Commandant Feuvrier,
OC French Personnel at 7SFTS.
Wing Commander J.H.M.Smith,
Chief Flying Instructor.
Wing Commander D.Kinnear,
OC RAF Sutton Bridge.
Wing Commander F. Stevens,
Chief Technical Officer.
Squadron Leader C.J.Rose,
Chief Ground Instructor.
Squadron Leader B.Ruffell,
OC No.1 Sqn 7SFTS
(RAF Peterborough).
Squadron Leader L.S.Holman,
OC No.2 Sqn 7SFTS
(RAF Sutton Bridge).

Graduates of 7 SFTS,
No.6(French) Course

No.1 Sqn (Harvard)

No.2 Sqn (Oxford)

Peterborough/Sutton Bridge
Sous/Lt J Regnier
Sous/Lt M.Carreras
Sgt G.Desseaux
Sgt P.L.Bex
Sgt J.Cave
Sgt M.Biskup
Sgt P.J.Cazaty
Sgt P.G.V.Bousquet
Sgt P.Chaucard
Sgt G.J.Combes
Sgt P.Guilland
Sgt C.A.Debono
Sgt J.J.P.Guilhemdebat
Sgt L.M.Giguelay
Sgt E.Mestre
Sgt R.L.V.Jourdain
Sgt J.Picard
Sgt M.F.Pedespan
Sgt R.L.B.Saint-Martin
Sgt J.M.E.Souillard
S/M H.Bartolomei
S/M P.G.Y.Bouchet
S/M R.L.M.Cadoux
S/M M.J.D.Caron
S/M Y. Guillou
S/M H.P.E.Hostachy
S/M A.M.Rolin

Percival Prentice T1, VR231, of 7FTS Cottesmore was destroyed in a crash near Bourne (Lincs) on 28/5/51. (A Pearcy Jr)

married-quarter housing was used by staff of Holbeach Range, which continued to operate as an air weapons range and indeed, together with Wainfleet, remains fully operational in its RAF and NATO capacity to the present day. It is true to say that since the end of WW2 the district has never lost its connection with aviation both through its attractiveness as a flying training area and through its proximity to The Wash ranges. In addition to military flying, the growth of private flying for pleasure and business flying for agricultural purposes in the second half of the 20th. century has meant Fenland skies are rarely still.

Business as usual

It is not intended at this point to address in detail the rich aviation history of the Fenland region relating to the second half of the twentieth century, as that is another story entirely in its own right. It is, however, appropriate to indicate the broad course of those events which bring this story up to date.

Although Sutton Bridge and Peterborough had closed to flying operations, there was no let-up in the post-war RAF pilot training programme throughout the region and in many ways, events of subsequent years brought with them constant reminders of days gone by. For example, back in 1926, until the airfield at Sutton Bridge had got into its stride, aircraft using Holbeach range originally operated directly from their home bases. This was how it would be in the future, with Range visitors coming not only from airfields all over the UK but also from mainland Europe. Other reminders of past eras came with Canadian and American pilots returning to use airspace around The Wash, as did pilots from RAF squadrons featuring

Originally designed around the Mamba turbo-prop engine, the chin radiator of the Merlin 35 used in the production T2 model ruined the good looks of the Boulton Paul Balliol. The Balliol became the 'in-between' trainer with 7FTS and RAFC Cranwell, replacing the Harvard and Prentice but soon being overtaken by the arrival of Vampire T11 jets. VR596 was on the strength of CFS at West Raynham and was written off in an accident near Kings Lynn on 14/8/52.

Left: The Forth Railway Bridge makes a fine backdrop for this formation of Gloster Meteor F4's of 222 Sqn. in 1950. Nearest to the camera, VT218, ZD-R passed from frontline service to 206 Advanced Flying School at Oakington, with whom it crashed on 16/12/52 at Holbeach Marsh.

Below: A brand new Meteor 8, WE912, which saw service with 616 Sqn. R Aux AF, pictured at Gloster's Hucclecote factory, with a T7 in the left background and a PR10 on the right...

...on a low-flying interception exercise over the Fens on 27/9/53, the pilot of WE912, Plt. Off. G. Furness died heroically when he delayed ejecting from his burning Meteor until it was clear of the town of Spalding.

(F.G.Swanborough)

earlier in this story, such as 1 and 23 Sqns., to name but two. To complete that sense of change and continuity the Range itself, now designated RAF Holbeach, became an RAF Station in its own right, as did Wainfleet, its partner just across The Wash.

Although Harvard aircraft had left Sutton Bridge and Peterborough their distinctive 'buzz-saw' drone could still be heard over the length and breadth of the Fens for the remainder of the 1940's. Harvard IIb's were operated by 3FTS at RAF Feltwell to the east, 7FTS at Cottesmore to the west and by the RAF College at Cranwell in the north, so Fenland skies were, as ever, the playground for student pilots.

Cross-country flights, low flying - authorised or unauthorised - aerobatics and weapons training continued unabated. Due to the fallibility of men and machines, the Fenland 'prairies' also continued to be littered with the results of students who had either "...temporarily misplaced their position" (i.e. lost!) or those whose aircraft had suffered engine failure. At the other extreme, though, sadly there were the results of collision or of forced landings which had gone wrong.

The Wash region in the 1950's was a veritable spotter's paradise. Growling Rolls Royce Merlin and Griffon engines gave way to the woosh of RR Derwent or DH Goblin and Ghost jet engines as the propeller age changed to the jet age. Still encircled by active airfields in the early 1950's, for a while, props would remain in evidence with the Flying Training Schools. Harvards for example gave way to the Percival Prentice T1 at Feltwell, Boulton-Paul Balliol T2's entered service with both 7FTS, CFS West Raynham and RAF College Cranwell, while the latter also operated DH Chipmunk and Percival Provost trainers, all of which graced Fenland skies day after day.

On the other hand, Meteor F4's and T7's were filtering through to Advanced Flying Schools such as 206AFS at RAF Oakington several of whose aircraft were lost in accidents in the early 50's. Later in that decade, the arrival of De Havilland's Vampire T11 and FB5, at Swinderby, Cranwell and Oakington extended jet training across the region. Meteor F8 day fighters were in front line service, for example, with 56 Sqn. at Waterbeach and 92 Sqn. Coningsby, while nightfighter Vampire NF10's of 253 Sqn. at Waterbeach and Venom NF2 aircraft from 23 Sqn. at Coltishall, were regular sights even in daytime. It is not surprising, therefore, that air activity around The Wash was as intense as ever.

A Canadian interlude.

Of course, the political climate, too, played its part in deciding what aircraft could be seen in the region. In the early 50's, for example, the Korean War occupied the attention and resources of both Britain and the USA. In order to strengthen NATO aircraft guarding

Above the clouds over The Wash these DH VenomNF2 nightfighters wear the livery of 23 Sqn. based at Coltishall in 1954. Below: Glistening in watery sunlight reflecting from RAF North Luffenham's rain soaked apron are Canadair Sabres of No.1 Wing RCAF. In the foreground is 19181, one of a pair of Sabres which were destroyed in a mid-air collision over The Wash on 15/4/52. (both MOD, Crown copyright)

Europe at this volatile time, the RCAF was called upon to deploy a number of squadrons to England and in February 1952 No.1 Fighter Wing RCAF took up residence at RAF North Luffenham, Rutland. Thus in addition to the usual RAF inventory an exciting new shape in the form of the swept-wing Canadair Sabre Mk2 - US North American F86 Sabres built under licence - could be seen frequently traversing the Fens and The Wash often at 40,000-plus feet altitude. The Canadians remained at Luffenham for almost three years, during which there was the inevitable crop of accidents before the Wing re-deployed to France and Germany at the end of 1954.

410(Cougar) Sqn. lost two pilots on 18 April 1952 when Flg. Off. J.A.L.Kerr in 19177 collided with Flg. Off. A.E.Rayner in 19181. Both Sabres fell onto Wainfleet Range and although one pilot managed to eject, both died as a result of the accident. Veteran WW2 pilot, Sqn. Ldr. A.R.McKenzie escaped unhurt from a wheels-up forced landing near Bourne (Lincs) on 12/6/52, when his Sabre 19189 suffered engine failure at 40,000 feet but a year later, Flg. Off. Ray Bedard of 439(Tiger) Sqn. was not so fortunate when 19193, suddenly disintegrated in mid-air during a training sortie over The Wash on 23/6/53.

The Yanks return.

Although US bombers had been based in England since

During the 1960's USAF fighter-bombers lost their brightly coloured image and wore drab green/brown camouflage. This F100D, 55-3655, of 77TFS, 20TFW based at Upper Heyford, Oxon., represents that base's long association with the Wash Ranges. On 28/5/70, 55-3655 suffered engine failure during a routine bombing practice but pilot Capt. Guy Baker ejected safely before the Super Sabre plunged into the sea.

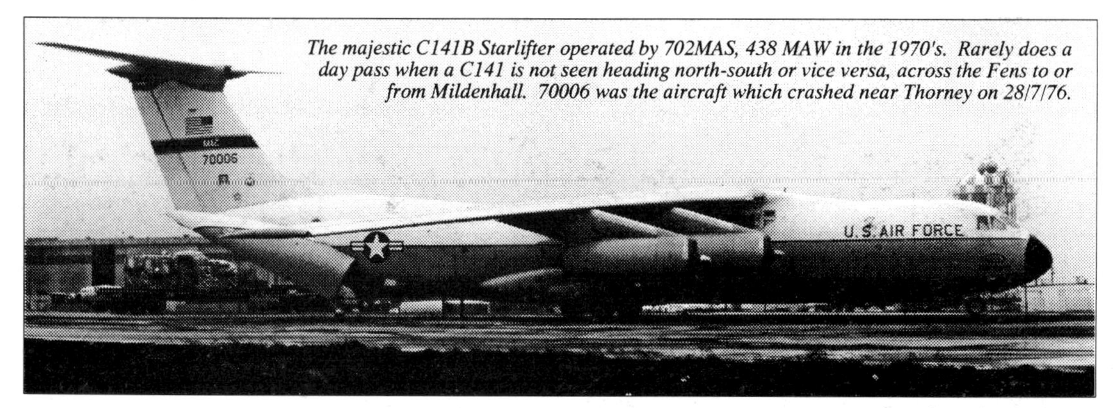

The majestic C141B Starlifter operated by 702MAS, 438 MAW in the 1970's. Rarely does a day pass when a C141 is not seen heading north-south or vice versa, across the Fens to or from Mildenhall. 70006 was the aircraft which crashed near Thorney on 28/7/76.

the early 1950's, it was not until about 1957 that the enforced removal of foreign aircraft from French soil meant US fighter types would once again grace Fenland skies. Thereafter the Wash ranges witnessed a procession of USAF fast jets, beginning, for example, with Republic F84F Thunderstreaks of 81 Fighter Bomber Wing (FBW) from Shepherds Grove. The catalogue of range users continues through the 1960's with F100D Super Sabres, principally those from 20 Tactical Fighter Wing (TFW) Wethersfield and 48TFW Lakenheath together with F101C Voodoos from 81TFW Bentwaters. Each of these units suffered losses due to air accidents in The Wash area during the 1960's.

By 1965, 10TRW, operating from Alconbury airbase, had traded in its RB-66's for the ubiquitous F4 Phantom and its RF4C models became a regular sight and sound for the next fifteen years as they smoked down the rivers Welland and Nene day and night, heading for Holbeach and Wainfleet ranges.

In contrast, many other US types can be observed tracking north to south or vice versa, heading into or climbing out of the massive USAF base at RAF Mildenhall on the southern edge of the Fens. Among the most frequent are Boeing KC135 Tankers, Lockheed C5 Galaxy and C141 Starlifter and in recent years, McDonnell-Douglas C17 Globemaster III, transports.

What should have been one of those routine flights for 67-0006, a C141B of 438 Military Airlift Wing, turned into disaster on the night of August 28, 1976. The Starlifter was carrying 27,000lbs of cargo, its own and a supernumary crew plus a handful of passengers, 18 people in all, from McGuire AFB, New Jersey. The weather was foul that night with electrical storms across the whole country. As it was descending through 2000 feet on a steady approach for Mildenhall the aircraft appeared, to a few eyewitnesses on the ground, to be struck by lightning. Whatever the cause, the Starlifter plunged to the ground and exploded on open farmland in Old Knarr Fen, near Thorney, killing all on board. By tragic coincidence another C141 from the same unit crashed in Iceland on the same day also due to bad weather.

The two Wittering-based Harriers involved in the mid-air collision near Thorney on 23/2/83 were T4, XW926/58 of 233 OCU (top) and GR1,(later a GR3) XV795/05 seen here with 1 Sqn.

Above: RAF Sutton Bridge is no longer in existance but as one of the most sophisticated air weapons ranges in the UK, RAF Holbeach - an RAF Station in its own right - is operator of the range located on that same area of Holbeach Marsh used by the biplanes of the 1920's and fulfils a vital NATO role. Here, Rapier surface-to-air missile batteries are seen atop the sea bank, set up to 'defend' the Range against attacking aircraft during Operation 'Elder Forest' in April 1988. In the centre background is the Range Control Tower and in the distance to the right is one of the quadrant huts.

Left: "Just aim at that little red square!" One of the regular users of the Range, before its withdrawal from the UK, a USAF Fairchild A-10 Thunderbolt II leaves a trail of gunsmoke as it fires a one-second, 80-round burst from its potent multi-barrelled 30mm cannon at ground targets on Holbeach Marsh Range in 1988.

Right: A Jaguar of 45 Sqn. from RAF Coltishall streaks across the salt marsh on a low level bombing run. Guided by lanes of red and white barrels it is about to release a practice smoke bomb at a 'tank' target. It is low tide and high and dry can be seen the ship used as a cannon and rocket target - known to the locals as 'The Pink Boat'.

Above: Near miss! A bright flash and puff of white smoke indicate the impact point of the practice bomb. Quadrant-tower staff quickly pass the co-ordinates to the control tower for relay to the pilot so that he can adjust his aim for the next bombing run.

Below: a line of canvas air-to-ground gunnery targets spread across the marsh. [all author]

MEANWHILE... OUT ON THE RANGE

During the 1980's, for low flying there was nothing to touch the antics of the USAF's Fairchild A-10A Thunderbolt II ground attack aircraft. This type roamed far and wide across the flat Fens in loose gaggles of three or four aircraft. This aircraft is 81-0987 from 509TFS, 81 TFW based at Bentwaters / Woodbridge in 1984. It was lost in an accident near Over, Cambs on 22/12/88.

Still operating from Upper Heyford, the 20TFW traded in its F100's for the General Dynamics F-111E. These long range bombers practiced day and night at low level, pounding the bombing, strafe and ship targets on Holbeach and Wainfleet ranges. 68-001 was one of these, until it fell victim of The Wash on Freiston Marsh on 5/2/90.

The Thorney area has witnessed more than its fair share of air accidents this century, with Super Sabre, Phantom, Harrier and Tornado aircraft joining those of the wartime era.

One example which received much press coverage, due to it mirroring a similar incident over Wisbech four years previously, was a collision which occurred on 23/2/83 between two BAe Harriers from 233 OCU based at RAF Wittering. Having fought with distinction in the aerial battles of the Falklands war, it was a cruel twist that Flt. Lt. John Leeming should die on a routine training sortie. He was instructing Flg. Off. David Haigh in Harrier T4, XW926 when it was involved in a collision with a single seat GR3, XV795, flown by Flt. Lt. David Oakley. Only Flt. Lt Oakley survived the accident in which both aeroplanes were destroyed.

Nearly four years elapsed before Thorney was the scene of another mid-air collision, this time involving two Tornado GR1 aircraft from 617(Dambuster) Sqn. Six minutes into a night training sortie bound for Scotland, ZA605 and ZA611 collided causing '605 to dive into open farm land near Thorney with the loss of both crewmen. ZA611 miraculously remained airborne and was able to return safely to its base at RAF Marham.

Rememberence.

It is a pity that misfortune has had to be one of the routes by which some of the course of this story is charted, for such incidents are often sensationalised by the media in a way which misrepresents the wider picture. The human price of defending the sky in such a professional way is high but Trenchard's legacy - that "...quality in men, machines, training and organisation" - mentioned at the beginning of this book, has stood the test of time and should not be forgotten.

As for the village of Sutton Bridge, it no longer echoes with the languages of foreign airmen nor are uniforms of different hues seen down that long main street or in the bars of local pubs. The airfield itself has slowly faded away under industrial development, although the sound of fast jets still crackles across its boundaries. Their crews are following the river to the range just like their predecessors more than seventy years ago, training to be - Combat Ready.

The Tornado here is ZA605 'O' of 617Sqn. when it was based at RAF Marham.

Ernest Mottram at the unveiling in 1993 of a memorial to those who served at RAF Sutton Bridge. As Aircraftman Mottram, Ernest was the first airman to arrive for duty when the Armament Practice Camp opened for 'business' in September 1926.

On September 1, 1993 former CGS Instrument Fitter, ex-LAC Roy Barker, stood on the spot where, fifty years before, he had passed many times on his way to and from the airfield. He was attending the unveiling of a memorial dedicated to all those who served at RAF Sutton Bridge. He recalled:

"I arrived early so that I could pay my respects to the many young pilots who are laid to rest in the village churchyard. One grave, that of a Polish pilot, had fresh flowers on it. Chatting to the gardener, an old RAF 'sweat' with a period of service himself at Sutton Bridge, it transpired that the niece of the pilot came from Poland every couple of years to visit the grave and had in fact just done so. Another stone marks the resting place of a Luftwaffe airman and I paid my respects to that young man too."

"At the new memorial site, between the Camp and Cross Keys Bridge, in the crowd of 200 people it was difficult to place the faces of 70-year old men with the fellows I knew half a century ago. But, when reminiscing, the years soon rolled away."

"In glorious sunshine, without a cloud in the sky, the memorial was blessed by the Padre of RAF Marham. Then Ernest Mottram, the first airman to arrive at RAF Sutton Bridge all those years ago in 1926, together with Martin Cowley, at 13 the youngest ATC cadet from 272 (Wisbech) Squadron, drew back a pale blue sheet to reveal the memorial. This is a plinth surmounted by a propeller blade, the product of a recovery dig by Fenland Aircraft Preservation Society, from 56 OTU Hurricane L2529 which crashed on 21/3/41,. Its pilot, Sgt Dick Read, survived and by coincidence, a lady claiming to be his sweetheart in those days attended the ceremony but Dick himself was not there."

"Now all heads turned sky-wards as the unmistakable growl of a Merlin grew ever louder, until a lone Spitfire MkV(AB910) swooped low over the assembly; the pilot making two passes over that Bridge so familiar to his forbears."

"Finally, another Sutton Bridge 'old-boy', Jack Flint, read the Act of Homage before a bugler played Last Post and Reveille."

Air Incidents in the Fenland region 1944 to 1946

Date	Aircraft	Serial	Unit	Location	Pilot	Fate
10/04/44	Lancaster	ND820	635	Bicker, Nr Boston	Flt. Sgt. D.J.Farrant	K
11/04/44	B17	N/K	379 BG	Barroway Drove	U/K	K
12/04/44	Master	DM177	7(P)AFU	1m NW Northborough	Sgt. G.E.Backaert	K
13/04/44	Master	DL889	16 SFTS	RAF Sutton Bridge	Lt. A.Ruschill	U
17/04/44	Master	AZ545	16 SFTS	RAF Sutton Bridge	AC2. Wropaj-Hordziejewic	U
18/04/44	Lancaster	ND475	57	Whittlesey	Plt. Off. A.E.O'Beary	K
18/04/44	Lancaster	LL667	115	Coveney Fen	Plt. Off. J.Birnie	K
18/04/44	Lancaster	LL867	115	Near Witchford	Flt. Lt. C.Eddy	K
21/04/44	Master	N/K	7(P)AFU	Bretton, Peterboro	Flg. Off. Bannister	K
22/04/44	Master	DM273	16 SFTS	RAF Sutton Bridge	AC2. H.Lebioda	U
23/04/44	Albemarle	V1610	42 OTU	Kirton Fen, Boston	Sgt. J.E.Hutchinson	K
25/04/44	Halifax	LK789	76	Welney Wash	Plt. Off. D.R.Dibbins	K
05/05/44	Mosquito	DZ646	139	Ramsey	Flt. Lt. G.C.Keys	K
09/05/44	Master	AZ366	16 SFTS	RAF Sutton Bridge	Lt. A.Ruschill	U
12/05/44	C47A Skytrain	42-92679	316 TCG	Benwick, March	Mjr. J.R.Ferris	K
12/05/44	C47A Skytrain	42-10887	316 TCG	Benwick, March	1/Lt. J.L.Sharber Jr.	K
13/05/44	Blenheim	L1139	12(P)AFU	Upwell	Flg. Off. R.J.Pope	U
16/05/44	Master	DM348	16 SFTS	RAF Sutton Bridge	AC2. R.Godlewski	I
16/05/44	Master	DK857	16 SFTS	Long Sutton	LAC. Z.Czaplicki	K
21/05/44	Lancaster	DS633	574	The Wash		
24/05/44	Halifax	DG403	1667 HCU	Butterwick	Plt. Off. P.Burke	I
28/05/44	Hurricane	KX409	84 GSU	Peterborough	Flt. Sgt. P.C.Mason	U
29/05/44	Mosquito	DD717	141	Clenchwarton	WO. A.L.Potter	K
02/06/44	P38 Lightning	N/K	N/K	New Leake	2/Lt. W.D.Jolly ?	K
08/06/44	B17G	42-97132	388 BG	Burnt Fen	2/Lt. C.H.Bryant	K
08/06/44	B24H Liberator	42-100261	392 BG	Silk Willoughby	2/Lt. H.A.White	U
12/06/44	A35B Vengeance	41-31384	1 TTGF	Castle Rising	2/Lt. M.J.Harper	I
14/06/44	Hurricane	LF313	28 OTU	Peterborough	Flg. Off. J.Wildy	U
17/06/44	Lancaster	W4851	3 LFS	Near Lakenheath	WO. R.E.K.Newman	K
17/06/44	Lancaster	ED376	3 LFS	Near Southery	Flg. Off. R.R.F.Whitby	K
19/06/44	Beaufighter	X7705	51 OTU	Stilton	WO. Kotiba	K
20/06/44	Master	AZ262	7(P)AFU	1m NE Sibson	Plt. Off. R.A.Jones	K
23/06/44	Lancaster	ME625	97	Postland	Flt. Lt. H.S.Van Raalte	K
23/06/44	Lancaster	ND981	97	Deeping St Nicholas	Flg. Off. E.L.Perkins	K
26/06/44	Wellington	MF528	29 OTU	Market Deeping	Sgt. T.Spencer	U
28/06/44	Stirling	BK654	1661 HCU	Gosberton Risegate	Flg. Off. C.B.White	U
06/07/44	Typhoon	JP496	3 TEU	West Pinchbeck	Flg. Off. T.H.Sharpe	U
07/07/44	Hellcat		NAFDU	Market Deeping	N/K	
08/07/44	B17	43-37799	447 BG	RAF Sutton Bridge	N/K	
08/07/44	C-47A Skytrain	43-15341	315 TCG	Tinwell, Stamford	1/Lt. J.G.Leonard	K
08/07/44	C-47A Skytrain	42-108873	315 TCG	Tinwell, Stamford	2/Lt. L.L.Byrne	K
10/07/44	Master	DL948	7(P)AFU	March To Wisbech Road	Plt. Off. A.Bamford	U
13/07/44	B24H Liberator	42-95103	392 BG	Wrangle Common	1/Lt. N.J.Hunt	K
16/07/44	Lancaster	ND464	83	New York, Boston	Flg. Off. D.J.Heggarty	K
21/07/44	Master	DK991	7(P)AFU	Thorney	Sgt. R.D.Stagg	K
24/07/44	Lancaster	PB294	207	The Wash	Flg. Off. P.C.MacIntosh	K
27/07/44	Master	EM330	7(P)AFU	2m N R.Nene Outfall	Plt. Off. H.A.McKill	K

Pictured in winter sunshine of late-1943 next to Lancaster ND501, OF-U of 97 Sqn., is back row from left: Sgt. F.E. Coxhead (FE); Flg. Off. E.L. Perkins (Pilot); Flg. Off. W. Hunt (Nav); Flt. Sgt. J. Fairbairn (GeeOp). Front from left: Sgt. Coman (WOp); Flt. Sgt. McBride (RG); Sgt. Russell (MUG). On 23/6/44 the places of McBride and Russell were taken by WO D.G. Partos and Flg. Off A. Ward for a daylight formation practice. Lancaster ND981 in which they were flying was in collision with ME625 south of Spalding and both aircraft crashed. Sgt. Coman was the sole survivor.

(R. Perkins)

27/07/44	Stirling	LJ451	1651 HCU	March	Plt. Off. J.W.Hocking	K
28/07/44	C-47A Skytrain	42-23334	61 TCG	Sleaford	1/Lt. T.A.Gall	K
28/07/44	C-47A Skytrain	43-15097	61 TCG	Sleaford	1/Lt. G.B.Hartzell	K
30/07/44	Lancaster	LM284	57	The Wash	Flg. Off. D.L.Davies	M
02/08/44	P-51D Mustang	44-13832	20 FG	Werrington	2/Lt.. S.J.Nelson	K
05/08/44	Avenger	JZ569	NAFDU	River Nene Outfall	Lt. A.J.Dundas RN	K
07/08/44	Mosquito	NT202	617	Wainfleet Range	N/K	K
10/08/44	Master	AZ705	7(P)AFU	RAF Sutton Bridge	Flt. Sgt. Nicholson	U
14/08/44	Lancaster	PD208	550	Wansford	Flt. Sgt. J.Hough	K
16/08/44	Master	DM111	7(P)AFU	Moulton Chapel	Flg. Off. H.T.Richardson	U
19/08/44	Master	AZ359	7(P)AFU	2m from Wansford	Plt. Off. A.K.Green	K
23/08/44	Wellington	MF520	24 OTU	Southery	Flt. Sgt. J.L.Murrey	K
01/09/44	Wellington	MF234	524	The Wash	Flg. Off. D.J.Paterson	I
02/09/44	Halifax	LW344	1656 HCU	Little Casterton	H.Garthwaite	K
08/09/44	B17G	42-31238	351 BG	Langtoft	2/Lt. J.C.Haba	K
09/09/44	B24J Liberator	42-50907	458 BG	Crowland Common	2/Lt. W. R.Frederick	K
12/09/44	Hurricane	AF986	7(P)AFU	Pinchbeck	Sgt. T.A.Hemingway	K
16/09/44	Master	EM387	7(P)AFU	Sutton Bridge	Flt. Sgt. W.G.Brady	U
16/09/44	Mosquito	KB211	1655 MTU	Moulton Chapel	Flt. Lt. A.W.Rutledge	K
19/09/44	Waco CG-4A	N/K	315 TCG	15m SE Peterborough		
23/09/44	Troop Glider			Deeping Fen		

Above: Lt. Robert R. Volkman USAAF aged 20 sustained links with the folks back home through his 8 year-old sister's name Mary Jane painted on the cowling of his Mustang. Robert was leading a formation of Mustangs from 376FS, 361FG on 29/10/44 when 44-14197 suffered engine failure and he had to force land near Peterborough.

(R.R. Volkman)

One of the famous Ball Boys from 511BS, 351BG, whose aircraft names always included the surname of their CO. 2/Lt. John Haba and 2/Lt. Clinton Cavett pose in front of B17G Flying Fortress, 42-31238, Devils Ball. This bomber crashed near Market Deeping on 8/9/44 during formation assembly for a mission to Ludwigshaven. Only tail-gunner Sgt. D.M. Holihan survived.

(D. Benfield)

25/09/44	Master	AZ833	5(P)AFU	West Pinchbeck	Sgt. J.O'Flynn	U
27/09/44	Mosquito	DZ521	627	Tilney All Saints	Flg. Off. A.Matheson	K
27/09/44	P-51 Mustang	N/K	N/K	Yaxley	N/K	K
01/10/44	P-51D Mustang	44-14561	361 FG	Manea	1/Lt. T.A.Dekle	I
03/10/44	Oxford	BG267	12(P)AFU	Helpringham	Flt. Sgt. Malaquin	U
06/10/44	Master	AZ381	7(P)AFU	RAF Sutton Bridge	Cpl. B.J.Lecluse	U
07/10/44	Master	AZ797	7(P)AFU	RAF Sutton Bridge	N/K	U
07/10/44	Master	DL197	7(P)AFU	RAF Sutton Bridge	Damaged by AZ797	
09/10/44	Mosquito	KB261	608	Wimbotsham	Flt. Lt. R.G.Gardner	K
10/10/44	Mosquito	KB404	608	West Of Downham Mkt	Flg. Off. J.A.Smith	U
10/10/44	Master	DL888	7(P)AFU	RAF Sutton Bridge	Flt. Sgt. Robertson	U
12/10/44	B17G	N/K	452 BG	Coates		
12/10/44	B17G	N/K	N/K	Fate Not Known		
13/10/44	Master	DM171	7(P)AFU	RAF Sutton Bridge	Sgt. G.Haywood	U
13/10/44	Fiesler Fi103 (V-1)			Bourne/Castle Bytham		
14/10/44	Hurricane	L1721	7(P)AFU	Eye, Peterborough	Flg. Off. W.J.E.Fawcett	U
14/10/44	Lancaster	ME788	12	The Wash	Flg. Off. C.H.Henry	U
15/10/44	Master	DM349	7(P)AFU	Wrangle	Cpl. P.M.Bertholle	U
16/10/44	Master	AZ662	7(P)AFU	RAF Sutton Bridge	Cpl. B.J.LeCluse	U
17/10/44	Oxford	HM603	7(P)AFU	RAF Sutton Bridge	Flt. Sgt. G.Whitelaw	U
17/10/44	Vengeance	41-3190	1 TTGU	RAF Sutton Bridge	N/K	U
19/10/44	Mosquito	KB215	627	Wainfleet Range	Flt. Lt. Bland	U
29/10/44	P-51A Mustang	44-14197	361 FG	Peterborough	2/Lt. R.R.Volkman	U
09/11/44	Master	DL949	7(P)AFU	RAF Sutton Bridge	Cpl. Guilmemdebat	U
09/11/44	Oxford	HM749	12(P)AFU	Horbling, Bourne	Flt. Sgt. T.D.Wragg	U
09/11/44	Hurricane	L2087	7(P)AFU	2m W of Crowland	Flt. Sgt. M.E.Quayle	U
09/11/44	P-47	N/K	N/K	Hilgay	N/K	N/K
10/11/44	Mosquito	KB360	608	Friday Bridge, Wisbech	Flt. Lt. S.D.Webb	K
14/11/44	Lancaster	PB702	83	The Wash		
22/11/44	Mosquito	DD736	1692 BSTU	Kings Lynn	Flg. Off. F.C.Preece	K
23/11/44	Master	DL541	7(P)AFU	RAF Sutton Bridge	Flg. Off. F.B.Moffat	U
26/11/44	Harvard	N/K	N/K	Wisbech	N/K (American)	U
02/12/44	Master	AZ801	7(P)AFU	RAF Sutton Bridge	Cpl. P.E.Gilbert	U
03/12/44	Wildcat	JV652	NAFDU	Near Stamford	Lt. A.Pickles RNVR	I
08/12/44	Lancaster	PB749	1651 HCU	Langtoft	Flt. Sgt. J.Hall	K
09/12/44	Stirling	EF208	1661 HCU	Wiggenhall St Peter	Flt. Sgt. B.A.C.Bear	U
11/12/44	Lancaster	NG270	1651 HCU	Ailsworth,P'boro	Flg. Off. C.L.Makewell	K
15/12/44	Lancaster	PD201	12	Holbeach Drove	Plt. Off. R.T.Gillingham	K
18/12/44	Lancaster	R5846	3 LFS	Hockwold Fen	Flt. Sgt. G.T.Jacobs	K
18/12/44	Lancaster	R5674	3 LFS	Hockwold Fen	Flt. Sgt. H.W.Harler	K
31/12/44	Mosquito	DZ589	PNTU	Benwick	Flg. Off. P.Germaine	U
2/1/45	P-51 Mustang	43-24808	361FG	1m from Sutton Bridge	2/Lt. M. C. Kelly	U

There is little here for the passer-by to recognise as a P51 Mustang. The pilot, 2/Lt. Marion C. Kelly of 361FG 'hit the silk' on 2/1/45 when he lost control and spun while practising an Immelmann turn at 30,000 feet over Sutton Bridge. The aircraft broke up in the spin and Kelly was thrown out at 8000 feet and parachuted to safety. (M.C. Kelly)

A heavily retouched image - almost making it an artists impression - of an air-launched Fiesler Fi-103 V1 flying bomb, similar to the one that fell on Castor and Ailsworth on 3 January 1945.

03/01/45	Fiesler Fi103 (V1)			Castor/Ailsworth		
04/01/45	Master	DM230	7 SFTS	RAF Sutton Bridge	Cpl. M.Brun	U
05/01/45	B-25 Mitchell	N/K	N/K	Tottenhill Row	N/K	N/K
05/01/45	C-47B Skytrain	43-48727	313 TCG	West Pinchbeck	1/Lt. H.R.Klaus	K
07/01/45	Lancaster	JB286	467	Eye, Peterborough	Flg. Off. W.A.McNamee	M
07/01/45	Oxford	P9811	7 SFTS	RAF Sutton Bridge	S/Lt. G.L.H.Riviere	U
10/01/45	Master	DL238	7 SFTS	RAF Sutton Bridge	Flt. Sgt.. D.Aitchison	U
15/01/45	Oxford	V4126	7 SFTS	RAF Sutton Bridge	Flt. Lt. W.J.White	U
15/01/45	Mosquito	MM194	128	Near Chatteris	Flg. Off. A.W.Hitman	K
16/01/45	B-24J Liberator	42-51471	491 BG	Deeping St Nicholas	2/Lt. F.C.Rose	U
22/01/45	Oxford	LX746	7 SFTS	Sutterton	Sgt. J.Jouet	U
01/02/45	P-51 Mustang	44-11233	364 FG	The Wash	2/Lt. E.A.Knapp	K
02/02/45	Mosquito	PZ245	239	Deeping St Nicholas	Plt. Off. P.O.Falconer	U
05/02/45	Mosquito	HX981	51 OTU	Emneth, Wisbech	Flt. Lt. A.E.Allsworth	I
06/02/45	B17G	42-37806	388 BG	Soham	1/Lt. Thompson	U
06/02/45	B17G	43-37894	490 BG	Prickwillow	1/Lt. J.V.Hedgcock	U
10/02/45	Mosquito	HR178	2 GSU	New York, Boston	Flt. Lt. T.H.Holdsworth	K
19/02/45	Mustang	N/K	479 FG	RAF Sutton Bridge	N/K	I
19/02/45	Oxford	LX333	7 SFTS	RAF Sutton Bridge	Damaged By Mustang	
19/02/45	Oxford	MP278	7 SFTS	RAF Sutton Bridge	Damaged By Mustang	
26/02/45	Lancaster	ME450	75	Chatteris	Flg. Off. N.H.Thorpe	K
02/03/45	Lancaster	ND572	57	Ruskington Fen	Flg. Off. R.J.Anscomb	K
02/03/45	Lancaster	ME473	207	Ruskington Fen	A/Flt. Lt. E.M.Lawson	K
03/03/45	Halifax	NR229	346	Friskney Church End	Plt. Off. Schrank	U
03/03/45	Halifax	NA680	347	Sleaford	Capt. Laucou	K
06/03/45	Lancaster	ME386	207	The Wash	Flg. Off. A.H.Wakeling	K

With its plexiglass nose and chin-turret missing and with bent props on the port inner, all the result of a mid-air collision, the pilot of 43-38859 leans out of the cockpit window to survey the damage and ponder his good luck. His buddy from 486BG, Lt. C.R. Simmonds was not so lucky as he and five of his crew perished in the accident during a training flight near Holbeach.

07/03/45	Oxford	PH413	7 SFTS	2m South Spalding	Flt. Sgt. J.E.Vaudrey	I
09/03/45	B17G	N/K	306 BG	The Wash	2/Lt.. W.E.Miessler	K
10/03/45	Master	DM171	7 SFTS	RAF Sutton Bridge	Cpl. P.Bosc	U
16/03/45	Lancaster	ND869	44	The Wash	Flt. Lt. W.H.Shepherd	M
18/03/45	Tiger Moth	T6160	N/K	Parson Drove	N/K	U
18/03/45	Mosquito	HJ926	13 OTU	Holbeach St Marks	Flg. Off. R.A.Hazell	U
20/03/45	Mosquito	NS998	85	Holbeach Range	Flt. Lt. G.H.Ellis	M
20/03/45	Lancaster	RA530	57	Stickney	Flg. Off. C.Coburn	K
21/03/45	Halifax	N/K	1665 HCU	4m SE Wittering	Plt. Off. P.E.Nettlefield	K
25/03/45	Master	DL250	7 SFTS	Terrington St Clements	Flt. Lt. A.H.Burr	K
26/03/45	Master	W9098	7 SFTS	Near Peterborough	Cpl. J.Dessenteaux	U
27/03/45	Master	DK918	7 SFTS	RAF Sutton Bridge	Flt. Sgt. C.E.Hookham	U
29/03/45	Master	DM336	7 SFTS	Thorney	Cpl. R.Debienkiewicz	K
29/03/45	Stirling	PW391	ORTU	Thorney, Coll With DM336	Flt. Lt. W.J.Howes	K
30/03/45	B17G	N/K	452 BG	Hilgay	N/K	
15/04/45	Oxford	HM676	18(P)AFU	Market Deeping	Flt. Sgt. R.D.Fishbourne	K
19/04/45	Lancaster	ME357	49	The Wash	Plt. Off. D. L.Hytch	U
19/04/45	Mosquito	HR216	1692 BSTU	Walpole St Andrew	Flg. Off. T.W.Jasper	K
24/04/45	P-51 Mustang	44-13646	361 FG	Eau Brink	2/Lt.. R.W.Hobbs	I
25/04/45	P-51 Mustang	N/K	N/K	Holbeach St Marks	N/K	U
26/04/45	B17G	44-8687	486 BG	Lutton Marsh	1/Lt. C.R.Simmonds	K
26/04/45	B17G	43-38859	486 BG	Damaged in collision with 44-8687		
28/04/45	Wellington	NA798	85 OTU	Whittlesey Wash	Flt. Lt. S.B.Dalmais	U
04/05/45	P-51 Mustang	N/K	N/K	The Wash	N/K	K
13/05/45	P-51D Mustang	N/K	20 FG	Peterborough	N/K	U
18/05/45	Oxford	PH418	7 SFTS	Wingland Marsh	Cpl. Chef. R.Parmentier	U
20/05/45	B-24M	44-50688	389 BG	Manea Common	1/Lt.. J.J.O'Brien	K
24/05/45	Oxford	R5952	17 SFTS	Scredington	WO. J.H.Stewart	U
03/06/45	Halifax	NA702	ORTU	Peterborough	Sgt. S.L.Cook	K
03/06/45	Wellington	LP906	81 OTU	Peterborough	Flt. Sgt. A.G.Collins	K
08/06/45	Harvard	FX433	7 SFTS	Spalding	WO. K.N.Doyle	K
22/06/45	P-51B Mustang	42-106638	361 FG	Hilgay Fen	Flg. Off. W.C.Ross	I
19/07/45	Oxford	LB446	7 SFTS	RAF Sutton Bridge	Matelot A.M.Rolin	U
08/08/45	Oxford	LX113	7 SFTS	RAF Sutton Bridge	Cpl. Chef. P.Bousquet	U
13/08/45	Oxford	PH414	7 SFTS	Clenchwarton	Matelot C.G.Moitessier	K
03/09/45	Wellington	LP657	26 OTU	Spalding	Flg. Off. L.Huygens	K
07/09/45	Oxford	HN129	7 SFTS	RAF Sutton Bridge	Sgt. N.Brunat	U
17/09/45	Oxford	HN735	7 SFTS	RAF Sutton Bridge	Cpl. G.Ledroff	U
18/09/45	Oxford	LX558	7 SFTS	RAF Sutton Bridge	Q/M. J.Guillou	U
02/10/45	Oxford	LX361	7 SFTS	RAF Sutton Bridge	Q/M. J.Stoeklin	U
20/10/45	Hurricane	PG470	521	Kings Lynn	WO. R.A.Fewkes	I
30/10/45	Oxford	HN324	7 SFTS	RAF Sutton Bridge	Matelot H.Bartholomei	U
06/11/45	Mosquito	MM222	105	Ramsey St Mary	Flt. Lt. E.J.Morgan	I
29/11/45	Oxford	PG954	7 SFTS	RAF Sutton Bridge	Matelot K.Merrett	U
02/02/46	Oxford	PG998	7 SFTS	RAF Sutton Bridge	Cpl. R.M.Dumont	U
12/02/46	Oxford	NM369	7 SFTS	RAF Sutton Bridge	Cpl. M.Rougier	U
21/02/46	Oxford	NM609	7 SFTS	RAF Sutton Bridge	Sgt. M.F.Allegrand	U

The forlorn tail unit of B24M Liberator, 44-50688, 389BG, which appeared to have broken away as the aircraft crashed at Manea Common in a violent storm. Outbound from Hethel on instruments, this aircraft carried 9 aircrew and 4 ground-crew passengers all returning Stateside at the cessation of hostilities in Europe. There were only two survivors. (I. McLachlan)

The memorial plinth and Hurricane propeller erected at the edge of the airfield and beside the Cross Keys swing bridge under which Flt. Lt. Atcherley flew in the incident described in chapter one.

INDEX

BIBLIOGRAPHY

Action Stations, Vol 1; Bruce Barrymore Halpenny, PSL, 1981.
Action Stations, Vol 2; Michael J.F.Bowyer, PSL, 1979.
Aircraft Of The RAF Since 1918; Owen Thetford, Putnam, 1957.
Aircraft Serial Registers(Various); Air Britain Historians Ltd.
Air Fighting, The Story of; AVM J.E.Johnson, Hutchinson, 1985.
Airfields Of Lincolnshire Since 1912; Blake, Hodgson and Taylor, Midland Counties, 1984.
Aviation In Northamptonshire; Michael Gibson, Northamptonshire Libraries, 1982.
Avro Aircraft Since 1908; A.J.Jackson, Putnam, 1965.
Battle Of Hamburg The; Martin Middlebrook, Alan Lane, 1980.
Battle Over Britain; Francis K.Mason, McWhirter, 1969.
Blitz Then and Now The; Ed. Winston Ramsey, After The Battle, Vol1 1987, Vol2, 1988.
Bomber Command War Diaries The; Middlebrook & Everitt, Viking, 1985.
Bomber County, T.N.Hancock; Lincolnshire Library Service, 1978.
Bomber Squadrons of the RAF and Their Aircraft; J.P.R.Moyes, Macdonald & Janes, 1976.
British Aviation Vols 1-5, Harald Penrose, Putnam 1969 and HMSO.
British Military Aircraft Serials 1878-1987; Bruce Robertson, Midland Counties, 1987.
Doodlebugs The; Norman Longmate, Hutchinson, 1981.
Duel In The Dark; G/C Peter Townsend, Harrap, 1986.
Eagle Squadrons The; Vern Haugland, David and Charles, 1980.
Fighter Aces of World War 2; Robert Jackson, Arthur Barker Ltd, 1976.
Fighter Leader, The Story of W/C I.R.Gleed DSO DFC; Norman Franks, Wiliam Kimber, 1978.
Fighter Squadrons of the RAF and Their Aircraft; J.D.R.Rawlings, Macdonald & Janes, 1976.
First Over Germany, A History of the 306th Bomb Group; Russell A.Strong, 1982.
Fortresses Of The Big Triangle First; Cliff T.Bishop, East Anglia Books, 1986.
Halifax, An Illustrated History of a Classic WW2 Bomber; K.A.Merrick, Ian Allen Ltd, 1980.
Intruders Over Britain; Simon W.Parry, Air Research Publications, 1987.
Jump For It, Stories of the Caterpillar Club; Gerald Bowman, Evans Bros Ltd, 1955.
Lancaster, Story of a Famous Bomber; Bruce Robertson, Harleyford, 1964.
Lincolnshire Air War, Books 1&2; S.Finn, Aero Litho Co, 1973/1983.
Men Of The Battle of Britain; Kenneth Wynn, Glidden Books, 1990.
Mighty Eighth The; Roger A.Freeman, Janes, 1970.
Number 1 Squadron; Michael Shaw, Ian Allen Ltd, 1986.
One More Hour; Desmond Scott, Hutchinson, 1989.
Pathfinder Force, A History of 8 Group; G.Musgrove, Macdonald & Janes, 1976.
Pride Of Unicorns A, (David and Richard Atcherley of the RAF); John Pudney, Oldbourne, 1960.
Reach For The Sky, Douglas Bader his life story, Paul Brickhill, Collins, 1954.
Royal Air Force 1939-1945, Vols 1-3; D.Richards and H.St.G.Saunders, HMSO, 1974.
Skegness Lifeboats, A century and a Half of; Lt/Cdr F.S.W.Major, B.S.Major.
Spitfire Crash Logs Vols1 & 2; D.J.Smith, 1978.
Squadrons of the RAF; James J. Halley, Air Britain, 1980.
Tales from the Bombers; Chas Bowyer, William Kimber, 1985.
Thousand Plan The, The Story of the First Thousand Bomber Raid on Cologne; Ralph Barker, Chatto & Windus, 1965.
Typhoon Pilot; Desmond Scott, Secker and Warburg / Leo Cooper, 1982.
V For Vengeance; David Johnson, William Kimber, 1981.
Valiant Wings; Norman L.R.Franks, William Kimber, 1988.
Years of Command; Sholto Douglas, Collins, 1966.